Quicken® 2015

FOR DUMMIES

A Wiley Brand

by Stephen L. Nelson, MBA, CPA

FOR DUMMIES
A Wiley Brand

Quicken® 2015 For Dummies®

Published by
John Wiley & Sons, Inc.
111 River Street
Hoboken, NJ 07030-5774
www.wiley.com

Copyright © 2014 by John Wiley & Sons, Inc., Hoboken, New Jersey

Published by John Wiley & Sons, Inc., Hoboken, New Jersey

Published simultaneously in Canada

For general information on our other products and services, please contact our Customer Care Department within the U.S. at 877-762-2974, outside the U.S. at 317-572-3993, or fax 317-572-4002.

For technical support, please visit www.wiley.com/techsupport.

Wiley publishes in a variety of print and electronic formats and by print-on-demand. Some material included with standard print versions of this book may not be included in e-books or in print-on-demand. If this book refers to media such as a CD or DVD that is not included in the version you purchased, you may download this material at http://booksupport.wiley.com. For more information about Wiley products, visit www.wiley.com.

Library of Congress Control Number: 2014946663

ISBN 978-1-118-92013-8 (pbk); ISBN 978-1-118-92014-5 (ebk); ISBN 978-1-118-92029-9 (ebk)

Manufactured in the United States of America

10 9 8 7 6 5 4 3 2 1

Contents at a Glance

Table of Contents

Introduction

· ·

You aren't a dummy, of course. But here's the deal: You don't have to be some sort of technogeek or financial wizard to manage your financial affairs on a PC. You have other things to do, places to go, and people to meet. And that's where *Quicken 2015 For Dummies* comes in.

In the pages that follow, I give you the straight scoop on how to use Quicken 2015 for Windows, without a lot of extra baggage, goofy tangential information, or misguided advice.

About This Book

This book isn't meant to be read from cover to cover like some Scandinavian crime thriller page-turner. Rather, it's organized into tiny, no-sweat descriptions of how to do the things you need to do. If you're the sort of person who just doesn't feel right *not* reading a book from cover to cover, you can, of course, go ahead and read this thing from front to back.

I can recommend this approach, however, only for people who have already checked the TV listings. There may, after all, be a *Grimm* rerun on.

To make the best use of your time and energy, you should know about the following conventions I use in this book.

When I want you to type something, such as **Hydraulics screamed as the pilot lowered his landing gear**, I put it in bold letters.

By the way, with Quicken, you don't have to worry about the case of the stuff you type (except for passwords, which are case sensitive). If I tell you to type **Hillary**, you can type **HILLARY**. Or you can follow e. e. cummings's lead and type **hillary**.

Whenever I describe a message or information that you see on the screen, I present it as follows:

```
Surprise! This is a message onscreen.
```

Sometimes I provide step-by-step descriptions of tasks. I feel very bad that I have to do this. So to make things easier for you, I highlight the tasks with bold text. That way, you'll know exactly what you're supposed to do. I also often provide a more detailed explanation in regular text. You can skip the regular text that accompanies the step-by-step descriptions if you already understand the process.

Here's an example that shows what I mean:

1. **Press Enter.**

 Find the key that's labeled Enter. Extend your index finger so that it rests ever so gently on the Enter key. In one sure, fluid motion, press the Enter key by using your index finger. Then release the key.

Okay, that's kind of an extreme example. I never go into that much detail. But you get the idea. If you know how to press Enter, you can just do that and not read further. If you need help — say, with the finger depression part or something — just read the nitty-gritty details.

Can you skip anything else? Let me see now. . . . You can skip the paragraphs with the Technical Stuff icons next to them. See the "Special Icons" section, later in this Introduction, for an example of the Technical Stuff icon. The information I stick in those paragraphs is really only for those of you who like that technical kind of stuff.

But a warning: Don't skip the Warnings. They're the text flagged with the picture of the 19th-century bomb. They describe some things you really shouldn't do.

Out of respect for you, I'm not going to put such stuff in these paragraphs as "Don't smoke." I figure that you're an adult. You can make your own lifestyle decisions.

So I'll reserve the Warnings for more urgent and immediate dangers — things akin to "Don't smoke while you're filling your car with gasoline."

Three Foolish Assumptions

I assume just three things:

- You have a PC with Microsoft Windows XP, Windows Vista, Windows 7, or Windows 8.
- You know how to turn it on.
- You want to use some flavor of Quicken 2015.

Oh, wait, I'm going to assume one more (fourth) thing: You own or somehow have access to a copy of Quicken.

You may be interested to know that Quicken comes in several versions. It doesn't really matter which one of the several versions you have. Each version works basically the same way, and this book applies to them all. But because each version has a few unique features, you may find that your screen doesn't look exactly like the screens shown in this book. You may, for example, have a few buttons that you don't see in the figures I show you. Don't worry if this happens. It probably means that you're working with a different version than I am.

Just to let you know, I used the super-duper, includes-everything version to write this book. You can tell this because the menu bar, which appears in some of the figures, sometimes shows both a Rental Property menu and a Business menu. If you have a different version, your menu bar will not show these menus. Your title bar (if you compare) will also show a different name.

The upshot here? Don't freak out if your version of Quicken 2015 looks a wee bit different from the figures shown in this book.

Beyond the Book

This book is packed with information about using and benefiting from Quicken. But you'll be glad to learn, I'm sure, that you can find additional relevant content at the www.dummies.com website:

- ✔ **Cheat Sheet:** (www.dummies.com/cheatsheet/quicken2015) supplies a handy reference that you'll use over and over, or refer to when you don't have the book handy.

- ✔ **Online articles covering additional topics at**

 www.dummies.com/extras/quicken2015

 Here, you'll find some tangential articles about simplifying your personal financial management and making stuff like your taxes and investing easier.

- ✔ **Updates to this book, if any, are at**

 www.dummies.com/extras/quicken2015

Special Icons

Like many computer books, this book uses *icons,* or little pictures, to flag things that don't quite fit into the flow of things. *For Dummies* books use a standard set of icons that flag little digressions, such as the following:

This icon points out nerdy technical material that you may want to skip (or read, if you're feeling particularly bright).

Here's a shortcut to make your life easier.

This icon is just a friendly reminder to do something.

And this icon is a friendly reminder *not* to do something . . . or else.

Where to Next?

If you're just getting started, flip the page and start reading the first chapter.

If you have a special problem or question, use the Table of Contents or the Index to find out where that topic is covered and then turn to that page.

Part I
Zen, Quicken, and the Big Picture

getting started with

Quicken

In this part . . .

✔ Set up the Quicken software quickly and correctly so you start off right and immediately enjoy all the benefits.

✔ Get a bird's-eye overview of how you'll turn Quicken into a powerful personal financial-management tool to create a road map for success.

✔ Maximize your income, your savings, and your net worth by tapping easy-to-use budgeting tools and techniques.

Chapter 1

Setting Up Shop

• •

In This Chapter

▶ Installing and setting up Quicken

▶ Setting up your bank (or other) accounts if you're a first-time user

▶ Providing a Quicken overview

▶ Solving setup problems

• •

*I*f you've never used Quicken, begin here. This chapter tells you how to install Quicken (if you haven't already) and how to start the program for the first time. You also find out how you go about setting up Quicken accounts to track banking activities — specifically, the money that goes into and out of a checking or savings account.

If you've already begun to use Quicken, don't waste any time reading this chapter unless you want the review. You already know the stuff it covers.

By the way, if you have Windows, I assume that you know a little bit about it. No, you don't have to be some sort of expert. Shoot, you don't even have to be all that proficient. You do need to know how to start Windows applications (such as Quicken). It also helps immensely if you know how to choose commands on menus and how to enter stuff in windows and dialog boxes. If you don't know how to do these kinds of things, flip to Appendix A. It provides a quick-and-dirty overview of how you work in Windows. Read the stuff in the appendix, or at least skim it, and then come back to this chapter.

When I say Windows, I mean a recent version of Windows — something Microsoft is either currently selling or has sold in the last few years. Quicken 2015 won't run on Windows versions earlier than Windows Vista (with Service Pack 2) so if you want to run the latest version and you're still white-knuckling with Windows XP, I'm afraid it's time to upgrade. By the way, I used Windows 8.1 on the computer I used to write this book.

Installing and Starting Quicken

You install Quicken the same way that you install any program in Windows. If you already know how to install programs, you don't need any help from me. Stop reading here; do the installation thing; start your newly installed Quicken program; and then start reading the next section, "Finishing Setup If You've Used Quicken Before."

If you need help installing Quicken, here are the step-by-step instructions. Installing Quicken from a CD is easy:

1. **Insert the CD into the CD-ROM drive.**

 In a short amount of time, Quicken should display the Quicken 2015 Install wizard window. I'm not going to show this window in a figure. There's really nothing in the window to talk about. The window just reads `Welcome to Quicken 2015!`

 Note: I should make a clarification here, I realize. If you're installing Quicken for the first time, there's really nothing in the welcome window to talk about. However, if you're *upgrading* to Quicken 2015 from an earlier version of Quicken, the Install wizard gets all chatty. For example, the Install wizard tells you that Quicken really cares about you and will automatically back up your existing data file. The wizard tells you it will not only install the new version of Quicken, but also uninstall the old version. Finally, the wizard tells you it'll convert your "old version of Quicken" data to a format that works with Quicken 2015.

2. **Click Next.**

 Quicken then displays a window that asks you a couple of questions:

 • Whether you accept the Quicken license agreement

 • Whether you're okay with having Quicken send anonymous usage statistics to Intuit

 You can answer the Install wizard's questions by selecting the check boxes in front of the questions.

3. **Click Let's Go.**

 Quicken displays the license agreement, which you should read, of course. But note that the license agreement window includes a couple of check boxes: one you check to indicate you agree to the license agreement, and one you check to indicate you and Quicken are "good" even if Quicken sends information about how you're using the program to the folks at Intuit.

4. **Click Next.**

 Quicken displays the next window of the Install wizard, which tells you things are about to start happening but which also, as a subtle aside,

asks where you want to install Quicken. You should accept the program's suggestion: a Quicken subfolder in your Program Files folder.

Note: If you do want to change the location Quicken uses to store your data, you click the installation location hyperlink (shown in the lower-left corner of the window), click the Change Install Location button when Quicken displays the next window, and then use the dialog box that Quicken displays next to choose a drive and folder for the file.

5. **Click Next.**

Quicken displays yet another window of the Install wizard, indicating that the wizard needs to install the Quicken software and may need to update the software, too. Assuming you're okay with all this — and you should be — click the Install button.

Quicken installs itself. This process takes a few minutes. Along the way, you may see other screenfuls of messages, including marketing information about the features new to Quicken and some progress reports on the installation itself.

After the installation is complete, Quicken displays an `installation complete` message.

6. **Click Finish.**

Congratulations. You're nearly done. You'll need to restart your computer, so verify that the Reboot Now box is checked inside the dialog box that displays the `installation complete` message. Then click Finish.

You can purchase Quicken from the `www.quicken.intuit.com` website. And if you do so, you don't grab the installation program files from a CD but rather you grab them from the Intuit website. If you're taking this approach, visit the website, click the Buy Now button, and then follow the onscreen instructions to download the installation program files.

Finishing Setup If You've Used Quicken Before

If you've used a previous version of Quicken, the Quicken program displays a window that asks about converting your old Quicken data file to the next Quicken 2015 file format. If you're okay with this — and you should be; Quicken saves a copy of the old file — click the Convert File button. Quicken then converts the file.

The Quicken setup process can usually tell whether you've used Quicken before. The setup process knows where the Quicken installation program usually puts the Quicken program and data files, and the installation program will

look there. If you've used Quicken before but Quicken can't see this, two possibilities exist:

- ✔ You may have put the Quicken data file someplace weird. (If that's the case, with any luck, you remember the weird place where you hid the Quicken data file. But if not, see the section "The mysterious case of the missing Quicken data files" at the end of this chapter.)
- ✔ Maybe you didn't do anything with the Quicken data file, but the data file has somehow gone missing. (If that's the case, I hope you backed up the Quicken data file to a CD or to some other disc from which you can restore the data file.)

Finishing Setup If You've Not Used Quicken Before

To finish the setup when you've not used Quicken before, the program displays a friendly welcome message (not shown here), which asks you to indicate whether you're a new Quicken user, want to start over from scratch as though you're a new user, or have used Quicken before and need to open a file from a previous version of Quicken.

You indicate your Quicken status by selecting the appropriate option button and then clicking the big blue Get Started button. What happens next depends on which button you click.

Already a Quicken user?

If you've used Quicken before and select the I've Used Quicken Before option, Quicken then displays another Get Started With Quicken 2015 window, which asks whether you want to open a Quicken file located on this computer, restore a Quicken data file you've backed up to CD or disc, or start over and create a new data file.

If you indicate that you want to open another Quicken data file located on the computer, Quicken displays a dialog box that asks where that file is. If you indicate that you want to grab a backup copy of the Quicken file, Quicken displays a dialog box that asks where that file is. Presumably, if either of these situations is your case, you'll know where the data file or backup copy of the data file is.

Are you new to Quicken?

If you indicate that you're a new Quicken user, Quicken automatically sets up a data file for you. (You don't need to worry about it.)

Registering Quicken

Quicken prompts you to register the first time you start the program. (You might as well do this. The registration takes only a few minutes. All you do, in a nutshell, is provide your name and address, a bit of information about how you use Quicken, and your e-mail address.)

Note: You will also be prompted to set up a Intuit ID when you register unless you've already created an Intuit ID for use with another Intuit product, such as Quicken.com or TurboTax.

After you register, Quicken displays the Add Account dialog box. (See Figure 1-1.) The Add Account dialog box walks you through the steps for setting up the account (bank accounts, for example) that you'll manage using Quicken. (You can find out much more on this process in the next section.)

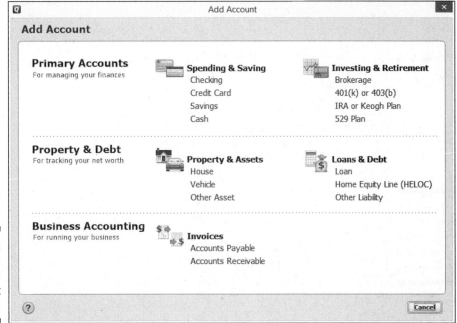

Figure 1-1:
The Quicken
Add
Account
dialog box.

Describing Your Banking

As mentioned in the preceding section, if you haven't used Quicken before or are starting from scratch, the first time you start Quicken 2015, the program shows the Add Account dialog box, which you use to tell Quicken about the accounts you'll track.

Click the Checking hyperlink (it appears at the top of the little list of accounts under the Spending & Saving heading) to provide information about your primary checking account and its current balance. Figure 1-2 shows the window that collects the first part of this information, but just so you don't get confused, here are the precise steps you take:

1. **Identify the financial institution — usually a bank — by typing your institution's name in the text box provided.**

 As you type, Quicken displays a list of financial institutions that match what you've typed so far. The more you type, the shorter the list of possible matching institutions. *Note:* When you start the Quicken program, it attempts to make an Internet connection so it can grab the most up-to-date version of this list of financial institutions.

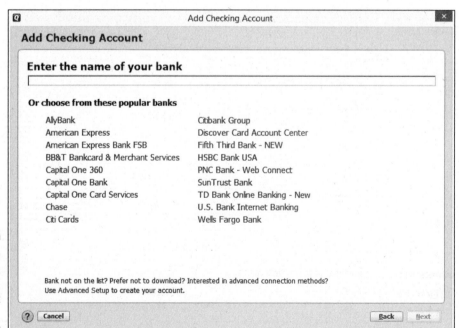

AllyBank	Citibank Group
American Express	Discover Card Account Center
American Express Bank FSB	Fifth Third Bank - NEW
BB&T Bankcard & Merchant Services	HSBC Bank USA
Capital One 360	PNC Bank - Web Connect
Capital One Bank	SunTrust Bank
Capital One Card Services	TD Bank Online Banking - New
Chase	U.S. Bank Internet Banking
Citi Cards	Wells Fargo Bank

Figure 1-2: The first Add Checking Account window.

2. **Tell Quicken whether you want to download transactions directly from your bank or enter transactions manually.**

 If your bank provides Internet access to your bank account — and most banks do — Quicken knows. And as a result, Quicken attempts to not so subtly push you into just grabbing data from the bank's website. I'm going to suggest, however, that you maintain your account manually. You have plenty of time later to find out how online banking works. (Online banking is really cool, though. See Chapter 6 for more information.)

 That said, however, if you see your bank listed and you want to use online banking, select the bank and click Next. When you click the Next button, Quicken displays another version of the Add Your Primary Checking Account window, which asks for the username and password required to access your bank account electronically. To download transactions and account balance information directly from your bank's website, you need to provide this information. After you provide this information, click the Connect button to test the username and password information.

 If you don't want to use online banking quite yet, and are happy to start slow and go manually at the beginning, click the Advanced Setup hyperlink at the bottom of the first Add Your Primary Checking Account window. Quicken won't quite believe you're bold enough to ignore its strong advice to go digital, so it displays another Add Your Primary Checking Account window that provides option buttons you can use to indicate that you want to be clever and just download transactions — or that you want to be ploddingly cautious (at least at the start) and enter transactions manually. By default, the I Want to Select the Connection Method option is selected. (See Figure 1-3.) But you don't want to be clever — or at least not quite yet — so select the I Want to Enter My Transactions Manually option.

 Note: Quicken may not get into this online banking stuff if it can tell that your bank doesn't support online banking.

3. **Tell Quicken the name you want to use for the checking account.**

 You do so by typing a name in the Account Name/Nickname text box, shown in Figure 1-4. Furthermore, if given the choice, click one of the option buttons that may appear below the Account Name/Nickname text box to indicate whether you're using the bank account primarily for business finances, personal finances, and so on. By the way, as far as the account name goes, you can be as general or as specific as you want. But brevity is a virtue here, so be concise: Quicken uses your account name to label stuff within the Quicken window and on Quicken reports. If you use a long account name, the name may not always fit on reports and screens.

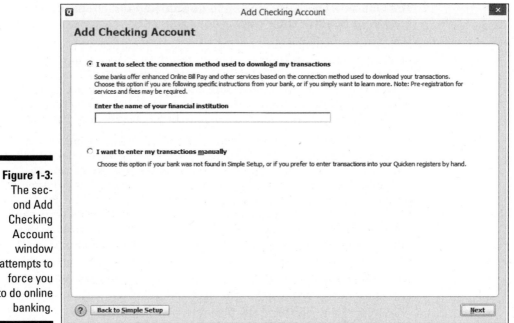

Figure 1-3:
The sec-
ond Add
Checking
Account
window
attempts to
force you
to do online
banking.

Figure 1-4:
The third
Add
Checking
Account
window.

4. **Enter the ending bank statement date by referring to your bank statement.**

 After you provide Quicken a name and general description of the account's transactions, click Next, and Quicken displays another account setup dialog box (shown in Figure 1-5) that asks about the account's ending statement date and ending statement balance. Enter the date of your last bank statement in the Statement Ending Date text box. This date, by the way, is the date forward from which you will start using Quicken. Enter the date in *MM/DD/YYYY* or *MM/DD/YY* fashion.

 "Geez, Steve," you're now saying to yourself, "what's *MM/DD/YYYY* fashion?" Okay. Here's an example: If your bank statement is dated August 30, 2015, type **8/30/2015**, or you can type **083015**.

5. **Enter the ending bank statement balance by referring to your latest bank statement.**

 This balance is whatever appears on your bank statement. This balance is also the amount of money in your account on the date you begin your financial recordkeeping. If you have $4.16 in your checking account, type **4.16** in the Statement Ending Balance text box.

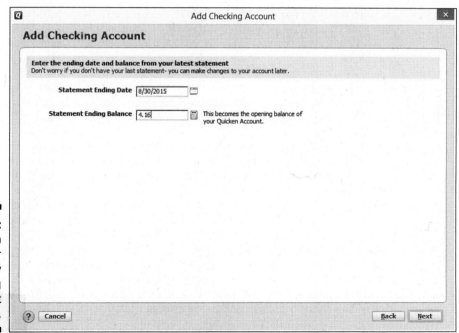

Figure 1-5:
The fourth
Adding Your
Primary
Checking
Account
window.

6. **After you type the bank statement balance, click the Next button to continue moving through the account setup.**

 Ultimately, you'll see an Account Added window that indicates you've successfully added your bank account. That window also provides a check box you can use to tell Quicken it should sync the account data you'll show for the just-added account with the Quicken Cloud so you can get balance data by using a mobile device like a smartphone. (Do check the box if you've got such a device.) The Account Added window also provides buttons you can click to add another bank account (including things like credit card accounts), as well as a button you can click to indicate that you're finished and just want to start using Quicken.

7. **If you have several other bank accounts that you want to set up within Quicken, repeat the preceding steps for each account.**

 Just click the button that refers to adding another bank account.

Slogging Through More Setup Stuff

Okay, from my perspective, after you've described your bank account(s), you're ready to start using Quicken. With Quicken, the key thing you want to do is track your bank account(s) so you can monitor and measure your income and your outgo — and so you know how much money you have in an account.

The folks at Intuit, however, allow you to provide the Quicken program a lot more information about your financial affairs. Specifically, the Intuit gang lets you describe in detail your income sources and your regular expenditures.

After you finish adding your accounts, Quicken displays its home page (see Figure 1-6). To tell Quicken all about your income and outgo, you click the Get Started button in the Stay on Top of Monthly Bills area of the home page.

When you do, Quicken displays the first Stay on Top of Monthly Bills window, shown in Figure 1-7. To describe a recurring bill (such as your rent check, car loan payment, and so on), you click the Add a Bill button. Then, when Quicken displays the Add Bill Reminder dialog box (not shown here), you describe the bill in detail, including who gets paid, when they should be paid, why they're paid, and so forth. (I'm not going to describe the Add Bill Reminder dialog box here because I talk about it in detail in Chapter 12, when the subject of loan payments comes up.)

Figure 1-6:
The Quicken
home page.

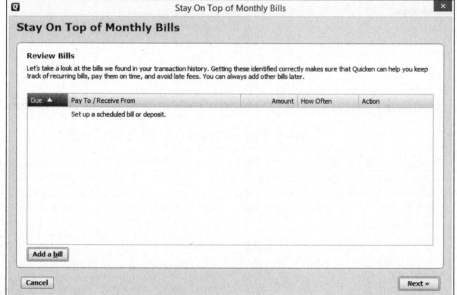

Figure 1-7:
The first
version of
the Stay
on Top of
Monthly
Bills
window.

If you click the Next button in the bottom-right corner of the Stay on Top of Monthly Bills window, Quicken displays a second version of the window, shown in Figure 1-8. The second version of the Stay on Top of Monthly Bills window provides an Add Income Reminder button.

Figure 1-8:
The second version of the Stay on Top of Monthly Bills window.

To provide information about your income to Quicken, click the Add Income Reminder button. Quicken displays dialog boxes that ask for the gory details.

The best way to get started

Quicken wants you to use your last bank statement to set up the bank account you track. This way, your financial records synchronize with the bank's records when you start using Quicken.

But I want to suggest something slightly different to you. Go back farther than just to the beginning of the preceding month (which is what you do when you use your most recent bank statement). Go back to the beginning of the year and use the last bank statement of the preceding year — even if it's now several months after the beginning of the year. Now, I'm not trying to waste your time. Let me point out two big advantages to having a complete year's data in Quicken: Tracking and tallying your tax deductions will be a snap, and planning your finances will be easier. When you enter the activity, be sure to enter any outstanding checks or deposits from the previous period — with their correct dates — as well. That way, they'll be there to check off when you do your first reconciliation.

Going back to the beginning of the year isn't as hard as you may think. Quicken provides a bunch of tools to help you enter several months' worth of data in a very short time, as you can see in this chapter and in the two or three that follow.

Steve's Overview

You don't need to know much about the mechanics of the Quicken *interface* —
the way its window looks and works — to begin working with Quicken, espe-
cially in any chapters in this book in which I cover the basics. I provide plenty
of detailed instructions, but I have a couple of quick comments now.

Using Quicken Qcards

If you click the View Guidance button in the upper-right corner of the Quicken
window (see Figure 1-6, for example), Quicken displays business-card-size
pop-up boxes in your Quicken program window, called Quicken Qcards. You
can remove these Qcards from your program window (as I did for shooting
the screen shots in this book). But you'll want to use the Qcards for at least a
little while if you're a new user. The Qcards provide all sorts of good informa-
tion and advice about getting going with Quicken. And you can page through
whole scads of tidbits and tips by clicking the Qcard Previous and Next buttons.
Finally, when you ultimately tire of the Qcards, no problem — just click the
Qcard Close button (the X in the upper-right corner of the box).

Starting Quicken for the second time

The second time you start Quicken — and every subsequent time — things
work pretty much the same way as the first time. Double-click the Quicken
icon on your start screen or desktop.

Using the Accounts bar

Along the left edge of the program window, just beneath the boldface word
Accounts, Quicken lists the accounts you've set up. In other words, if you set
up a single checking account, the Accounts bar shows just that single checking
account. If you set up 13 bank accounts because that's just the sort of person
you are, the Accounts bar shows the 13 checking and savings accounts.

You can display the transactions you've entered for an account shown in
the Accounts bar by clicking the account name. (I talk more about this in
Chapter 4.)

You can collapse the Accounts bar by clicking the arrowhead symbol that appears in front of the word *Accounts.* If you've previously collapsed the Accounts bar, you can expand the bar by clicking the arrowhead symbol again. The arrowhead symbol points right if the list is collapsed, and it points down if the list is expanded.

Navigating with tabs

Quicken arranges all its features — whistles, bells, or whatever else you want to call them — by using navigation tabs that appear near the top edge of the window. For example, if you look closely at Figure 1-6 (shown earlier), you can see tabs labeled Home, Spending, Bills, Planning, and Rental Property.

If you're still confused, click the buttons and bits of text in the area of the Quicken window that I'm talking about. You'll clearly see how things work.

If you click the Home or Bills tab and you haven't yet set up enough of Quicken to use the features provided by the tab, you encounter a blue Get Started button. If you click the Get Started button, Quicken steps you through setting up the tab's features.

Solving Tricky Setup Problems

I want to quickly go over a handful of semitricky or possibly slightly annoying setup problems that new Quicken users may encounter. If you have Quicken set up and are ready to roll, skip this stuff.

Using the Quicken Mobile App

If you have a mobile device like an Android or Apple smartphone, you can and should download the (currently) free Quicken 2015 app. By providing the app with your Intuit ID information (essentially, your e-mail address and a password), you can view account balances and transactions for any of the accounts you told Quicken to sync to the Quicken Cloud.

Did somebody say Macintosh?

You can use existing old Quicken files if you're working with a new version of Quicken. In fact, if the Quicken installation program can find a version of old Quicken files on your computer, it gives you the option of skipping all the

Quicken setup stuff. In this case, you just begin using your existing files. (I mention this point earlier in this chapter, in fact.)

If you've been using Quicken for Macintosh, however, you have to export your data from the Macintosh before you can read it in the Windows version. And I can think of about a million things more fun to do than exporting Quicken data from a Mac to Windows. See the section in Chapter 17 on importing data from an old accounting system for a brief discussion of the procedure (and some suggestions of better ways to spend your time).

The mysterious case of the missing Quicken data files

If Quicken doesn't find the old files, you need to open the specific files. But if you have this problem, you should be able to solve it yourself. What has happened, if you find yourself in this boat, is that you've moved or messed around with the Quicken files with some other program, such as Windows. If you did that, presumably you had a reason. And more to the point, you should know where you put the files.

Migrating from Microsoft Money

Suppose that you're moving from Microsoft Money to Quicken. The question of the hour is this: Can you reuse your old or existing Money files in Quicken? The answer is yes, sort of.

First of all, the Quicken File menu includes an Import command that lets you import files from Microsoft Money 2007 or 2008. So far, so good.

Further, if you've got an older version of Microsoft Money that you want to convert data from, you can follow instructions provided at the `http://quicken.intuit.com` website for migrating the data. To get to the actual page of instructions for how you do this, use Bing or Google and enter *Intuit. com Importing Your Microsoft Money File into Quicken* as your search term. The instructions, just so you know, require you to download the Microsoft Money Plus Sunset Deluxe software so you can upgrade your *really* old Microsoft Money data file to the nearly-as-old Money 2008 data file format — and then direct you to import that data file into Quicken. The bottom line? Theoretically, you can move old Microsoft Money data files to Quicken.

Practically, however, moving financial information from Quicken to Money or vice versa doesn't seem to work all that well. Transactions seem to get lost. Account balances get messed up. People ruin their lives. Well, maybe that last comment is a slight exaggeration. But aside from that, no kidding: Migrating is problematic. If you do want to move data from one program to another, I suggest making sure that you have a really good reason for doing so — and that you allow yourself enough time to track down and correct any errors that might creep in along the way.

Chapter 2

Introduction to the Big Picture

· ·

In This Chapter

▶ Distilling Quicken to its very essence

▶ Setting up additional bank accounts

▶ Adding, removing, and modifying categories

▶ Understanding tags

· ·

*B*efore you spend a bunch of time on Quicken, you have to understand the big picture. You need to know what Quicken can do. You need to know what you want to do. And, as a practical matter, you need to tell Quicken what you want it to do.

Boiling Quicken Down to Its Essence

When you boil Quicken down to its essence, it does six things:

✔ **It lets you track your tax deductions.**

This feature makes preparing your personal or business tax return easier for you or your poor accountant, Cratchit.

✔ **It lets you monitor your income and outgo using your computer, a mobile device like a smartphone, or printed reports.**

Usually, this stuff is great fodder for discussions about the family finances. And if you're running a business or investing in real estate rental properties, this income-and-expense information becomes more than just great conversation fodder; the information also helps you manage your business better.

✔ **It lets you print checks (and sometimes other forms too).**

This device is mostly a time-saver, but it can also be useful for people who are neatness freaks.

✔ **It lets you track the things you own (such as bank accounts, investments, and real estate) and the debts you owe (such as home mortgage principal, car loan balances, and credit card balances).**

These things are really important to know.

✔ **It helps you make better personal financial planning decisions about such matters as retirement, your children's future college costs, and your savings and investments.**

I think this stuff is really neat.

✔ **It gives you the opportunity to pay bills electronically and, in some cases, even do all your banking electronically.**

This stuff is pretty neat, too. No, let me amend that: Online bill paying and banking are *really* neat. I do have some minor (very minor) reservations that I discuss in Chapter 6, which deals with online banking in depth.

Tracking tax deductions

To track your tax deductions, make a list of the deductions you want to track. To do so, pull out last year's tax return. Note which lines you filled in. (Perhaps mortgage interest, property taxes, state income taxes, and charitable contributions?) This method works because there's a darn good chance that the tax deductions you claimed last year will also be the tax deductions you'll claim in the future.

I cover the Quicken categories, which you use to track your tax deductions, a little later in this chapter.

Monitoring spending

At our house, we (my wife [Sue] and I, your humble author) use Quicken to monitor our spending on the mundane little necessities of life: groceries, clothing, dog food, cable television, and. . .well, you get the picture. To keep track of how much we spend on various items, we also use the Quicken categories.

If you want to monitor a particular spending category, decide up front what the category should be before you begin recording your data.

Your list of spending categories, by the way, shouldn't be an exhaustive list of super-fine pigeonholes, such as *Friday-night Mexican food, Fast food for lunch,* and so on. To track your spending on eating out, one category named something like *Meals* or *Grub* usually is easiest.

In fact, I'm going to go out on a limb. You can probably start with a dozen categories, more or less:

- Car
- Clothing
- Entertainment and vacation
- Groceries
- Household expenses (besides food)
- Insurance
- Medical and dental
- Rent (or mortgage payments)
- Taxes
- Utilities (electricity, water, cable television)
- Work expenses

If you want to, you can expand this list, and you can do so over time. Heck, you can create dozens and dozens of categories. My experience, though, is that you'll probably use only a handful of categories.

Printing checks (and other forms)

You can use Quicken to print checks. This little trick provides a couple of benefits: It's really fast if you have several checks to print, and your printed checks look very neat and darn professional.

To print checks, you need to do just two things. First, look through the check supply information that comes with Quicken, and pick a check form that suits your style. Then order the form. (The check forms that come with *remittance advices* — or check stubs — work well for businesses.)

Preprinted check forms aren't cheap. If you're using Quicken at home with personal-style checks (such as those that go in your wallet), using computer checks may not be cost effective. Even if you're using Quicken for a business, and you're used to buying those outrageously expensive business-style checks, you'll still find computer checks a bit more expensive.

I'm pretty much a cheapskate, so I don't use printed checks at home (although I do use them in my business). I should admit, however, that I also don't write very many checks.

By the way, I've "checked" around. Although you can order Quicken check forms from other sources (such as your local office-supplies store), they're about the same price from Intuit (the maker of Quicken). If you want to order from Intuit, you can refer to the catalog that came in the Quicken packaging. You can also visit www.quicken.com.

One other comment here about printing checks: If you're going to pay bills electronically, you don't need to print checks with Quicken. Oh, sure, you can print checks if you want. But you won't want to. Paying a bill electronically is easier and cheaper than paying a bill with a Quicken-printed check.

A general comment about printing other forms: If you run a business, and the business needs to produce invoices, you can use Quicken Home & Business and Quicken Rental Property Manager (two business-y flavors of Quicken) to produce invoice forms, too. (You can add both of these features by choosing the appropriate command — Add Home & Business or Add Rental Property Manager — from the Help menu.)

Tracking bank accounts, credit cards, and other stuff

You must decide which bank accounts and credit cards you want to track. In most cases, you want to track each bank account you use and any credit card on which you carry a balance.

You may also want to track other assets and liabilities. *Assets* are just things you own: investments, cars, a house, and so on. *Liabilities* are things you owe: margin loans from your broker, car loans, a mortgage, and so on.

Shoot, I suppose that you could even track the things your neighbor owns — or perhaps just those things you especially covet. I'm not sure that this is a very good idea, though. (Maybe a healthier approach is to track just those things that you've borrowed from your neighbor.)

Planning your personal finances

Your computer's computational horsepower makes it the ideal tool for doing complicated calculations. So maybe you're not surprised that Quicken comes with five powerful calculators that let you make smarter borrowing choices, better mortgage-refinancing decisions, more accurate savings and investment calculations, and extremely helpful retirement and college savings calculations.

I believe that these financial planning tools are the most valuable features that Quicken offers. If you don't want to wait to find out more about them, flip to Chapter 10. I'll wait.

Banking online

If you want, you can tell Quicken that it should do the work of paying some person or merchant electronically. In other words, at the same time that you describe some check to Quicken — you do so by entering stuff in a window — you can say to Quicken, "I not only want you to record this check for me, but I also want you to pay it for me."

If your bank supports online banking, you may also be able to move money between your accounts and get up-to-date statements electronically. Ask your bank for details about this service if you're interested.

To perform this sort of online banking, you need to have an Internet connection, and you need to do a little bit of paperwork. But the Quicken online banking features can save you scads of time. And the features are easy to use. Basically, all you do is use Quicken in the usual way — which is what I talk about in the chapters that follow — and then click a couple of extra buttons.

Setting Up Additional Accounts

When you first began working with Quicken — and this may have been only a few minutes ago or several years ago — you were prompted to set up an account. And you probably set up at least a checking account because this is probably your most active bank account. If you want to track any additional accounts — for example, a savings account — you must set them up, too.

Setting up another banking account

To set up an additional checking, savings, or money market account, you give the account a name and then its balance as of a set date. Here's how:

1. **Click the Add an Account button.**

 Quicken displays the Add Account window, shown in Figure 2-1.

 The Add an Account button is located near the bottom of the Accounts bar, which appears along the left edge of the Quicken program window. You can collapse and expand the Accounts bar by clicking the small arrow button just left of the Accounts label. If the arrow button points down, clicking the button collapses the Accounts bar. If the button points right, clicking the button expands the previously collapsed Accounts bar.

2. **Click either the Checking or Savings hyperlink.**

 Quicken displays a version of the Add Account window, shown in Figure 2-2, that asks for the bank name.

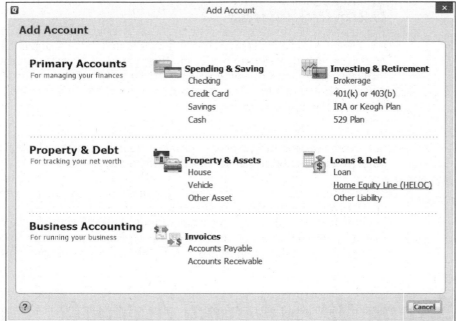

Figure 2-1:
The Add
Account
window.

3. (Optional) Identify the financial institution and then click Next.

To identify the bank and (simultaneously) set up the account for online banking, enter the bank's name in the Enter the Name of Your Bank text box. As you type the bank name, Quicken creates a list of banks that match what you're typing. When you see your bank listed, select its name. Quicken then asks you to enter the bank's online sign-on information for the account. (This information probably includes a username and password or equivalent information.) If you want to enable online access to the bank account information, provide the requested information and then click the Connect button. Alternatively, if you don't want to identify your bank, you can click the Advanced Setup link (near the bottom of the window) to display a second Add Account window (not shown) that asks whether you want to connect to your bank automatically so you can download transactions or want to enter transactions manually.

4. Indicate whether you want to download transactions or manually enter transactions and then click Next.

When Quicken asks whether you want to download account activity and balance information directly from your bank or enter the information manually, indicate that you just enter transactions manually. (Quicken asks the "manual versus online" questions if you select a financial institution that allows for online banking.)

Figure 2-2:
The first Add
Checking
Account
window
used for
a bank
account.

5. **Name the account and then click Next.**

 When Quicken displays the first Add Checking Account dialog box (see Figure 2-3), move the cursor to the Account Name/Nickname text box and type a name in that box. Then, if you're working with some versions of Quicken, you may get a chance to indicate how you'll use Quicken by selecting one of those "This account is primarily used for" buttons so Quicken can start you off with a good beginner set of categories. Click Next after you do this. You're almost done.

6. **Enter the account balance date.**

 When Quicken displays the Add Checking Account dialog box, shown in Figure 2-4, enter the date that you're going to start keeping records for the bank account with Quicken. (Quicken wants you to start your record keeping for an account on a bank statement date because on a bank statement date, you have a really good balance from the bank.) Move the cursor to the Statement Ending Date text box, and type the month number, a slash, the day number, a slash, and the year number. If you start on July 1, 2015, for example, type **07/1/2015**. Or, if this seems way too complicated for you, click the button at the end of the Statement Ending Date text box so that Quicken displays a pop-up calendar. Then click the date. Use the << and >> buttons to move back and forth a month at a time.

Figure 2-3:
The Add Checking Account dialog box.

Figure 2-4:
The Statement Date and Balance dialog box.

Note: If you want to keep your transaction records for tax purposes, of course, it makes sense to track whatever accounts you can from the first of the year, assuming that you have all the necessary statements or your own records of all the transactions.

7. **Click inside the Statement Ending Balance text box and enter the bank account balance.**

Use the number keys to enter the balance. The folks at Intuit, by the way, really want you to use the balance from your bank statement. If you have terrible financial records — for example, if you haven't reconciled your account since either George Bush left the White House — this idea is probably good advice. If you have neat, accurate financial records, go ahead and use your check register's balance.

If you do use the bank statement balance as your starting balance, be sure to enter all the transactions that have cleared or will clear after the bank statement balance date. (This should make sense, right? If a check or deposit isn't reflected in the bank statement figure, you must enter it into Quicken with its correct date.)

8. **Click Next and then click the Finish button.**

Quicken redisplays the Home tab.

Hey, Quicken, I want to use that account!

In Quicken, you work with one account at a time. The logic is simple: You record income and expenses for a particular account (a specific checking account, savings account, and so on). That makes sense, right?

Here's the next thing you want to know about using these accounts: In general, you work with an individual account by using the *register window,* shown in Figure 2-5. I talk about using the register window a lot more in the chapters that follow, but in a nutshell, it's where you enter account transactions in the register. Entering transactions in a register is the basic Quicken recordkeeping task.

Here's another thing you need to know about working with a particular Quicken account. You use the Accounts bar, which appears along the left edge of the Quicken program window (shown in Figure 2-5), to tell Quicken which account you want to work with in a register window.

To use the Quicken Accounts bar, you click its hyperlinks. In other words, select the account you want by clicking the account name. Quicken displays the register window for that account.

Figure 2-5:
The register
window.

You can collapse and expand the Accounts bar by clicking the small arrow-head button marked that's just to the left of Accounts. If the arrowhead button points down, clicking the button collapses the Accounts bar. If the arrow-head button points right, clicking the button expands a previously collapsed Accounts bar.

Whipping Your Category Lists into Shape

Quicken supplies categories to. . .well, categorize your spending. For example, you would probably use the Rent category to categorize all the checks you write to pay rent.

The predefined categories list may be just what you want. Then again, it may not. Table 2-1 shows the all-inclusive Personal Income and Personal Expenses category list.

Your category list may vary somewhat from the one shown in Table 2-1. Quicken may customize your starting category list based on the version of Quicken you install. For example, if you install the version of Quicken that supports tracking rental property, the category list may include Rental Property Income and Expense categories.

Take a minute to look through the category list. If you find categories you don't need, cross them off the list in the book. You can delete them from Quicken in a minute or so. If you need categories you don't see, add them at the bottom of the list. You can add them in about two minutes or so.

✔ To track a certain income or spending item for income tax purposes — wages, property taxes, and so on — you need a Quicken category.

✔ To track a certain income or spending item because you're just interested in knowing how much you spend on it (for example, renting DVDs), you need a Quicken category.

✔ To budget by categories (because you need a category for any income or spending item that you want to budget), you need a Quicken category.

Table 2-1	The Category List
Categories	*Descriptions*
Income Categories	
Div Income	Dividends earned from stocks you own
Interest Inc	Interest income on bank accounts and so on
Net Salary	Your net-of-taxes income from a job
Net Salary Spouse	Your spouse's net-of-taxes income from a job
Other Inc	Income that doesn't fit into another category
Expense Categories	
Auto & Transport	The big catch-all category for auto and transportation expenses
Auto Insurance	Car insurance premiums
Auto Payment	Car loan or lease payments
Car Wash	Car washes (and maybe detailing?)
Gas & Fuel	Gas, diesel, biodiesel, and so on
Parking	Parking and (ideally, no) parking tickets
Public Transportation	Bus, subway, elevated and commuter trains, and rickshaws (in some areas)
Registration	Vehicle registration fees
Service & Parts	Services and repairs expenses
Tolls	Toll charges
Bills & Utilities	The big general category for regular bills and utilities expenses
Credit Card Payment	Amounts paid on your credit card when you're not tracking this stuff in granular detail
Home Phone	Landline phone
Internet	Internet service provider
Mobile Phone	Cellphone (and text messaging?)

(continued)

Table 2-1 *(continued)*

Categories	*Descriptions*
Television	Cable television
Utilities	Water, sewer, electricity, and gas
Cash & ATM	Pocket spending via ATM and mad money
Deposit to Savings	Not a real spending category, but a shortcut for people who don't want to set up a savings account
Education	The general category for education
Books & Supplies	Books and other school supplies
Student Loan	Student loan payments
Tuition	Tuition and lab fees
Entertainment	Catch-all parent category for entertainment spending
Amusement	Hey, whatever spins your propeller
Arts	Catch-all subcategory for stuff that follows
Movies & DVDs	Movie rentals and purchases as well as cinema tickets
Music	Music CDs, music downloads, street-musician payments
Newspaper & Magazines	Periodical subscriptions
Fees & Charges	Catch-all parent category for bank, credit card, and similar fees
ATM Fee	Cash machine charges
Bank Fee	Bank fees, penalties, and service charges
Late Fee	Late fees charged by vendors
Service Fee	Miscellaneous service charges
Trade Commissions	Broker commissions
Financial	Catch-all parent category for financial services and products
Financial Advisor	Investment advisor fees
Life Insurance	Life insurance premiums
Food & Dining	Another catch-all parent category
Alcohol & Bars	Yeah, I wanted to talk to you about this
Coffee Shops	Caffeine expenditures
Fast Food	What you should eat less of
Groceries	What you should eat more of
Restaurants	Restaurant charges, including gratuities
Gifts & Donations	The giving parent category

Categories	*Descriptions*
Charity	Gifts to nonprofit, religious, and similar organizations
Gift	Usually for gifts to family members and friends
Health & Fitness	The parent category for all your medical and fitness-related expenses
Dentist	Dentistry expenses
Doctor	Physicians' fees
Eyecare	Optometrist fees, eyeglasses, contact lenses, and similar items
Gym	Fitness club and gym expenses and fees
Health Insurance	Health insurance premiums
Pharmacy	Expenses for prescription and over-the-counter medicines
Sports	Sporting expenses and similar activities
Home	Household-expenses parent category
Furnishings	Furniture and accessories
HOA Dues	Homeowners' association dues
Home Improvement	Home repairs and improvements
Home Insurance	Homeowners' and renters' insurance
Home Services	Home cleaning and maintenance services
Home Supplies	Home cleaning and maintenance supplies
Lawn & Garden	Landscaping-type expenses
Mortgage	Mortgage payments (for people who aren't tracking mortgage loan balances)
Rent	Rent payments
Interest Exp	Interest expense on personal lines of credit and other consumer debts
IRA Contribution	Individual Retirement Account contributions
Kids	Catch-all parent category for kids-related subcategories
Allowance	Kids' allowance money
Baby Supplies	Diapers and so forth
Babysitter & Daycare	Costs of childcare
Child Support	Child-support payments
Kids' Activities	Little League, dance classes, karate summer camp, and so forth
Toys	Toys, games, computer games

(continued)

Table 2-1 *(continued)*

Categories	*Descriptions*
Misc.	Stuff you can't categorize someplace else
Not Sure	Stuff you can't categorize someplace else and yet feel oddly uncomfortable putting into the Misc. category
Personal Care	The catch-all parent category for the personal-care subcategories
Hair	Haircuts, colorings, extensions, weaves, and other such follicle finances
Laundry	Dry cleaning and other laundry services
Spa & Massage	Spa treatments, massage therapy
Pets	The catch-all parent category for pet-related expenses
Pet Food & Supplies	What you feed Rover and Twinkle the cat
Pet Grooming	Dog shampoos, cat shampoos, nail clippings
Vet	Veterinarian bills
Shopping	The catch-all shopping category
Books	My personal weakness
Clothing	Work and casual clothing, including shoes
Electronics & Software	Electronics (including computer) gear and software
Hobbies	Hobby and craft expenses and activity costs
Sporting Goods	Sporting and recreational equipment
Tax	Personal tax expenses parent category
Fed	Federal income, Social Security, and Medicare taxes
Property	Real estate and personal property taxes
State	State income and related payroll taxes
Travel	Personal travel expenses
Air Travel	Airplane tickets
Hotel	Hotel and other lodging charges
Rental Car & Taxi	Rental cars, taxis, and similar costs (including airport transfers)
Vacation	Personal and family vacation expenses

Subcategories . . . yikes, what are they?

You surely didn't buy Quicken so that you could spend all day Saturday sitting at your computer instead of taking the kids to the zoo. I realize this and want to make Quicken easier for you to use. To do so, I figure I should tell you which Quicken features you can ignore if you're feeling a bit overwhelmed. Subcategories are among those things I think that you can ignore.

"Subcategories?" you ask. "Yikes! What are they?"

Subcategories are categories within categories. If you look at the Auto & Transport expense category in Table 2-1, for example, you'll notice a bunch of categories that follow the category: Auto Insurance, Auto Payment, Car Wash, Gas & Fuel, Parking, Public Transportation, Registration, Service & Parts, and Tolls.

When you use subcategories, you can subcategorize a transaction that pays, for example, auto and transportation expenses; you can further break down this category into subcategories such as Insurance, Fuel, Service, and so on. If you want to see a list of the ways you've spent your money, Quicken summarizes your spending both by category and, within a category, by subcategory. On a Quicken report, then, you might see this level of detail:

Category	*Expense*
Auto & Transport	
Auto Insurance	900
Gas & Fuel	100
Service & Parts	700
Total taxes	1,700

No doubt about it: Subcategories are useful tools. But they make working with Quicken a little more complicated and a little more difficult. As a practical matter, you usually don't need them as you start off. If, later, you want to track a spending category in fine, granular detail, you can go ape on the subcategory thing then, okay? For these reasons, I'm not going to get into subcategories here.

If you get excited about the topic of subcategories later — after you have the hang of Quicken — you can peruse the Quicken documentation for more information.

If you *do* want to use the Quicken subcategories, don't delete the subcategories shown in Table 2-1. If you *don't* want to use the subcategories, go ahead and delete them. (I tell you how to remove categories in "Removing categories you loathe," later in this chapter.)

Category groups . . . double yikes!

Category groups, which were known as *supercategories* in a previous version of Quicken, combine categories into sets that you can use in reports and in your budgeting. Sure, they're sort of cool, but you don't need to worry about them if you're just starting with Quicken.

If you're dying to know more about category groups, you can refer to Quicken online Help. Quicken Help works like Help in other Windows programs. If you don't know Windows all that well — or at least not well enough to use Help comfortably — see Appendix A.

Four tips on categorization

I have just four tips for categorizing:

✔ **Cross off any category you won't use.**

If you don't pay state income taxes in the state you live in, for example, get rid of the State Tax category. Extra, unneeded categories just clutter your list. I think it's great if you can get down to just a handful of categories.

✔ **Don't be afraid to lump together similar spending categories.**

Take your utilities expenses, for example. If you pay water, natural gas, electricity, and sewer, why not use a single Utilities category? If you pay different utility companies for your water, natural gas, electricity, and sewer, you can still see what you spend on just electricity, for example, even with a single catch-all category for utilities.

✔ **Be sure to categorize anything that may be a tax deduction.**

Categorize alimony, educational, medical, and dental expenses; state and local income taxes; real estate taxes; personal property taxes; home mortgage interest and points; investment interest; charitable contributions; casualty and theft losses; moving expenses; unreimbursed employee expenses; and all those vague, miscellaneous deductions. (By the way, the foregoing is a pretty complete list of itemized deductions in the United States at the time this book was written.)

✔ **Don't sweat this category stuff too much.**

In spite of the preceding three tips, don't let these category lists or the work of customizing them scare you. If you want to spend a few minutes cleaning up the list, hey, that's great. If not, or if you're starting to get anxious, just skip to Chapter 3.

Ch-ch-changing a category list

You should now be ready to fix any category list problems. Basically, you need to do three things: add categories, remove categories, and change category names and descriptions.

Adding individual categories you'd love to use

Adding individual categories is a snap. Here's all you have to do:

1. **Choose Tools⇨Category List.**

 Quicken displays the Category List window (shown in Figure 2-6). This window lists the categories available and the accounts you've set up. Careful readers may notice that the categories shown in Figure 2-6 include those shown in Table 2-1.

Figure 2-6:
The
Category
List window.

2. Click the Add Category button in the Category List window.

The Add Category button, by the way, appears in the upper-right corner of the window. Quicken dutifully displays the Set Up Category dialog box (shown in Figure 2-7). You probably aren't surprised that you use this puppy to describe the new category.

Figure 2-7:
The Set Up
Category
dialog box.

3. Enter a short name for the category.

Move the cursor to the Category Name text box and type a name. Although you can use up to 15 characters, use as short a name as possible to clearly identify the category. Why? Because you use this category name every time you want to tag a transaction to fall into the category.

4. Enter a description for the category.

Move the cursor to the Description text box and then describe the category. Quicken uses the category description on reports that show the category. If you don't add a description, Quicken just uses the category name. You don't need a description, obviously, if your category name is. . .well, adequately descriptive.

5. (Optional) Identify the category group.

If you disregarded my earlier suggestion to *not* worry about category groups, click the Options button at the bottom of the Category List window and choose Assign Category Group from the menu that Quicken displays. When Quicken displays the Assign Category Groups dialog

box, click the Add Custom Groups button to create a new category group. Then, with the Assign Category Groups dialog box still displayed, select the category you want to group from the Find the Category You'd Like to Re-Assign list box (shown on the left half of the dialog box) and then the category group you want to use from the Assign It to a Custom Category Group list box (shown on the right half of the dialog box). Click Done when you're. . .well, done.

6. **Indicate whether the category is an income category or an expense category.**

 Select the appropriate Income, Expense, or Subcategory Of option button; just select the appropriate option button with your furry little friend, the mouse. If you've totally blown off my admonition not to use subcategories just yet, use the dialog box's drop-down list to indicate into which income or expense category a new subcategory falls.

7. **Indicate whether the category tracks an amount you will use on an input line on next year's tax return.**

 By *line,* I mean the actual tax-return line — such as the line on the U.S. 1040 form that tracks alimony.

 If a category does track a tax deduction, click the Tax Reporting tab of the Set Up Category dialog box, move the cursor to the Tax-Related check box, and then *select the check box* if the category is tax-related or *deselect the check box* if the category isn't tax-related. Just to clear up any confusion, vacationing in Hawaii probably isn't a tax deduction — even if your neighbor promises that it is. Then identify the form and line by opening the Tax Line Item drop-down list box and selecting one of its entries.

8. **Click OK.**

 Quicken adds the new category in the Category List window (refer to Figure 2-6) and then redisplays the window. Now that you understand the stuff in the Category List window, note that it shows the category name; its type; notations concerning the category's tax-reporting status; and, golly darn, even its description and group. (The tax information about on which tax-return line a category gets reported appears only if the Show Tax Line Item choice below the option button is selected.)

Adding categories from a situational list

Quicken keeps lists of categories that are standard for people in certain situations, including Quicken users who are married, homeowners, real estate investors, and business owners.

To use these situational lists as a source of new categories, follow these steps:

1. **Choose Tools⇨Category List.**

 Quicken displays the Category List window (refer to Figure 2-6).

2. **Click the Options button and then choose the Manage Categories command from the menu.**

 Quicken displays the Manage Categories dialog box. This window lists the categories that may be useful in certain situations.

3. **Select one of the situational lists.**

 Open the Available Categories drop-down list box (you can do this simply by clicking the box) and select the situational list of categories you want to display: standard, business, investment, or rents and royalties. Quicken displays the categories from the situational list selected.

4. **Select the categories you want to add.**

 Click the categories in the Categories list that you want to add. Quicken marks the categories you select with a check. You can, by the way, mark all the categories shown in the situational list by clicking the Mark All button. You can unmark all the "marked" categories by clicking the Clear All button.

5. **Add the selected categories.**

 After you mark the categories you want to add, click the Add button. Quicken adds the categories to the Categories to Add list. To complete the addition of the categories, click Add.

Removing categories you loathe

Removing categories takes only a couple of keystrokes. With the Category List window displayed, follow these steps:

1. **Click the category you want to remove and then choose the Delete button that appears.**

 If no transactions are in the category, Quicken displays a message that asks you to confirm your decision. You can't remove any categories you're using for some old transaction. Accordingly, you may first need to recategorize transactions that use a category you want to nuke.

2. **If you want to remove the selected category, click OK.**

 Otherwise, press the Esc key or click the Cancel button.

Changing category names and descriptions

You can change a category name, its type, its description, and its tax-related setting if you later discover that you made some mistake, such as misspelling a word in a description.

To change a category name, follow these steps:

1. **Display the Category List window (refer to Figure 2-6).**

2. **Use the arrow keys or click to select the category you want to change. Click an Action button, and then click the Edit button.**

 Quicken displays a dialog box that has text boxes and option buttons describing the selected category's information: its name, description, type, and tax-related settings.

3. **Make the changes you want by replacing text box contents or changing option-button settings.**

4. **Click OK to save your changes and return to the Category List window.**

Want to Play Tag?

Using categories isn't the only way that you can summarize your financial records. Quicken provides tools called *tags* that let you summarize transactions in addition to the way you summarize transactions with categories. (In previous versions of Quicken, tags were known by another name: *classes*.)

Now, typically, tags aren't something you need to worry about — especially if you're just using Quicken to regain control of your personal finances. However, tags can be very useful if you're using Quicken in a business or if you're investing in rental real estate.

For these reasons, I want to quickly describe how you set up tags.

To set up a tag (or several tags), take these steps:

1. **Display the Tag List window.**

 To do this, choose Tools⇨Tag List. Quicken displays the Tag List window (not shown).

2. **Click the New button in the Tag List window.**

 Quicken displays the New Tag dialog box (shown in Figure 2-8).

Figure 2-8:
The New Tag
dialog box.

New Tag

New Tag

*Required fields

Name *

Description

Copy number ☐ Tell me more

OK Cancel

3. Enter a short name for the tag.

Move the cursor to the Name text box, and type a name. Use as short a name as possible to clearly identify the tag. You use this tag name every time you want to tag a transaction. (If you're using tags to identify real estate rental properties, which is probably their most common use, you may want to use the street name as the tag: *Winston* as the tag for the duplex on Winston Street, *Roosevelt* as the tag for the cottage on Roosevelt Avenue, and so on.)

The reason real estate investors tag transactions is straightforward. When you tag each income or deduction transaction with (for example) the property name, Quicken easily produces a profit-and-loss statement for each property, using the categories and tags to slice and dice the data.

4. Enter a description for the tag.

Move the cursor to the Description text box and then describe the tag. Quicken uses the tag description on reports that show the tag. If you don't add a description, Quicken just uses the tag name. You don't need a longer description if your tag name is descriptive enough.

The technical editor, David (who's also a CPA), wants me to tell you that you should just ignore the Copy Number box. He's probably right. But if you're just dying to know what this box does, click the Tell Me More link.

5. Click OK.

Quicken adds the new tag in the Tag List window and then redisplays the window. And that's that.

Chapter 3

Maximum Fun, Maximum Profits

● ●

In This Chapter

▶ Deciding whether you need a budget

▶ Discovering tips for personal and business budgets

▶ Setting up and reviewing a budget

● ●

I don't think that a budget amounts to financial handcuffs, and neither should you. A budget is really a plan that outlines the way you need to earn and spend your money to achieve the maximum amount of fun — or the way a business needs to earn and spend its money to make the most profit.

Should You Even Bother with a Budget?

A *budget,* as you probably know, is a list of the ways you earn and spend your money. If you create a good, workable category list with Quicken (see Chapter 2), you're halfway to a good, solid budget. (In fact, the only step left is to specify how much you earn in each income category and how much you spend in each expense category.)

Does everybody need a budget? No, of course not. Maybe at your house, you're already having a bunch of fun with your money. Maybe in your business, you make money so effortlessly that you really don't plan your income and outgo.

For the rest of us, though, a budget improves our chances of getting to wherever it is we want to go financially. In fact, I'll stop calling it a budget. The word has such negative connotations. I know — I'll call it a *Secret Plan.*

Serious Advice about Your Secret Plan

Before I walk you through the mechanics of outlining your Secret Plan (your budget), I want to give you a few tips.

Your personal Secret Plan

You can do four things to make your Secret Plan more likely to work:

✔ **Plan your income and expenses as a family.**

With this sort of planning, two heads are invariably better than one. What's more, though I don't really want to get into marriage counseling here, a family's budget — oops, I mean *Secret Plan* — needs to reflect the priorities and feelings of everyone who has to live within the plan. Don't use a Secret Plan as a way to minimize what your spouse spends on clothing or on long-distance telephone charges talking to relatives in the old country. You need to resolve issues regarding your clothing and long-distance charges before you finalize your Secret Plan.

✔ **Include some cushion in your plan.**

In other words, don't budget to spend every last dollar. If you plan from the start to spend every dollar you make, you undoubtedly have to fight the mother of all financial battles: paying for unexpected expenses when you don't have any money. (You know the sorts of things I mean: car repairs, medical expenses, or that cocktail dress or tuxedo you absolutely *must* have for a special party.)

✔ **Regularly compare your actual income and outgo to your planned income and outgo.**

This part of your plan is probably the most important and also the part that Quicken helps you with most. As long as you use Quicken to record what you receive and spend, you can print reports showing what you planned and what actually occurred.

✔ **Make adjustments as necessary.**

When you have problems with your Secret Plan — and you will — you'll know that your plan isn't working. You can then make adjustments, for example, by spending a little less on calling the old country.

A Secret Plan for your business

The tips for personal Secret Plans also apply to businesses, but I have a special tip for small businesses using Quicken. (I'm going to write very quietly now so that no one else hears....)

Go to the library, ask for the RMA (Risk Management Association) survey, and look up the ways that other businesses like yours spend money. If your library doesn't have the RMA survey, see whether it has the Dun & Bradstreet survey or Troy's Almanac of Business and Industrial Financial Ratios survey.

These surveys are really cool:

✔ The **RMA** surveys bank-lending officers, creates a summary of the information these bankers receive from their customers, and publishes the results.

✔ **Dun & Bradstreet** collects and summarizes its proprietary financial information.

✔ **Troy** (who's actually a business Ph.D.) collects Internal Revenue Service data and publishes the same sort of financial results.

In the preceding surveys, you can get really useful information about what businesses like yours spend, make, and own. For example, you can look up what percentage of sales the average tavern spends on beer and peanuts, the average profit your CPA makes, and the profit a car dealer makes on the average car sale. (Isn't that all kinds of interesting stuff?)

By the way, the surveys won't actually have a line on the taverns page labeled *beer and peanuts.* It'll be called *cost of goods sold* or some similarly vague accounting term.

Two things that really goof up Secret Plans

Because I'm talking about you-know-what, let me touch on a couple of things that really goof up your financial plans: windfalls and monster changes.

The problem with windfalls

Your boss smiles, calls you into his office, and then gives you the good news. You're getting a $5,000 bonus! "It's about time," you think. Outside, of course, you maintain your dignity. You act grateful but not gushy. Then you call your husband.

Here's what happens next. Bob (that's your husband's name) gets excited, congratulates you, and tells you he'll pick up a bottle of wine on the way home to celebrate.

On your drive home, you mull over the possibilities and conclude that you can use the $5,000 as a big down payment for that new family minivan you've been looking at. (With the trade-in and the $5,000, your payments will be a manageable $300 per month.)

On his way home, Bob stops to look at those golf clubs he's been coveting; charges $800 on his credit card; and then, feeling slightly guilty, buys you the $600 set. (Pretend that you're just starting to play golf.)

You may laugh at this scenario, but suppose that it really happened. Furthermore, pretend that you really do buy the minivan. At this point, you spent $6,400 on a van and golf clubs, and you've signed up for what you're guessing will be another $300-per-month payment.

This turn of events doesn't sound all that bad now, does it?

Here's the problem: When you get your check, it's not going to be $5,000. You're probably going to pay roughly $400 in Social Security and Medicare taxes, and maybe another chunk in federal and state income taxes. Other money may be taken out, too, for forced savings plans — such as a 401(k) plan — or for charitable giving. After all is said and done, you get maybe half the bonus in cash — say, $2,500.

Now you see the problem. You have $2,500 in cold, hard cash, but with Bob's help, you've already spent $6,400 and signed up for $300-per-month minivan payments.

In a nutshell, you face two big problems with windfalls:

- ✔ You never get the entire windfall, yet spending as though you will is quite easy.

- ✔ Windfalls, by their very nature, tend to get used for big purchases (often as down payments) that ratchet up your living expenses: boats, new houses, cars, and so forth.

Regarding windfalls, my advice to you is simple:

- ✔ Don't spend a windfall until you actually hold the check in your hot little hand. (You're even better off to wait, say, six months. That way, Bob can really think about whether he needs those new golf clubs.)

- ✔ Don't spend a windfall on something that increases your monthly living expenses without first redoing your budget.

The problem with monster income changes

If your income changes radically, planning a budget becomes really hard. Suppose that your income more than doubles. One day you're cruising along making $50,000, and the next day you're suddenly making $100,000.

(Congratulations, by the way.) I'll tell you what you'll discover, however, should you find yourself in this position: You'll find that $100,000 a year isn't as much money as you may think. (By the way, this business about monster income changes is true no matter what your income level. Like, if you're cruising along making $500,000 and see your income rocket to $1,000,000, everything I'm saying here still applies.)

Go ahead. Laugh. But for one thing — if your income doubles, your income taxes almost certainly more than quadruple.

One of the great myths about income taxes is that the rich don't pay very much or that they pay the same percentage. But that's not actually true. If you make $50,000 per year (roughly the average household income in the United States), and you have a spouse and a couple of kids, you might pay about $1,000 in federal income taxes. If you make $100,000 a year (roughly the 90th-percentile household income), though, you pay about $10,000 per year. So if your salary doubles from $50,000 to $100,000 (perhaps your spouse gets a really nice job), your income taxes increase almost tenfold, going from $1,000 to $10,000. I don't bring this fact up to get you agitated about whether it's right or fair that you should pay a bunch of any extra income you make in taxes. I bring it up so that you can better plan for any monster income changes you experience. If your income spikes, your income taxes really spike. And don't even get me started on state and local taxes. . .

Another thing — and I know it sounds crazy — is that you'll find it hard to spend an extra $50,000 wisely when you've been making a lot less. And if you start making some big purchases, such as houses and cars and speedboats, you'll not only burn through a great deal of cash, but also ratchet up your monthly living expenses.

Monster income changes that go the other way are even more difficult. If you've been making, say, $100,000 a year and then see your salary drop to a darn respectable $50,000, it's going to hurt, too, and probably more than you think. That old living-expense ratcheting effect comes into play here. Presumably, if you've been making $100,000 a year, you've been spending it — or most of it.

But other reasons contribute — at least initially — to making a monster salary drop very difficult. You've probably chosen friends (nice people, such as the Joneses), clothing stores, and hobbies that are in line with your income.

Another thing about a monster salary drop is sort of subtle. You probably denominate your purchases in amounts related to your income. Make $50,000, and you think lots of the time in terms of $10 purchases. But make $100,000 a year, and maybe you often easily think in terms of $20 purchases. This observation makes perfect sense. But if your income drops from $100,000 down to $50,000, you'll probably still find yourself thinking of those old $20 purchases.

So what to do? If you experience a monster income change, redo your Secret Plan. And be particularly careful and thoughtful.

Setting Up a Secret Plan

Okay, now you're ready to set up your budget — er, I mean, Secret Plan.

Introducing the Budgets window

To get to the window in which you enter your budget, click the Planning tab and if necessary click the Budgets button. This causes Quicken to display the Budgets window — though the window won't show any budgeting information because you won't yet have created any budgets.

If you click the Get Started button, which appears in the middle of the Budgets window if you haven't created a budget, Quicken displays the Create a New Budget dialog box (shown in Figure 3-1). You now can begin the process of creating a budget. With the sort of kindness you often don't expect from strangers, Quicken even suggests a name for your budget and enters it in the Budget Name text box. The name will be something really clever like Budget 1 or Budget 2, but you can replace Quicken's idea of clever.

Figure 3-1:
The Create
a New
Budget
dialog box.

Automatic budgets are easy but rough

When you click the OK button in the Create a New Budget dialog box, most versions of Quicken automatically create a starting budget, using any existing financial data. (This rough-hewn approach, obviously, doesn't work unless you've already been using Quicken and so have some existing financial data.)

When Quicken finishes with these tasks, it suggests and displays budgeted amounts in the Budgets window for your biggest spending categories (see Figure 3-2).

Figure 3-2:
The Budgets window with automatically created budget amounts.

To change an automatically budgeted amount, click the budget value you want to change. Quicken then opens a text box for the value and also adds little buttons you can use to fiddle with the budgeted amount.

If you do select a category to budget, Quicken adds little buttons to the Budgets window that let you do stuff with that line item's budgeted amount:

✔ **Rollover Unused Amounts button:** Quicken lets you control how unused budget amounts either get or don't get rolled over into the next budgeting period. When you click the Rollover Options button (which looks like two entwined arrows), Quicken supplies a menu with commands you can use to

- Turn off the rollover of unused budget amounts.

- Turn on the rollover of unused budget amounts.

- Roll over only positive amounts.

- Display help about the whole science and art of budget rollovers.

Note that by default, rollovers don't occur. In other words, if you underspend in Month 1, Quicken doesn't automatically add your Month 1 underspending to your Month 2 budget.

✔ **Apply Amounts button:** If you click the button that shows a gear, Quicken displays the Apply Amounts menu with commands that let you

- Use the budgeted amount for the current month as the budget for the rest of the months remaining in the year.

- Use the budgeted amount as the budget for all the months in the year.

- Edit the yearly budgeted amount

- Calculate the average budget

- Indicate that you want the month's budget set to the average spending for the category.

- Get more information with a "Help me, I'm in terrible trouble" command.

✔ **Category History button:** If you click the button that shows a tiny column chart, Quicken displays a pop-up box with two tabs: History and Transactions. The History tab graphically depicts your monthly spending for the category over the last year in a column chart. The Transactions tab (shown in Figure 3-3) lists the transactions that make up the category total.

✔ **Calculator button:** Quicken also displays a little calculator icon when you've selected a text box that accepts a value in both the Graph View and Grid View. Click the Calculator icon to display a pop-up calculator to make computations on the fly.

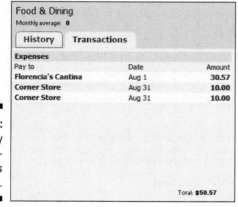

Figure 3-3:
The History and Trans-
actions
pop-up box.

Advanced budget settings for your calendar

You can click the Advanced Budget Settings button (the arrowhead that appears just in front of the label Advanced Budget Settings) in the Create a New Budget dialog box (refer to Figure 3-1) when you want to use a non-calendar year for your budget. When you do this, Quicken adds two option buttons to the Create a New Budget Window (see Figure 3-4). You select the Use My Current Calendar Setting option to specify that you want the calendar year used as a budgeting year. You select the Use a Different Calendar button to choose a budget year that starts some time other than January.

Figure 3-4:
The Create a New Budget window with the Advanced Budget Settings options showing.

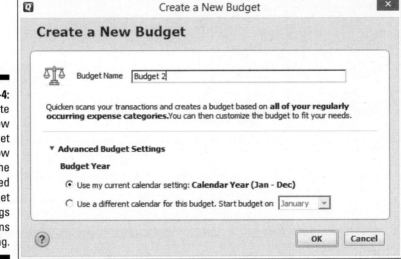

Specifying categories for budgeting

You can add a category to the Budgets window when you're budgeting by clicking the Select Categories to Budget link (see lower-left corner of window) and then choosing the categories you want to budget from the Select Categories to Budget dialog box (shown in Figure 3-5). Click OK when you finish with the Select Categories to Budget dialog box.

Budgeting different monthly amounts

If you want to set specific amounts for each month of the year, click the Budget Actions button and choose the Switch to Annual View command. Then enter the budget amount for January in the January Budget column, the amount for February in the February budget column, and so on (see Figure 3-6).

Figure 3-5:
The Select
Categories
to Budget
dialog box.

Figure 3-6:
An annual
view of the
Budgets
window.

As you enter amounts, Quicken updates any subtotals and grand totals that use those amounts. Note that you don't have to do anything special to save your budgeting work. Quicken automatically saves your budget for you. When you're done working on your budget, for example, you can just exit the Quicken program or click a tab to see another Quicken window.

Reviewing the options

If you click the Budget Actions button (which appears in the upper-right corner of the Budgets window), Quicken displays a menu with eight commands that are useful for working with your budgets:

- **Select Categories to Budget:** Displays the Select Categories to Budget dialog box, discussed earlier in the chapter and shown in Figure 3-5.

- **Switch to Graph View/Annual View:** Toggles the display view of your budget between a just-the-budgeted-month view and a month-by-month-spreadsheet of the entire year.

- **Budget Reports:** Displays a submenu that lists the two Quicken reports that summarize budgeting information: Budget Report and Monthly Budget Report. These reports are also available on the Reports menu, as discussed in Chapter 7.

- **View Options:** Displays a menu of formatting options for the budget, including check boxes you can use to show cents, include reminders, and short parent categories, as well as an Edit Budget Name command that you can use to change the name of the budget.

- **Duplicate This Budget:** Creates a copy of the currently displayed budget and then prompts you to give the copy a name.

- **Delete This Budget:** Deletes the currently displayed budget.

- **Create New Budget:** Displays the Create a New Budget dialog box (refer to Figure 3-1) so you can begin the process of creating yet another budget.

- **Budget Preferences:** Displays the Budget Preferences dialog box (not shown), which you can use to control how Quicken treats transfers between savings accounts and how Quicken accounts for savings goals transactions.

Reviewing your budget

After you complete your budget, you'll want to review your handiwork, of course. And you perform your review by using the Budgets window and its unnamed, unlabeled drop-down lists and boxes (refer to Figures 3-2 and 3-6). Which drop-down lists and boxes Quicken displays and what order these items appear in, however, depends on factors like the number of budgets you've created. But you'll see some or all of the following:

- **Budget name:** If you've created several budgets, Quicken supplies an unlabeled drop-down list box in the top-left corner of the Budgets window. You use this drop-down list box to select the budget you want to review.

- **Graph View/Annual View:** The Graph View/Annual View drop-down list box lets you flip between the Graph View and the Annual View.

- **Interval:** The unlabeled budgeting interval drop-down list box in the top-left corner lets you select the interval you're budgeting for: monthly, quarterly, yearly, quarter to date, year to date, and so on.

- **Calendar:** Finally, you use the unlabeled calendar box to select the specific month for Graph View.

Can I make a suggestion? If you have any questions about what the unlabeled drop-down lists or boxes do, just experiment with the various budgeting drop-down list and box options. You'll pretty quickly figure out on your own how they work.

If a careful review of your budget shows that things have become rather a mess, click the Budget Actions button and choose the Delete This Budget command. Then you can start your work over.

What to do after you enter your budget

After you create your Secret Plan, you don't have to do anything special to save your work. When you create a budget, Quicken automatically saves your work for you.

I talk more about using the budget in later chapters (Chapter 7, for example). If you want to print a *hard copy* (computerese for *paper)* of the budget, choose Reports➪Spending➪Budget. If you have a printing question, go to Chapter 5.

You're not going to use the Secret Plan for a while. But don't worry; in Chapter 7, I explain how to print reports, including a report that compares your actual spending with. . .uh, your budget.

Part II
The Absolute Basics

Get techniques and tricks for your Quicken 2015 setup in "Three Tricks to Make Your Quicken 2015 Setup Fast and Easy" at www.dummies.com/extras/quicken2015.

In this part . . .

- ✔ See how to use Quicken to make keeping your checkbook not only less of a grind, but also a tactic for handling your finances better.

- ✔ Get tips and tricks for printing and producing checks, as well as for creating reports based on the financial data you collect with Quicken.

- ✔ Simplify your finances by tapping the power of Quicken's and your bank's online banking tools and systems.

- ✔ Glean true insight into your personal finances, your investments and businesses, or rental properties you own by using reporting and graphing features.

- ✔ Improve the accuracy and precision of your banking and financial records by employing automated account reconciliation tools.

- ✔ Protect your data by using Quicken's backup and restoration utilities and its powerful-but-friendly security features.

- ✔ Gain huge personal financial planning insights by working with Quicken's retirement, savings, college planning, and investment calculators.

Chapter 4

Checkbook on a Computer

. .

In This Chapter

▶ Recording checks, deposits, and transfers

▶ Splitting categories

▶ Deleting and voiding your transactions

▶ Understanding the register phenomenon

▶ Discovering Quicken's calculators and calendars

▶ Attaching an image, a flag, or a note to a transaction

. .

This is it. The big time. You're finally going to do those everyday Quicken things: entering checks, deposits, and transfers. Along the way, you also use some of the neat tools that Quicken provides for making these tasks easier, more precise, and faster.

Getting Started

Okay. I'm going to start at the very beginning.

As you start working with Quicken, you probably want to work from the Spending tab (shown in Figure 4-1). Basically, it looks and works (sort of) like a web page that provides clickable hyperlinks to some of the most popular banking and bookkeeping features of Quicken, and also supplies interesting tidbits of financial trivia. But initially, before you start entering data, the tab looks pretty sparse. (This is how Figure 4-1 looks.)

Figure 4-1:
The Spending tab, or window.

Finding Your Checkbook

To enter checkbook transactions, look for the bank account you want to work with listed in the Accounts bar. When you see the bank account, you can click it to display that account's transactions in a register (shown in Figure 4-2).

Figure 4-2:
The account transactions showing in a register window.

Figure 4-2 shows the account name — Checking — highlighted in the Accounts bar and in the Quicken window's title bar.

The starting balance you specified as part of setting up the account is the first amount that Quicken lists. In Figure 4-2, for example, the starting balance is $4.16. Bummer.

Recording Checks

First things first: You can enter checks by using the Spending tab and its register window (refer to Figure 4-2) or the Write Checks window, which I describe in Chapter 5.

You use the Spending tab's register window for the checks that you don't want to print or pay electronically with Quicken; you use the Write and Print Checks command and the Write Checks window the command displays to enter the checks that you do want to print or pay electronically with Quicken. (This rule isn't etched in stone, but it does make things easier, so it's the rule that I follow.)

Entering a check in the register

Entering a check in the register is a simple matter of describing to whom you wrote the check and how much you paid. Suppose that you paid $85.95 to the cable television company for your monthly cable service. Here's how you enter this check:

Interested in online banking and bill payment?

If you want to know more about how Online Bill Payment and online banking work, read Chapter 6. For now, just pay attention to how the Quicken register works. Everything you read about in this chapter will help you use the Quicken Online Account Access feature more easily.

1. **Enter the check date.**

 Move the cursor to the Date field in the next empty row of the register (if it isn't already there) and type the date by using MM/DD format. To enter August 31, 2015, for example, type **8/31**. You usually don't have to type the year because Quicken retrieves the current year number from the little clock inside your computer.

 You can adjust the date in a Date field by using the + and – keys on your keyboard. The + key adds one day to the current date; the – key subtracts one day from the current date.

2. **Enter the check number.**

 Move the cursor (or tab) to the Check # field and type the check number. Alternatively, move the cursor to the Check Number field and then, when Quicken displays a list box of entries (such as ATM, Deposit, EFT, Next Check Num, Print Check, Send Online Payment, and Transfer), select Next Check Num if you want. Quicken then fills in the number with its guess as to the new check number — one more than the preceding check number you entered. If this guess is right, you can just leave it in place. If it isn't right, type over what Quicken guessed with the correct number or use the + or – key to increase or decrease the check number.

3. **Enter the payee.**

 Move the cursor to the Payee field. Type the name of the person or business you're paying. If the cable company's name is Movies Galore, for example, type **Movies Galore**. (In the future, you can probably select payee names in the Payee list box.)

4. **(Optional) Enter a memo description.**

 Move the cursor to the Memo field, and describe the specific reason that you're paying the check. You may identify the cable payment as the June payment, for example. If you're using Quicken for a business, use this field to identify the paid invoice — usually by entering the invoice number you're paying. You don't have to enter anything in this field, by the way.

5. **Enter the category.**

 Move the cursor to the Category field. Quicken displays a drop-down list box of category names from your category list. You can select one of these categories by using the arrow keys or the mouse. Or, if you're the independent type, just type the name yourself. For example, if you use the standard Quicken categories list, you may categorize a payment to your cable company as Bills & Utilities:Television. The first part of this entry, Bills & Utilities, is the category. The second part, Television, is the subcategory.

 If you go with the typing approach and you're not a super-fast typist, Quicken can probably guess which category you're entering before you enter it. When you start typing **Bi**, for example, Quicken fills in the rest of the category name — *lls & Utilities* for you (*Bi + lls & Utilities = Bills &*

Utilities). This feature is called *QuickFill,* and I talk about it in more detail in the section "Working with a kooky (and clever) little thing named QuickFill," later in this chapter.

6. **(Optional) Tag that transaction.**

 If, after reading about tags in Chapter 2, you decided to use tags and have turned this feature on, you can also enter a tag in the Tag field. Just to make this a bit clearer, suppose that you're using tags to segregate expenses by house because you actually own two homes: your principal residence and a cabin in the mountains. If you've set up two tags — *principal* and *cabin* — you record utilities expenses for your principal residence by entering **utilities** in the Category field and **principal** in the Tag field. You record utilities expenses for your cabin by entering **utilities** in the Category field and **cabin** in the Tag field.

7. **Enter the check amount.**

 Move the cursor to the Payment field, and type the check amount — **85.95** for this example. You don't have to type the dollar sign, but you do need to type the period to indicate the decimal place and cents.

8. **Click the Save button.**

 Click the Save button that appears in the transaction's row of the register. This option tells Quicken that you want to record the transaction in your register. Quicken beeps in acknowledgment, calculates the new account balance, and moves the cursor to the next slot (or row) in the register.

Figure 4-3 shows the cable television check recorded in the register. You can't see it in this black-and-white figure, but the $81.79 in the Balance field is in red after the $85.95 check is recorded. This red number indicates that you've overdrawn your account. I don't need to tell you what that means: overdraft charges.

Figure 4-3:
The Quicken register after recording the check to Movies Galore.

A neat little trick

You can expand and edit the list box of Check Number entries that Quicken displays. If you want to add some new entry to the Check Number drop-down list box, for example, do the following:

1. Click the Edit List button, which appears at the bottom of the Check Number drop-down list.

Quicken displays the Edit Num List dialog box.

2. Click the New button and then complete the dialog box that Quicken displays.

You can also remove any new Num entries you add by using the Edit Num List dialog box.

I won't spend any more time describing how this works, so if you want to figure it all out, just experiment. You can't hurt anything.

Changing a check you've entered

What if you need to change a check that you've already entered? Suppose that you make a terrible mistake, such as recording a $85.95 check as $89.55. Can you fix it? Sure. Just use the arrow keys or click the mouse to highlight the check transaction that you want to change. Use the Tab and Shift+Tab keys to move the cursor to the field you want to change. (You can also select the field by clicking in it with the mouse.) Then make your fix. Click the Enter button when you finish or press Enter on the keyboard.

Packing more checks into the register

Normally, Quicken displays a single row of information about each check that you enter. It also displays a single row of information about each of the other types of transactions you enter. The single-row approach is often pretty illegible, unfortunately. If you want to show more transaction information, click the Actions button (which shows a picture of a little gear and appears near the top-right corner of the register) and then choose the Two-Line Display command from the menu that Quicken displays. After you do, Quicken displays all the same register information (though arranged in slightly different order) in a double-line format (shown in Figure 4-4). To return to the single-line format, click the Actions button and choose the Two-Line Display command again.

Figure 4-4:
How the register looks with the Two-Line Display format.

Sorting transactions

If you click the Actions button, you notice that it also displays a bunch of commands in addition to the Two-Line Display command that I talk about in the preceding section. I talk about most of these commands elsewhere in this book, but let me mention one set of the commands here. If you choose the Sorting Options command, Quicken displays a submenu of commands that begin with *By.* These commands all work the same basic way. They let you reorganize the transactions shown in the register in some new way: by date, amount, check number, and so on.

Don't worry. I'm not going to waste your precious time by telling you (say) that the By Date command sorts transactions by their dates or that the By Category command sorts transactions by category. You knew that.

If you point to the column heading for the Payee field, the Payment field, or the Cleared Status field (labeled *Clr*), Quicken displays a pop-up command that you can use to re-sort the transactions in the register. These options are self-explanatory. The one that appears when you point to the Payee field is Sort by Payee, and the one that appears when you point to the Cleared Status field is Sort by Cleared. You get the picture.

Memorized payees

Quicken provides another feature — memorized payees — that's almost irrelevant to day-to-day Quicken use now that the QuickFill feature exists. But because you may hear about this tool, I briefly describe how it works.

A *memorized payee* is one that you've stored or that Quicken has stored in a special list. (To store the transaction, you select it in the register and choose Edit⇨Transaction⇨Memorize Payee.)

To later use or abuse a memorized transaction, choose Tools⇨Memorized Payee List to display

a list of previously memorized payees. When Quicken displays the list, select the payee you want to reuse and then click Use.

A list of memorized payees is a handy tool. But if you're feeling a little overwhelmed, don't spin your wheels trying to get up to speed on this feature. QuickFill almost always does the job for you because — get this — it automatically grabs memorized payees from the list.

Working with a kooky (and clever) little thing named QuickFill

Here's kind of a funny quirk about Quicken: If Quicken can guess what you're typing in a field, it fills in the rest of the field for you. Earlier in this chapter, I mention how this QuickFill feature works when you type category names. But it gets even better than that.

The second time you use a payee name, for example, Quicken knows that it's the second time. Quicken also figures, "Hey, some stuff from the last Movies Galore transaction will probably be the same for this transaction." When you type the first few letters of the payee name, Quicken supplies a payee name for you. After you press the Tab key to accept the name, Quicken uses the last transaction's information to fill in all the current transaction's fields.

This feature is a real time saver. Suppose that you did write a $85.95 check to Movies Galore for your August cable television bill. When you type **Movies Galore** to record September's cable television check, the amount will probably be the same. The complete payee name will certainly be the same, and the category will also be the same. So Quicken fills in all these fields, too.

QuickFill doesn't do everything for you, however. You still need to make sure that the date and check number are correct. If Quicken QuickFills a field with the wrong information, just replace the wrong information with the right information.

Recording Deposits

Recording a deposit works almost the same way as recording a check. The only difference is that you enter the deposit amount in the Deposit field rather than enter the check amount in the Payment field.

Entering a deposit into the register

Suppose that you receive $100 as a birthday gift from your elderly Aunt Enid and deposit it into your checking account. Here's how you record this deposit in the register:

1. **Enter the deposit date.**

 Move the cursor to the Date field of the next empty row of the register (if it isn't already there) and type the date. Use MM/DD format. You enter August 31, 2015, for example, as **8/31**. As with check dates, you have to enter the year only if the current year number, which Quicken retrieves from the little clock inside your computer, is wrong.

 You can adjust the date in a Date field in Quicken by using the + and – keys. The + key adds one day to the current date; the – key subtracts one day from the current date.

2. **Type the code** DEP **(for *deposit*) in the Check Number field.**

 Are you the meticulous type? Then go ahead and move the cursor to the Check Number field. Open the Num drop-down list box and select Deposit.

3. **Type the name of the person from whom you received the deposit.**

 In this case, move the cursor to the Payee field and type **Aunt Enid**. (I don't mean to sound presumptuous, but the next time Aunt Enid sends you birthday money, you can select her name in the Payee drop-down list box.)

4. **Enter the deposit amount.**

 Move the cursor to the Deposit field and type **100**. Don't type the dollar sign — or any other punctuation. (If Aunt Enid sweats money and sometimes passes out $1,000 gifts, for example, you record the deposit as **1000** — not 1,000 or $1,000.)

5. **(Optional) Enter a memo description.**

 Move the cursor to the Memo field and describe something, such as the reason for the deposit. Aunt Enid's money may be described as **birthday gift**. If you're a business depositing a customer's check, use this entry to identify the invoice the customer is paying.

6. Enter the category.

You know how this works by now. Move the cursor to the Category field. Open the Category drop-down list box, if necessary, and select the appropriate category. Alternatively, if you like living on the edge, try typing the category name. You might describe Aunt Enid's check as **Gift Received**.

To add a category, type a name in the Category field and move to another field. When Quicken doesn't recognize the category name, it asks you whether you want to add the category. Click Yes, and Quicken displays the Set Up Category dialog box. See Chapter 2 if you have questions about how this works.

7. (Optional) Enter a tag.

If you're tagging transactions because categories don't provide you enough detail about transactions, enter a tag in the Tag box. If you don't know what tags are and want to find out more, refer to the Chapter 2 discussion on using tags.

8. Click the Save button.

This command tells Quicken that you want to record the transaction in your register. Quicken beeps in protest but then adds the transaction.

Figure 4-5 shows the Checking register (in the Two-Line Display format) after you enter Aunt Enid's thoughtful gift. Your account is no longer overdrawn, so you have that going for you. Maybe before you go any further, you should call Aunt Enid to thank her.

Figure 4-5:
A Checking register as you record your first deposit.

See the ending balance given at the bottom in the register window? The Ending Balance shows the account balance after every register transaction. If you enter future-dated transactions, the register window shows both a *current balance* — the balance as of the current date — and an *ending balance,* which is the balance after all the transactions.

Quicken also includes a Paycheck Setup Wizard that you can use to describe the taxes withheld from your paycheck and categorize the deductions from your paycheck. That much said, you probably don't need to keep track of these amounts unless, for some reason, you want precise estimates of the income taxes you pay. Remember that your employer already does this accounting. Also remember that you must use the employer's data, which appears on your W-2 form — and not your Quicken data — when you prepare your U.S. taxes. If you do decide to use the Paycheck Wizard, click the Planning tab, the Tax Center button, and then the Add Paycheck button. When Quicken displays the Paycheck Setup dialog box, use its buttons and boxes to describe your payroll check and any deductions. Note that you may need to scroll down the Tax Center tab to see the Add Paycheck button. The button appears at the bottom of the tab.

Changing a deposit you've already entered

Big surprise here — changing a deposit works just like changing a check. First, use the arrow keys or click the mouse to select the deposit. Use the Tab and Shift+Tab keys to move the cursor to the field you want to change. Tab moves the cursor to the next field. Shift+Tab moves the cursor to the preceding field. (You can also select the field by clicking in it.) Then make your fix and click the Save button.

Recording Account Transfers

Account transfers occur when you move money from one account, such as your savings account, to another account, such as your checking account. But jeepers, why am I telling you this? If you have one of those combined savings and checking accounts, you probably do this sort of thing all the time.

Oh, now I remember why I brought this up: Quicken makes quick work of account transfers as long as you already have *both* accounts set up.

If you don't have the second account set up, you need to do that first. If you don't know how, flip to Chapter 2.

Entering an account transfer

Buckle up. I speed through the steps for recording an account transfer. For the most part, you record an account transfer the same way you record a check or deposit.

Suppose that you want to record the transfer of $10 from your checking account to your savings account. Maybe you want to set aside a little money to purchase a gift for your generous Aunt Enid — perhaps a Macklemore CD.

Say that you're working with your checking account and want to record a transfer to your account. Here's what you need to do:

1. **Enter the transfer date.**

 Move the cursor to the Date field. Then type the date that you move the money from one account to another.

2. **Flag the transaction as a transfer.**

 Move the cursor to the Check Number field. Open the drop-down list box and select the Transfer entry. Quicken abbreviates *transfer* as *TXFR*.

3. **(Optional) Enter a description of the transaction.**

 You don't have to do this, but you may want to use the Payee field to describe the transfer — for example, **Birthday**. You know how this works by now, don't you? You just move the cursor to the field. Then you pound away at the keyboard. Bang. Bang. Bang.

4. **Enter the transfer amount.**

 You enter amounts that you transfer out of an account in the Payment field, and you enter amounts that you transfer into an account in the Deposit field. So move the cursor to the right field (*right* as in *right and wrong,* not *right and left*) and then enter the transfer amount.

5. **(Optional) Enter a memo description.**

 Enter more information about the transaction (if you need to) in the Memo field. Perhaps a gift idea for Aunt Enid?

6. **Indicate the other account.**

 Move the cursor to the Category field, which has a modified name of Xfer Acct (standing for *Transfer Account*). When Quicken drops down a list box of accounts, select the other account. In Figure 4-6, I show the transfer as going to an account named Savings. I set up this account secretly, while you weren't watching. But note that the steps for setting up a second bank account parallel those for setting up a checking account. (See Chapter 2 for more information.)

7. **Click the Save button.**

 This command tells Quicken that you want to record the transfer transaction in your register.

 Figure 4-6 shows the Checking register after you transfer money from your checking account to your savings account so that you'll have money to purchase something nice for Aunt Enid's next birthday. (Seriously, think about the Macklemore CD idea. I'm sure your aunt will love rap.)

Figure 4-6:
The Checking register after you enter the transfer transaction.

Take a look at the Category field. Notice that Quicken uses brackets — [] — to identify the Category field entry as an account, not as an income or expense category.

Working with the other half of the transfer

Here's the cool thing about transfer transactions: Quicken automatically records the other half of the transfer for you. Figure 4-6 shows the $10 reduction in the checking account because of the transfer. Quicken uses this information to record a $10 increase in the savings account. Automatically. Biddabam. Biddaboom.

To see the other half of a transfer transaction, right-click the transfer transaction and choose the Go To Matching Transfer command on the More Actions menu. Quicken displays the other account in a new register window, shown in Figure 4-7.

Figure 4-7:
The other
half of the
transfer
transaction.

Changing a transfer you've already entered

Predictably, this activity works just like changing a check or a deposit:

1. **Select the transfer by using the arrow keys or by clicking the mouse.**

2. **Use the Tab and Shift+Tab keys to move the cursor to the field that you want to change.**

3. **Make your fix, click the Save button, and then go to lunch.**

Splitting Transactions

Here's a sort of Quicken riddle for you: Suppose that you have a check that pays more than one kind of expense. You trot down to the grocery store, for example, and pick up $10 worth of junk food and junk beverages (which you should categorize as a Groceries expense) and $10 worth of 10W-40 motor oil (which you should categorize as an Auto expense). How do you categorize a transaction like this? Well, I'll tell you. You use a *split category*.

Here's how a split category works: When you're ready to categorize the check, you click the Split button, and Quicken displays the Split Transaction window, shown in Figure 4-8. The Split button shows two arrows that look like a warning sign for a fork in the road.

Q Split Transaction ×

Split Transaction

Enter multiple categories to itemize this transaction; use the Memo field to record more details.

	Category	Tag	Memo	Amount
1.				
2.				
3.	Business Income	**Auto & Transport**		
4.	Business Expenses	Auto Insurance		
5.	Personal Income	Auto Payment		
6.	**Personal Expenses**	Car Wash		
7.	Rental Property Income			
8.	Rental Property Expenses	Gas & Fuel		
9.	Transfers	Parking		
10.	All Categories	Public Transportation		
11.		Registration		
12.				
13.		Service & Parts		
14.		Tolls		0.00
15.				0.00
16.		Add Category		0.00

Add Line

? | OK | Cancel

Figure 4-8:
The Split
Transaction
window.

Steps for splitting a check

Being a clever sort, you probably already know how the Split Transaction
window works. I go through the steps anyway. Suppose that you want to cat-
egorize a $20 check that includes $10 for groceries and $10 for motor oil.

To categorize a check in the Split Transaction window, do the following:

1. **Enter the first category name in the first Category field.**

 Move the cursor to the Category field (if it isn't already there). Activate
 the drop-down list box by pressing Alt+↓ arrow or by clicking the down
 arrow and then selecting the category name.

 (Despite what a dietitian may say, you can call the soda and candy
 Groceries.)

2. **(Optional) Tag the first categorized portion of the check.**

 If you're using tags to further classify your spending, move the cursor
 to the first Tag field and then type the tag. If you have no idea what I'm
 talking about here, either just forget I said anything or see the final para-
 graphs of Chapter 2.

3. **Enter a memo description for the first categorized portion of the check.**

Move the cursor to the first Memo field and then type whatever you want. (Maybe a description of the food you bought. Er, then again, maybe if you're buying real junk, you should just leave this blank.)

4. **Enter the amount spent for the first category.**

Move the cursor to the first Amount field and then type. . .well, the amount. If the first category is what you're calling Groceries, and you spent $10 on this, you type **10**.

5. **Repeat Steps 1–4 for each spending category.**

If you spent another $10 on motor oil, for example, move the cursor to the second Category field and enter the category and, optionally, the subcategory you use to summarize auto maintenance expenses. In Figure 4-9, for example, I use the category–subcategory combination Auto & Transport:Service & Parts. Optionally, tag the transaction. Optionally (again), move the cursor to the second Memo field and enter a memo description of the expenditure, such as **motor oil**. Move the cursor to the second Amount field and enter the amount of the expenditure, such as **10**.

Figure 4-9 shows a Split Transaction window that's complete. A split transaction can have up to 30 pieces. Use the scroll bar or PgUp and PgDn keys to scroll through the list of split amounts.

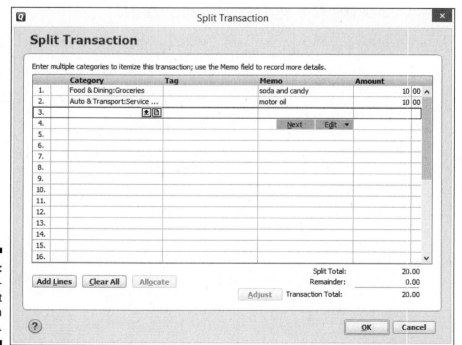

Figure 4-9:
The completed Split Transaction window.

6. **Verify that the Split Transaction window shows no uncategorized spending.**

 If you find extra spending — this shows up as the Remainder amount — either add the category you need or delete the split transaction line that's uncategorized. To delete a split transaction line, move the cursor to one of the fields in the line and choose Edit⇨Delete. You can also click the Adjust button to get rid of the Remainder amount — but in this case, Quicken adjusts the amount originally entered into the register so that it agrees with the details you've supplied in the Split Transaction window.

 If you want to insert a new line, move the selection cursor to the line above where you want to make your insertion and choose Edit⇨Insert. If you're fed up and want to start over from scratch, choose Edit⇨Clear All (which causes Quicken to erase all the split transaction lines).

7. **Click OK.**

 After you complete the Split Transaction window — that is, after you completely and correctly categorize all the little pieces of the transaction — click OK. Quicken closes the Split Transaction window. If you didn't enter an amount in the Payment column of the register before opening the Split Transaction window, Quicken displays a dialog box that asks whether the transaction is a payment or a deposit. You select an option button to make your choice known.

 To let you know that the transaction is one that you've split, the Category field shows --Split-- when you select the split transaction to show that you've split a transaction among categories or tags. Take a peek at Figure 4-10 to see for yourself.

Figure 4-10:
The Checking register. Can you find the boxes labeled Split?

8. **Click the Save button.**

 This command tells Quicken that you want to record the transaction in your register.

Editing and deleting split categories

You can delete or change any individual line of a split category. To do so, first select the transaction (to display the Split Transaction window) and then click the check-mark button, which appears in the register's Category field after you record the transaction. After Quicken dutifully displays the Split Transaction window, you can edit a field by selecting it and then typing over its contents. You can delete any line of the split transaction by choosing Edit⇨Delete. (If you want to delete all the lines of the split transaction so that you can start over, choose Clear All instead.)

If you want to unsplit the transaction so that you can assign it to a single category, you need to use a little trick: Click the X button that appears in the register's Category field after you record the transaction.

Splitting hairs

Quicken assumes that any transaction amount you enter in the register should agree with the total of the individual split transaction amounts entered in the Split Transaction window.

If you're not sure what the split transaction amount's total is, your best bet is to NOT — I repeat, *NOT* — enter the amount on the Transactions tab. Instead, enter the individual split transaction amounts in the Split Transaction window. When you leave the Split Transaction window, Quicken totals your individual split amounts and then prompts you to see whether the total is a payment or a deposit. Then it plugs this total into either the Payment or the Deposit field.

If you've already entered either a payment amount or a deposit amount, but you're not sure that the split transaction amounts agree with what you entered, you can tell Quicken to adjust the Payment or Deposit amount on the Transactions tab to whatever the individual split transaction amounts total. To do so, click the Split Transaction window's Adjust button. Quicken then adds the split transaction lines and plugs the total into the register. (This approach may best be called "I don't care if it's a round hole; I want to pound this square peg into it.")

By the way, Quicken shows any difference between the amount shown on the Transactions tab and the individual split transaction amounts. It shows this difference as the last split transaction line, so you can tell whether the individual splits agree with the payment or deposit amount shown in the register.

Sort of a voiding bug . . .

When you mark a transaction as void — you do this by selecting a transaction and choosing Edit⇨Transaction⇨Void Transaction(s) — Quicken does three things: It sticks VOID in the start of the Payee field, it marks the transaction as cleared, and it erases the amount in the Payment or Deposit field. So far, so good. But if you later fill in the Payment or Deposit field and don't pay attention to the warning from Quicken that you're editing a reconciled transaction, Quicken uses the payment or deposit amount that you enter to adjust the account balance — even though Quicken still shows the transaction as void. I keep thinking the folks at Intuit will fix this bug, but they haven't — at least, not yet. The bottom line is that you need to make sure that you don't edit transactions after you void them. Otherwise, you can all too easily foul up your account balance — perhaps even overdraw your account. I won't tell you about how I happened to learn this. . . .

Steps for splitting deposits and transfers

Wondering whether you can split deposits and transfers? Well, you can. The steps for doing so work just like the steps for splitting categories for a check transaction. The basic trick — if you can call it a trick — is to use the Split Transaction window to list all the category names and amounts.

One other point I should make here is that you can mix and match categories and transfers in the Split Transaction window. Some of the splits, for example, can be categories, and some can be transfer accounts. This type of transaction is common in a business setting. (See Chapter 15 for more information.)

Deleting and Voiding Transactions

You can delete and void register transactions by using the More Actions button's Delete and Void Transaction(s) commands. If you've looked at the More Actions button — it appears just below the selected transaction when you're entering data — you've probably already guessed as much. The More Actions button looks like a compass. Or something.

Using either command is a snap: Just highlight the transaction you want to delete or void by using the arrow keys or by clicking the mouse. Then click the More Actions button and choose the command. And that's that.

Use the Void Transaction(s) command any time you void a check. Quicken leaves voided transactions in the register but marks them as void and erases the Payment or Deposit amount. So by using the Void Transaction(s) command, you keep a record of voided, or canceled, transactions.

Use the Delete command if you want to remove the transaction from your register.

The Big Register Phenomenon

If you start entering a bunch of checks, deposits, and transfers into your registers, you'll soon find yourself with registers that contain hundreds — even thousands — of transactions. You can still work with one of these big registers by using the tools and techniques I talk about in the preceding paragraphs. Nevertheless, let me give you some more help for dealing with . . . (drumroll, please) . . . the big register phenomenon.

Moving through a big register

You can use the PgUp and PgDn keys to page up and down through your register a screenful of transactions at a time. Some people call this *scrolling*. You can call it whatever you want.

You can press Ctrl+Home to move to the first transaction in a register and Ctrl+End to move to the last transaction in a register.

You can also use the vertical scroll bar along the right edge of the Transactions tab. Click either above or below the square scroll-bar marker to page back and forth through the register. Or, if you have no qualms about dragging the mouse around, you can drag the scroll-bar marker up and down the scroll bar. If you drag the scroll-bar marker to scroll through the register, Quicken displays a pop-up box that shows the transaction date you've scrolled to.

Finding that darn transaction

Want to find a specific check, deposit, or transfer? No problem. The Find command provides a handy way for doing just that. Here's what you do:

1. **Choose Edit⇨Find or press Ctrl+F.**

 Quicken, with restrained but obvious enthusiasm, displays the Quicken Find dialog box (shown in Figure 4-11). You use this dialog box to describe, in as much detail as possible, the transaction you want to find.

Figure 4-11:
The Quicken
Find
dialog box.

2. **Specify which pieces, or fields, of the register transaction you want Quicken to search.**

 Click the down arrow to the right of the first Find box; then, in the drop-down list, select the field that Quicken should look at during the search: Amount, Cleared Status (the Clr field), Memo, Date, Check Number Category, Tag, or Payee. Or get truly crazy and pick the Any Fields list entry so that Quicken looks both high and low.

3. **Tell Quicken whether you're using a shotgun or a rifle.**

 (Metaphorically speaking, of course.) Specify how closely the text or value you're searching for must match the data stored in the register. To do so, open the second Find box and select the appropriate matching rule:

 - *Contains:* Select this rule if the field or fields you're searching just need to use a piece of text. If you enter **Aunt** in the Find text box and use this matching rule to search Payee fields, Quicken finds transactions that use the payee names *Aunt Enid, Aunt Enid and Uncle Joob, Uncle Harry and Aunt Edna,* and. . .well, you get the idea.

 - *Exact:* Select this rule if the field you're searching needs to exactly match your Find text-box entry. If you enter the Find text-box entry as **Aunt**, for example, and you're searching Payee fields, Quicken looks for transactions where the Payee field shows *Aunt* — nothing more and nothing less.

 - *Starts With:* Select this rule if the field you're searching for just needs to start with what you entered in the Find text box. For example, if you enter **Aunt** in the Find text box, and you're searching the Payee fields, Quicken looks for transactions where the

Payee field starts with the word *Aunt* — such as *Aunt Enid* or *Aunt Enid and Uncle Joob.* (Uncle Joob and Aunt Enid wouldn't cut the mustard in this case, though.)

- *Ends With:* Select this rule if the field you're searching for just needs to end with what you entered in the Find text box.

- *Greater:* Select this rule if the field you're searching for needs to hold a value that exceeds the number you entered in the Find text box. This makes sense, right? Like you're looking for checks you wrote for more than $100?

- *Greater or Equal:* Select this rule if the field you're searching for needs to hold a value that either exceeds or equals the number you entered in the Find text box.

- *Less:* Select this rule if the field you're searching for needs to hold a value that is less than the number you entered in the Find text box.

- *Less or Equal:* Select this rule if the field you're searching for needs to hold a value that is less than or equal to the number you entered in the Find text box.

4. **Enter the piece of text or number that identifies the transaction you want to locate.**

 Move the cursor to the third Find text box. Then type the text or number you want to find. By the way, the case of the text doesn't matter. If you type **aunt**, for example, Quicken finds *AUNT* or *Aunt.*

5. **Tell Quicken whether you want it to search forward or backward from the selected transaction.**

 Select the Search Backwards check box if you want to look backward starting from the selected transaction.

6. **Let the search begin.**

 You click either the Find or the Find All button to begin the search. If you click Find, Quicken looks through the register, and if it can find a transaction like you describe, it highlights the transaction.

 If you click Find All, Quicken looks through the register and builds a list of all the transactions that are like the one you describe. Then it displays the list in an expanded version of the Search Results window (shown in Figure 4-12). To edit a found transaction, select the transaction and click the Edit Transaction(s) button.

Quicken supplies another command that is similar to Find. The Edit menu's Find/Replace command lets you both locate and modify transactions that look like the one you describe. (To use the Find/Replace command, choose

Edit⇨Find/Replace.) For example, you may want to locate transactions show-ing Aunt Enid as the payee so that you can replace *Aunt* with *Great Aunt*. The Find/Replace command works in a similar fashion to the Find command except that you need to describe what you want to modify in the found transactions. After you complete the initial dialog box that Quicken displays when you choose the command, Quicken displays a window listing the trans-actions it has found. (This window looks like the one shown in Figure 4-13.) You mark — by clicking — the transactions you want to modify, describe the replacement information, and then click the Replace button.

Figure 4-12:
The Search
Results
window
with a trans-
action that
matches
the search
criteria.

You can use the Find/Replace command to find and replace categories, which is kind of a handy trick. For example, you may want to recategorize all your cable television payments as the Entertainment category (where earlier, you placed them in the Utilities category). To recategorize, use the Find/Replace command to search the Quicken register for the transactions you want to recategorize. Mark the transactions you're sure you want to recategorize. Then click the arrow button next to the With box so that Quicken displays a list of categories (see Figure 4-14) , select the category and click Replace All.

Figure 4-13:
The Find and Replace dialog box.

Figure 4-14:
The pop-up categories box you can use to recategorize.

Pop-Up Calendars and Calculators

Can I tell you just a couple more things? (If not, skip this section. If so, read on.) Quicken provides a pop-up calendar any time you move the selection cursor to a Date field. To get to the calendar, click the button that appears at the right end of the Date field. Quicken displays a calendar for the current month (shown in Figure 4-15). All you have to do is select the day you want as the date. (If you want to see a calendar for a different month, click the << and >> buttons.)

Figure 4-15:
The pop-up
calendar.

Quicken also provides a pop-up calculator any time you move the selection cursor to an Amount field. (See Figure 4-16.) To get to the calculator, click the button that appears at the right end of the Amount field.

Quicken displays a calculator like the one shown in Figure 4-16 when you choose the Tools⇨Calculator command. This baby works like a regular hand-held calculator. You just type the math you want to perform. Quicken displays the calculation result in the Amount field.

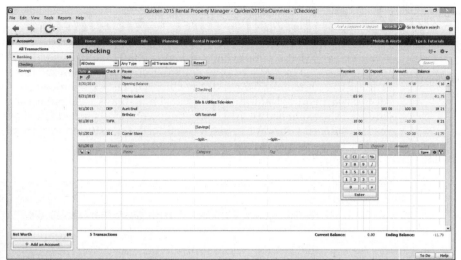

Figure 4-16:
The pop-up calculator.

Do the calculator keys make sense? Table 4-1 shows how they work.

Table 4-1 A Handyman's Guide to the Quicken Calculator Keys

Key Name	Operation
/ (slash)	Division
X	Multiplication
– (minus)	Subtraction
+ (plus)	Addition
. (period)	Indicates the decimal point
%	Indicates that the number you just typed is a percentage and should be converted to a decimal value
= (equal sign)	Calculates the amount and removes the pop-up calculator
<-	Removes, or clears, the last digit you entered
CE	Clears the last number entered into the calculator
C	Clears the Amount field
MC	Clears the calculator's memory
MR	Enters the number stored in the calculator's memory
MS	Stores the displayed value in the calculator's memory

 If you type a number in the Amount field and then type any one of the math operand keys (+, −, /, *), Quicken pops open the calculator to continue the calculation. You don't have to click the calculator button first.

Attaching Flags, Notes, and Images

Quicken provides a couple of handy though easy-to-miss buttons inside the register window just below the Date field: a Flag button and an Attach button. If you wouldn't mind, take a minute to see whether you can find these babies. The Flag button shows a little flag. The Attach button shows a picture of a paper clip.

The Flag button, if clicked, displays the Transaction Notes and Flags dialog box, which lets you append a note to a transaction; tell Quicken you want to flag the transaction in your register (by making the flag appear in a different color); and, just possibly, command Quicken to display an alert message about the transaction on some specified future date.

When you click the Attach button, Quicken displays the Transaction Attachments dialog box, which you can use to attach an image of the check or some document to the transaction. You can attach images from a variety of sources, including files, scanned images, or the Clipboard.

Chapter 5

Printing 101

. .

In This Chapter

▶ Printing a check

▶ Recovering from a mistake after you've printed the check

▶ Printing a register

. .

I bet you can't guess what this chapter describes. Gee, you guessed it — how to print checks and reports.

Printing Checks

Printing checks in Quicken is. . .well, quick. All you basically need to do is enter the information you want to print on the check form and the number you want Quicken to use to identify the check. Sounds simple enough, doesn't it? It is, as you can read in the steps that follow.

To enter the information on a check form, follow these steps:

1. **Display the Write Checks window.**

 You can display the Write Checks window in a bunch of ways. For example, you can choose the Tools⇨Write and Print Checks command. And when the Spending tab displays an account register, you can also click the Actions button (the button in the top-right corner of the tab that shows a gear) and choose the Write Checks command. You can also use the command shortcut Ctrl+W. Figure 5-1 shows the Write Checks: Checking window.

2. **Select the account on which you want to write the check.**

 This step is very important! To select the account you want to use, open the Write Checks From drop-down list at the top of the window. (You can do this by clicking the arrow button that's just to the right of the box.) When Quicken displays the list of accounts, choose the one you want to use.

Figure 5-1:
The Write
Checks:
Checking
window.

3. **Enter the check date.**

 First, use the mouse or Tab key to move the cursor to the Date field. Then type the date that you're going to print the check (probably today's date). Remember to type the date in MM/DD/YYYY format; enter September 1, 2015, as **9/1/2015**. You don't need to enter the year if the year number that Quicken retrieves from your computer's internal system clock is correct. You can adjust the date by a day by using + and – on the numeric keypad. You can also click the button at the end of the Date field to display your friend the pop-up calendar.

4. **Enter the name of the person or business you're paying.**

 Move the cursor to the Pay to the Order Of field and type away. For example, to write a check to me, type **Steve Nelson**. (Feel free to do so, by the way. If you send me a check, I'll even cash it as a sort of public service.) If you've written a check to the payee before, when you start to type the name, Quicken recognizes it and fills in the rest for you.

5. **Enter the amount of the check.**

 Move the cursor to the $ text box and type the amount. (If you're sending a check to me, be sure to make the amount nominal — for sure, not more than $10 or $20. . . .) When you press the Tab key, the cursor moves down to the next field, and Quicken writes the amount in words on the line under the payee name and before the word `Dollars`.

6. **Enter the payee's address.**

 If you plan to mail the check in a window envelope, move the cursor to the Bill Pay Address field. (You can do this by clicking in the field.) Then enter the name and address of the person or business you're paying.

TIP

Here's a little address entry trick: You can copy the payee name from the Pay to the Order Of text box to the first line of the Bill Pay Address field. Select the payee name and press Ctrl+C. Then click the mouse in or select the first line of the address field and press Ctrl+V. Now fill in the rest of the address block, including the street number and name, city, state, and ZIP code. After you enter this, Quicken memorizes these address details for the next time you use this payee.

7. (Optional) Enter a memo description of the check.

Move the cursor to the Memo field and enter a description (such as an account number or an invoice number) of why you're sending your money to this person or business. Or if you're sending someone a check because you didn't have time to go out and buy a real gift, type **Happy Birthday** in the Memo field. It's the little things that make a difference.

8. Enter the category.

Move the cursor to the Category field and type the category name for the expense you're paying with the check. If you don't remember the category name, scroll down the category list to find the category. Figure 5-2 shows the completed window for a check payable to Movies Galore, the local cable TV company.

![Write Checks: Checking window]

Figure 5-2:
A completed check.

You can assign a check to more than a single category by using the Split Transaction window. Using the Split Transaction window with the Write Checks window works the same way as using the Split Transaction window with the Transactions tab. (I describe using the Split Transaction window

with the Transactions tab in Chapter 4.) Okay. So why do I bring this up? You use the Split Transaction window when a check pays more than one type of expense or is transferred to more than one account.

For example, if you're writing a check to pay your mortgage, with part of the check paying the actual mortgage and part of the check going into an escrow account for property taxes, you can use the Split Transaction window to describe the transaction's individual components. To split a check amount so that the amount is assigned to multiple spending categories, click the Split button (which looks like a sign for a fork in the road) or press Ctrl+S. Either way, Quicken displays the Split Transaction window for you to indicate the categories and categorized amounts that make up the check total. If you have questions about how split transactions work, see Chapter 4.

9. **Click the Record Check button.**

 Quicken records the check. It displays the current account balance and the ending account balance, and it even adds a Checks to Print total in the bottom of the window. If you're working with a monitor that supports a high screen resolution, you'll also see a Checks to Print window that lists all the nitty-gritty about the checks you have to print. Shoot, when you're finished with one check, Quicken even scrolls the completed check off the screen and replaces it with a new, blank check that you can use to pay your next bill. It doesn't get much better than this, does it?

What if you make a mistake entering a check?

Don't worry. If you haven't yet printed the check, fixing mistakes is easy. If you press the PgUp and PgDn keys with the Write Checks window displayed, Quicken pages you through the check transactions. That way, you can display any check that you wrote — but have not yet printed — in the Write Checks window. An even easier way, if you have a lot of checks, is to double-click the check in the list that appears below the check form. (Quicken adds a check to this list when you click the Record Check button.)

With the check redisplayed, you can fix the mistake in two ways:

- ✓ If you incorrectly entered some bit of check information, move the cursor to the field with the incorrect data and just type over the data.

- ✓ If you're really mad or frustrated, you can delete the entire check by clicking the Delete button. (I should 'fess up here and suggest that you delete the check if you accidentally entered a check to me, for example.) Then you can re-enter the check — only this time, correctly.

Don't use this method to delete a check that you've already printed. Instead, void it. To void a check that you've already printed, follow these steps:

1. **Go into the Spending tab.**

2. **To display the register, click the Accounts-bar hyperlink for the account.**

 The Accounts bar appears along the left edge of the Quicken program window.

3. **Find the check in the register, select the check, and void it by clicking the More Actions button and then choosing the drop-down list's Void Transaction(s) command.**

4. **Write something, such as** VOID, **in large letters across the face of the printed check.**

Printing a check you've entered

Printing checks is easy. Here's what you need to do:

1. **Load the checks into your printer.**

 You do so the same way you load any other paper into your printer. If you have questions about it, refer to your printer documentation. (Sorry I can't help more on this process, but with a million printers on the market, I can't guess which one you have.)

2. **Click the Print button at the bottom of the Write Checks window and then choose the Checks command on the menu Quicken displays (or choose File⇨Print Checks).**

 If you haven't yet saved the check, Quicken asks whether you want to save the check. Then Quicken displays the Select Checks to Print: Checking dialog box shown in Figure 5-3. At the top of the dialog box, Quicken shows how many checks you have to print and the total dollar amount for those checks.

Figure 5-3:
The Select
Checks
to Print:
Checking
dialog box.

3. **Enter the first check number.**

 Move the cursor to the First Check Number text box and type the number printed on the first check form you'll print. Figure 5-3 shows 1001, for example, so the first check form is numbered 1001. To quickly increase or decrease the check numbers, use + or – on the numeric keypad.

4. **Indicate which checks Quicken should print by selecting one of these options:**

 • *All Checks:* Select this option button if you want Quicken to print all the checks you've entered by using the Write Checks window, which is the usual case. (If you select this option, skip to Step 6.)

 • *Checks Dated Through:* Select this option button if you want to print all the checks through a certain date; then type that date in the text box. (If you select this option, skip to Step 6.)

 • *Selected Checks:* Select this option button if you want to pick and choose which checks to print.

5. If you want to select which checks to print, click the Choose button.

Quicken, with some annoyance, displays the Select Checks to Print window, shown in Figure 5-4. Initially, Quicken marks all the checks dated on or earlier than the current date by placing a check mark in the Print column. If you don't want to print a check, either leave the Print field for that check clear (deselected) or click in the field to remove the check mark. When only the checks you want to print are marked to be printed, click Done to continue with this crazy little thing called check printing. Quicken, happy with your progress, redisplays the Select Checks to Print: Checking dialog box (refer to Figure 5-3).

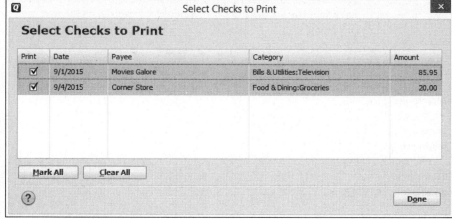

Figure 5-4:
The Select Checks to Print window.

6. Indicate which Quicken check form you're using.

Move the cursor to the Check Style drop-down list box; click the arrow so that the list drops down; and then select the check form you purchased: standard, voucher, or wallet checks.

7. Tell Quicken if you're printing a partial page.

If you're printing a partial page, use the Checks on First Page option buttons to indicate the number of check forms on the partial page. Select the Three option button if you have three checks, the Two option button if you have two checks, or the One option button if you have one check.

8. Indicate whether you want extra copies of the check form.

Type the number of copies you want in the Additional Copies text box. (This text box appears only if you're set up for the voucher check style.)

If you use Quicken for business to keep accounts payable files, make copies of checks to attach to the invoices that the checks pay. Then, if a vendor calls later, starts hassling you, and asks which check paid an invoice, you can easily check your accounts payable files, quickly answer that question, and basically cover your *derrière*.

9. Click OK and let the games begin.

A couple of quick tips: First, if you're unsure about how your checks feed through your printer, you can click the Print First Check button (see Figure 5-3) to tell Quicken to print only a single check. (This will let you confirm in another way that you've got things lined up correctly.) Second, if you're using a partial starting page of forms, your printer may prompt you to feed the first page of forms manually. When it finishes, Quicken asks whether it printed your checks correctly, as shown in Figure 5-5.

Figure 5-5:
The Did
Check(s)
Print OK?
dialog box.

Did Check(s) Print OK? ✕

Did Check(s) Print OK?

If checks 1001 through 1002 printed correctly, click
to continue. Otherwise, type the number of the first check
which printed incorrectly and then click OK.

First Incorrectly Printed Check: |

(?) OK

10. Do one of the following:

- If the checks printed correctly, click OK. You're done.

- If the checks didn't print correctly, enter the number of the first check that printed incorrectly and click OK; then repeat Steps 3–9.

11. Sign the printed checks.

Then — and I guess you probably don't need my help here — put the checks in the mail.

What if you discover a mistake after you print the check?

This problem isn't as big as you may think.

If you've already mailed the check, you can't do a whole lot. You can try to get the check back (if the person you paid hasn't cashed it) and replace it with the correct check. (Good luck on this one.)

If the person has cashed the check, you can't get the check back. If you overpaid the person by writing the check for too much, you need to get the person to pay you the overpayment amount. If you underpaid the person, you need to write another check for the amount of the underpayment.

If you printed the check but haven't mailed it, void the printed check. First, write **VOID** in large letters — in ink — across the face of the check form. (Use a ballpoint pen if you're using multipart forms so that the second and third parts also show as VOID.) Second, click the Register tab, highlight the check, click the More Actions button, and then choose the Void Transaction command. (This option marks the check as one that has been voided in the system so that Quicken doesn't use the voided check in calculating your account balance.)

A few words about check printing

Check printing is kind of complicated at first, isn't it?

For the record, I'm with you on this one. But you'll find that printing checks does get easier after the first few times.

Pretty soon, you'll be running instead of walking through the steps. Pretty soon, you'll just skate around things like check-form alignment problems. Pretty soon, you'll know all this stuff and never have to read *pretty soon* again.

Oh where oh where do the unprinted checks go?

The register stores *unprinted checks* — those you've entered by using the Write Checks: Checking window but haven't yet printed. To identify them as unprinted checks, Quicken sets their check numbers as Print. After you tell Quicken to print the unprinted checks, Quicken prints the checks in your register that have **Print** in the check number field and replaces the word *Print* with the actual check number.

This information is of little practical value in most instances, but it results in several interesting possibilities. For example, you can enter the checks you want to print directly in the register; all you need to do is enter the check number as **Print**. (Notice that you can't enter an address anywhere in the register, so this process isn't practical if you enter addresses that will be printed on your checks.) You also can cause a check you've printed once to print again by changing its check number from, say, **007** to **Print**. I can't think of many good reasons why you would want to change a check number. The only one I can think of is that you accidentally printed a check on plain paper and want to reprint it on a real check form.

Printing a Check Register

You can print a check register or a register for any other account. To print a register, follow these magic steps:

1. **Display the register by clicking the Accounts-bar hyperlink for the account.**

2. **Choose the File⇨Print [account name] command.**

 The File menu command you choose, by the way, names your account. If the account you displayed in Step 1 is named Checking, for example, the File menu command is Print Checking. After you choose the File menu command, of course, Quicken displays the Print Register dialog box, shown in Figure 5-6.

Figure 5-6:
The Print
Register
dialog box.

3. **(Optional) Customize the printed register.**

 You can use the Print Register dialog box to give the printed register a title (just enter something in the Printed Title box) and to specify the range of transactions. If you select the Print Split Transactions check box, Quicken prints the details of split transaction data.

4. **Print the register.**

 Click the Print Register dialog box's Print button. Quicken displays the Print dialog box, shown in Figure 5-7. You don't have to fool around with this dialog box. If you want to print a register pronto, just click OK. Then again, if you're the sort of person who likes to fool around with this kind of stuff, carry on with the rest of these steps.

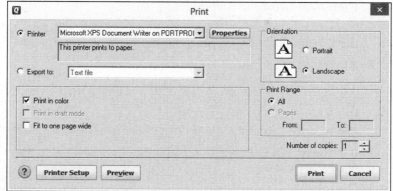

Figure 5-7:
The Print
dialog box.

5. (Optional) Export the report to disk if you want.

To print the report to disk as a text file, choose one of the following options from the Export To drop-down list:

- *Text File* if you want to create a text file, such as when you want to import the register into a word-processing program.

- *Tab-Delimited (Excel Compatible) Disk File,* such as when you want to import the register into a spreadsheet or database program. (Oooh . . . fancy. . . .)

- PRN *(123-compatible) Disk File,* such as when you want to import the register into any spreadsheet program that will open 1-2-3 files (which, basically, means any spreadsheet program, including Microsoft Excel). Lotus 123, by the way, was basically the first, super-popular spreadsheet program and widely used two decades ago.

If you indicate that you want a disk file, after you click the Export To button to start the ol' exporting process, Quicken displays the Create Disk File dialog box (not shown). This dialog box asks for the filename that Quicken should create as part of printing the file to disk and asks where you want to store the file. Just enter the filename you want in — you guessed it — the File Name text box. (Use a valid filename, of course.) Use the Save In text box to indicate where you want to store the file. And what do you do with the disk file? You're on your own here. . . .

6. (Optional) Tell Quicken which pages to print.

Use the Print Range option buttons and text boxes to limit the pages Quicken prints (refer to Figure 5-7). How? Select the Pages option button and then type the range of page numbers you want to print. That's simple enough, right?

7. **(Optional) Color your world.**

 If you have a color printer and want to print your register in color, select the Print in Color check box in the Print dialog box (refer to Figure 5-7).

8. **(Optional) Trade speed for quality.**

 You can select the Print in Draft Mode check box to tell Quicken it should print faster and spend less time worrying about the quality of the printing job (refer to Figure 5-7). In other words, you can use this check box to trade print quality for print speed. Life is full of trade-offs, isn't it?

9. **(Optional) Tell Quicken to scrunch the information so that it fits across the page.**

 Click the Fit to One Page Wide check box to tell Quicken that you want its register information to fit across the width of the page (refer to Figure 5-7).

10. **Click OK.**

 Quicken finally prints the register. I'm not going to show a printed copy of the register here. All it is, really, is just a printed copy of the same account detail information you see on the Transactions tab.

Should you save a printed copy of your register?

Here's a question for you: Should you save a printed copy of your register? I don't know. The case for printing a copy of your register and then having it handy in case...well, just in case is this: If your computer goes haywire and you need to re-enter your transactions, or if you need a hard-copy record of your transactions and for some reason don't have access to Quicken, having a printed register will make things much easier for you. You know what, though? I think that most people, if they religiously back up their Quicken data files (something I describe in Chapter 9), don't really need to print copies of their registers.

Now, I should say that if you're someone who likes to keep meticulous records of your income and spending, and you always double-check to make sure that you haven't left the iron on or even plugged in whenever you leave your house, you could print a copy of the register. And what I would suggest is that you print a copy of the register at the end of the year and then file this report away with your tax return.

By the way, I've been using Quicken since 1988 and have never needed a printed copy of my register. I've made frequent use of other reports. But never have I needed a hard, paper copy of my register. Any time I have had a question, I've simply looked through the online version of my current register or archived files from previous years.

Chapter 6

Online and In Charge

. .

In This Chapter

▶ Defining Online Account Access and Online Bill Payment

▶ Paying bills with Online Bill Payment

▶ Transferring money and downloading statements with Online Account Access

. .

*M*ost banks now offer some form of electronic banking service. And some banks even provide a pretty impressive variety of online services to the general consumer (you and me). This chapter briefly covers the Online Account Access and Online Bill Payment features that Quicken comes with so you can fully exploit the power of online banking.

What Are Online Account Access and Online Bill Payment?

I'm going to start with the basics — a definition of these two services.

Online services allow you to connect your computer to your bank's computer electronically through your Internet connection. You may think that doing so sounds scary, but Online Account Access and Online Bill Payment provide some very neat benefits:

✔ With **Online Bill Payment,** you can tell your bank or (in a pinch) the Intuit online financial services unit to make payments to specific individuals or businesses. In other words, rather than providing all this information in the usual way (on checks), you send the same information — the payees' names, their addresses, the amounts, and so on — and then the bank writes the checks. You can tell the bank to make automatic

recurring payments for bills that you pay on a regular basis, such as a rent or mortgage payment. You can use Online Bill Payment at any bank.

✓ With **Online Account Access,** you can get transaction information — such as information about which checks and deposits cleared your account and what bank service fees you've been charged — from the bank's computer. You can also transfer money between accounts — such as from your savings account to your checking account and from your checking account to your credit card account (to pay a credit card bill). To use Quicken for Online Account Access, you must make sure that your bank supports the Quicken Online Account Access service.

Wise Whys and Wherefores

Neither Online Account Access nor Online Bill Payment is difficult to use. And despite the nightmares that people with delusional paranoia may develop about electronic banking, the service is safe, secure, and very solid. Nevertheless, before you, too, jump onto the Online Account Access and Online Bill Payment bandwagon, you should probably consider these points:

✓ As I note in the preceding section, if you want to use the Online Account Access feature, your bank must be part of the Quicken Online Account Access program. (See the next section for details on how to find out whether your bank qualifies.)

✓ To sign up for and use Online Account Access or Online Bill Payment services, you need an Internet connection.

✓ You should be fairly comfortable with Quicken, especially with account transactions and transferring money between accounts. (Therefore, if you're new to Quicken, you should at least record a handful of checks, make some deposits, and reconcile your account before venturing into Online Account Access. This ramping up of your Quicken skills should take. . .oh, I don't know, about two weeks.)

✓ Make sure that your records are completely up to date and reconciled with the last statements you received from the bank.

This stuff usually ain't free. I can't tell you how much these two services will cost because your bank sets the charges. A good guess is $10 to $20 per month — and that adds up over the course of a year. But in choosing to use Online Account Access or Online Bill Payment, do consider all the hidden costs of the normal way of banking and paying bills. Gasoline, time, and postage can all add up, and these almost-hidden costs may make the costs of the

online services appear more reasonable. (Besides, you won't have to deal with all that nasty glue on your tongue from licking envelopes.)

My personal experience with online banking goes like this: The online banking stuff is great for any bank account you use a lot. But for those accounts with very low activity, the service (at least at the banks I use) is just too darn expensive.

Banking with Online Account Access and Online Bill Payment

To begin using either the Online Account Access or the Online Bill Payment service, you have to sign up. If you want to use Online Account Access, you sign up with your bank. Just visit your bank's website or call your local branch and ask someone whether the bank supports Online Account Access with Quicken. (If your bank doesn't support Online Account Access, you can still sign up with Intuit for Online Bill Payment; choose Tools⇨Quicken Bill Pay⇨Learn About Quicken Bill Pay for details.) Then do whatever the folks at the bank tell you to do to sign up. You'll probably have to fill out an application, agree to pay some extra fees, and then wait a few days for a customer identification number and a PIN (personal identification number).

After the bank does its preparation and sends you its welcome letter, you can set up Quicken for Online Account Access. To set up Quicken to use Online Account Access or Online Bill Payment services, display the account for which you want to activate online services. You can do this, for example, by following these steps:

1. **Click the account's hyperlink on the Accounts bar.**

2. **Tell Quicken you want to set up online banking or bill payment.**

 Click the Actions button and choose the Set Up Online command, shown in Figure 6-1. Quicken begins asking for information about the account (such as the name of the bank), and it may display an Account Setup dialog box that asks which version of your bank's online banking service you're already set up to use. You answer the questions Quicken asks. Then you click Next.

Figure 6-1:
Choose
the Set
Up Onlne
command
for initiating
online
banking.

3. **Identify yourself.**

When Quicken displays the Quicken Account Setup dialog box that asks for your login information, supply your customer identification number and PIN.

Let me say a couple more quick things about setting up Online Account Access or Online Bill Payment. Your bank or the Quicken folks may, as part of the application process, send you a letter asking for more information, a canceled check, or a signature. (If they do, of course, be sure to respond.)

Using Online Account Access and Online Bill Payment is extremely easy. You pay bills in pretty much the usual manner. You make account transfers in the same manner. And then you reconcile transactions with a mouse click.

Finding an online bank — online

You can determine which banks support Online Account Access by using your Internet connection. To do so, open your web browser and then enter the following web address in the browser's address bar:

```
https://quickenonline.intuit.com/quickenweb/external/fi-select.jsf
```

Enter the first part of the bank's name in the text box provided. You can enter a partial name to get a list of potential matches.

Honest Steve's evaluation of online services

I hate making financial record keeping more complicated. I like things simple. But all that said, I think Online Bill Payment and (in particular) Online Account Access are slick.

If you're using Quicken to keep your financial records, you get to pay your bills and reconcile your bank accounts for basically no extra work. Well, okay, you have to click your mouse an extra time. And initially, you need to provide addresses and account numbers for your payees (which takes about five minutes). So you do have to do a little extra work at the beginning. But Online Account Access saves you time and hassle when it comes to bill paying and banking.

The only catch — and this is a big one for some Quicken users — is that to use Online Account Access, your bank needs to have its act together. (Note that if your bank doesn't support Online Account Access with Quicken, you can still use Online Bill Payment by signing up for online payment with Intuit, as detailed at `http://quicken.intuit.com`.)

Now, all that said, I want to close with two caveats. Here's the first one: Online Account Access

isn't worth it if it means you end up banking at some poorly run bank. I, er, well, yeah, you see, I've been there. And it isn't pretty. To make a long, sorry story short, a long time ago, I had the experience of moving my banking from a well-run bank that didn't have Online Account Access to a poorly managed bank that did. Online Account Access is not — I repeat, is not — such a cool tool that you'll be happy banking at First National Idiots.

And now a second caveat: I have to tell you that making online payments isn't, in my experience, as reliable as writing a regular check and then sending that check through the mail. I don't know why this is. But it's been my experience that online payments more frequently get lost, and they sometimes get delayed. I've been using online banking and bill payment for maybe a dozen years now, and a time or two a year, people or businesses call and say, "Dude, we never got your payment" or, "Dude, we got your check late — you owe us a late fee." By comparison, my experience is that the U.S. Postal Service almost never loses my mailed payments.

Paying bills

You have three ways to record online payments. If you're comfortable using the Write Checks window, you write a check in the usual way. You enter the payee name, an amount, probably a category, and so on. Just make sure that you select the Online Payment check box. The Online Payment check box appears in the lower-right corner of the onscreen check form after you set up online banking for the account.

If you have questions about how the Write Checks window works, Chapter 5 shows you — among other things — how to use the Write Checks window

to describe checks you want to print. You use the same basic procedure to describe online payments that you want to make.

If you're more comfortable using the register to record payments, you can make online payments with that, too. In the Num column, just specify the payment number as **Send**.

If you have questions about how the register works, you may want to read Chapter 4. Chapter 4 describes — in some detail, I might add — how the Quicken register works.

By the way, the first time you make an online payment to someone, Quicken asks for some information in the Set Up Online Payee dialog box: where the person lives or where the business is located, and what account number Quicken can use to identify you or your business to the person or business you pay. You can also describe online payees by choosing Tools⇨Online Payee List, which displays a list of online payees. Then click the New button, which displays the Set Up Online Payee dialog box.

After you record a payment, you send it to the bank. To do so, choose the Tools⇨One Step Update command.

Quicken connects, through the Internet, to your bank's computer. As part of making this connection, you need to provide a PIN. When Quicken finishes sending your payment instructions to your bank, it displays a summary that basically says you've connected to the bank's computer and sent it some payment instructions. At this point, you're done.

Note: The first time that you use Online Account Access, Quicken asks you to change your PIN.

Note: You can have Quicken update your account information regularly. To do this, choose the Tools⇨Schedule Updates command and follow the onscreen instructions.

I need to make an important point here: You must send your payment instructions to the bank several days in advance of the time the bill needs to be paid. For obvious reasons, the bank needs a day or two to process the bill. And then the check very possibly has to go through the U.S. Postal Service. (I say "possibly" in the preceding sentence because some of your payments get made electronically and then some get turned into paper checks that get mailed.)

Are you still with me?

Okay, I'm going to take a little breather here — just to make sure that you understand what's going on. When you boil everything down to its essence, online payments are really just payment instructions you send to your bank. And when you make an online transfer, you're effectively just calling the bank and saying, "Please transfer money from one account to that other account."

This makes sense, right? You're really just giving instructions to the bank. And then the bank (actually, the bank's computer) goes off and does whatever you've told it to do. It's pretty simple.

Is Online Account Access anything to get all excited about? Is it really as slick as some people think? I think so. Sure, it's not always cheap. But after you get going, you get away from that business of finding your checkbook, signing checks, finding stamps, and on occasion running down to the post office to drop off some overdue bill.

Transferring money between accounts

As you may expect, you record Online Account Access transfers the same way that you record regular transfers — or at least in almost the same way. For online transfers, you can use the register in the normal way, but you need to specify that the transaction is an online transfer. You do this by activating the Num drop-down list box and selecting the Online Transfer entry.

If you have a credit card with a bank that supports Online Account Access, and if you also set up the credit card for Online Account Access, you can pay your credit card bill by transferring money from a bank account to your credit card account. You probably already thought of this if you have a credit card account. But I thought I'd mention it anyway. (For more information about credit card accounts, see Chapter 11.)

Updating your Quicken accounts

One major advantage of Online Account Access is that you can get the most up-to-date information regarding your accounts. Let me explain: When you use the Tools menu's One Step Update or Schedule Updates command, your bank automatically sends current transactions to your computer. If Quicken can match the bank's records with your records, no problem. Everything is fine.

If Quicken can't match the bank records with your records, however, it lists the mystery transactions on the Downloaded Transactions tab of the account register window. Then you can examine them before they go into your records. You can add downloaded transactions from the bank's list to your register by clicking the transaction and then clicking the Add to Register button.

By regularly downloading transactions into your online accounts and matching transactions between your Quicken records and the bank's records, you make reconciling your bank accounts a snap. In effect, by downloading and matching transactions, you get information about checks and debit card transactions that you've forgotten to record much earlier (because you don't have to wait until the end of the month). Note, however, that you should still reconcile your account n the usual way (described in Chapter 8).

Chapter 7

Reports, Charts, and Other Cool Tools

*Q*uicken enables you to summarize, slice, and dice register and account information in a variety of ways. This chapter describes how to use reports and produce graphs easily. This stuff is much easier to understand if you know how to print a transaction list first (a trick I describe at the end of Chapter 5).

Creating and Printing Reports

After you know how to print checks and transaction lists, all other printing in Quicken is easy, easy, easy.

Printing the facts, and nothing but the facts

The transactions you enter in the transaction-list window or a transaction form and the checks you enter in the Write Checks window determine the information in a report. To print a report, just choose the Reports menu and tell Quicken which report you want to print.

Quicken produces a bunch of reports. To make sense of what may otherwise become mass confusion, Quicken arranges all its reports into groups: Banking, Comparison, Investing (available when you've set up investment accounts), Net Worth & Balances (if you've set up any loans or credit card accounts), Spending, Tax, Rental Property (if you're using Quicken Rental Property Manager), and Business (if you're using Quicken Home & Business).

To see the reports in one of these groups, click the Reports command and then choose the report group from the Reports menu. As you may know, those little triangles to the right of menu commands tell you that another menu follows.

Figure 7-1 shows the Banking group of reports. Pretty exciting stuff so far, don't you think?

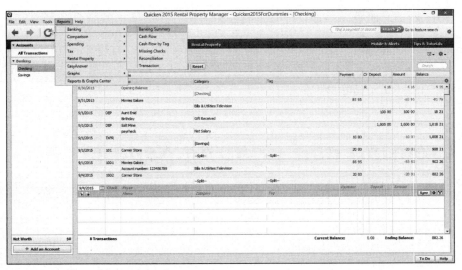

Figure 7-1:
The Banking group of reports.

To create a Cash Flow report (or any other report, for that matter) on the fly, choose the report from the appropriate menu. To create the Cash Flow report, for example, choose the Reports➪Banking➪Cash Flow command.

Quicken creates the report, placing it in a newly opened window. Figure 7-2 shows the Cash Flow report. After you create a report, you can change the report date or date range by using the text boxes at the top of the report.

Figure 7-2:
The Cash
Flow report.

To find out what type of information a report includes before you create the report or to preview a report, choose Reports⇨Reports & Graphs Center. This command displays the Reports and Graphs window, shown in Figure 7-3. Select a report group by clicking a topic on the left side and then selecting the report with the report group that you want to create. (In Figure 7-3, the Spending report group is selected and therefore shown. Within the Spending report group, the Spending by Category report is selected and therefore shown.)

You can change the report date or date range by using the text box(es) provided. Click the Show Report button to create the report. If you don't enter a new range of dates, Quicken assumes that you want to include transactions from the start of the current calendar year through the present date.

Reports that show account balances — such as the Account Balances report, the Net Worth report, the Balance Sheet report, and the Portfolio Value report — don't need a range of dates because these reports show account balances as of a specific date. In these cases, if you don't enter a date, Quicken assumes that you want account balances for the current system date from your computer's internal clock.

You can't see the entire onscreen version of a report unless your report is very small (or your screen is monstrously large). Press the PgUp and PgDn keys to scroll up and down, and press Tab and Shift+Tab to move right and left. If you're a mouse lover, you can click and drag various pieces of the scroll bars.

Figure 7-3:
The Reports
and Graphs
window.

To print the report Quicken shows, follow these steps:

1. Click the Print button.

Quicken displays the Print dialog box (see Figure 7-4).

Figure 7-4:
The Print
dialog box.

2. **To accept the given specifications — which are almost always fine — just click Print.**

 You'll never guess what happens next: Quicken prints the report!

3. **(Optional) To modify the default printing suggestions, use the option buttons and text boxes in the Print dialog box to mix it up a bit and then click Print:**

 • *Print To:* The Print To option buttons let you tell Quicken where it should send the report it produces: to the printer or to a disk file. If you choose to print it to a file, Quicken displays another dialog box, which you use to specify where the print file should be located and what the print file should be named. (I describe how this print-to-file option works in Chapter 5, so I won't repeat the discussion here. If you want the scoop, refer to the section about printing a check register.)

 • *Print Range:* Printing a long report? Consider using the Print Range option buttons and text box to specify that you want to print only a specified range of pages. As you might guess (if you're a clever person), select the Pages option button and then specify the individual pages (separating pages with commas) or the range of pages (separating the start and end page range with a hyphen). The following example page-range specification says, "Hey, Quicken, print pages 1, 4, and 5 and — oh, shoot, I don't know; maybe the page range 34 through 41 as well." For this, you would type the following:

 1, 4, 5, 34–41

 • *Copies:* As you've probably guessed, use the Number of Copies text box to tell Quicken to print multiple copies of a report.

 • *Page Scaling:* For some reports — although not all — you can use the Page Scaling option buttons and text boxes to tell Quicken that it should try to squish the report onto a smaller number of pages. Ever the thoughtful software program, Quicken provides two squishing methods. You can select the Page Scaling Adjust To option button and then enter a squishing percentage. Or you can select the Page Scaling Fit To option button and then specify the report size as a certain number of pages wide by a certain number of pages tall.

 • *Print What:* The Print What check boxes let you flip-flop between printing a graph and printing a report of the Quicken data you've said you want to see a report on. The easiest way to see what this report option does is to select and deselect.

 • *Orientation:* The Orientation option buttons allow you to specify how Quicken prints a report on pages: vertically (Portrait) or horizontally (Landscape). Again, if you're confused about this option, experiment by selecting the different buttons.

Note: When you click a Print dialog box button or enter some value in a Print dialog box field, Quicken redraws the Preview window (on the right) to show you what the report looks like with your new specification.

- *Ink Color:* If you use a color printer, Quicken provides Ink Color option buttons, which let you choose whether you want to print the report in expensive colored ink, in cheap black ink, or in gray-scale so that you can go all *film noir* about your finances.

- *Fonts:* The two Change Font buttons let you customize the look of your report by changing the font settings (point size, font, style, and so on) of the text used for your report's header text and body text. I feel kind of like a broken record saying this, but dude, seriously — the way to most easily figure out what these options do is simply to experiment. You can't foul up or corrupt your Quicken data by fiddle-faddling with the Print dialog box settings. And this is true even if you do something truly visually outrageous.

- *Adjust Margins:* Click the Adjust Margins button (upper right) to add margin-setting boxes to the Preview area in the Print dialog box. After Quicken adds these margin-setting boxes, you can change the printed report's margins by changing the margin settings.

Reviewing standard reports

Tables 7-1 through 7-8 describe the Quicken reports by group. Some of these babies won't make sense unless you understand how to collect the information that goes into the report, as I describe in Chapters 13, 14, 15, and 16. Also, I should tell you that some of these report groups won't be visible unless you've got the small-business or rental-property-manager version of Quicken.

Table 7-1	Quicken Banking Reports
Report	*Description*
Banking Summary	Summarizes spending totals by category.
Cash Flow	Summarizes the money that flows into and out of an account by income and expense categories and by transfers. Cash is king, dude, so this report includes only those transactions that you record in your bank, cash, and credit card accounts.
Cash Flow by Tag	Summarizes the money that flows into and out of an account not only by income and expense categories and by transfers, but — get this — also by tags. Perfect for the active real estate investor.

Report	Description
Missing Checks	Lists all the checks you've written and flags any gaps in the check-number sequence. This report helps you identify missing checks.
Reconciliation	Summarizes an account reconciliation that you've performed. You don't need this report, really, unless you have a clinical anxiety disorder and need to prove to yourself or your accountant that you really did reconcile your account.
Transaction	Lets you list transactions in multiple accounts chronologically.

Table 7-2	Quicken Comparison Reports
Report	**Description**
Current Spending vs. Average Spending by Category	Summarizes spending by category and compares category totals with the average category total over the past six months.
Current Spending vs. Average Spending by Payee	Summarizes spending by payee and compares payee totals with the average payee total over the past six months.
Cash Flow Comparison	Lets you compare category totals from two periods. You can use this report to compare January's activity with February's activity, for example. *Remember:* Because you're comparing two periods, you need to enter two transaction date ranges.
Income and Expense Comparison by Category	Summarizes spending totals by category for two time periods.
Income and Expense Comparison by Payee	Summarizes spending totals by payee for two time periods.
Profit and Loss Comparison	Compares one period's income and expense with a previous period's income and expense. Note that this report appears only after you unlock the Business Tools features of Quicken.

Table 7-3	Quicken Investing Reports
Report	**Description**
Capital Gains	Lists all the realized gains on individual investments you hold. (A *capital gain* occurs when an investment is worth more than you paid for it. When you sell the investment, you realize the gain.)
Investing Activity	Shows investment transactions grouped by activity.
Investment Asset Allocation	Shows investments by asset class.
Investment Income	Summarizes income and expense categories for the transactions you record in your investment accounts.
Investment Performance	A power-user report that calculates the internal rates of return delivered by each of the individual investments in your portfolio.
Investment Transactions	Lists recorded transactions for all your investment accounts.
Maturity Dates for Bonds and CDs	Produces a report that lists your bonds and certificates of deposit by maturity or redemption date.
Portfolio Value	Lists the current value of all securities in your investment accounts.
Portfolio Value & Cost Basis	Lists the current value and cost of all securities in your investment accounts.

Table 7-4	Quicken Net Worth & Balances Reports
Report	**Description**
Account Balances	Lists all accounts, their balances, and the difference between the sum of the asset accounts and the sum of the liabilities accounts, which the report identifies as your *net worth*.
Net Worth	Lists all accounts and their balances.

Table 7-5	Quicken Spending Reports
Report	**Description**
Itemized Categories	Lists transactions by category.
Itemized Payees	Lists transactions by payee.
Itemized Tags	Lists transactions by tags.
Spending by Category	Graphs spending and lists transactions by category.
Spending by Payee	Graphs spending and lists transactions by payee.
Current Spending vs. Average Spending by Category	Summarizes spending by category and compares category totals with the average category total over the past six months.
Current Spending vs. Average Spending by Payee	Summarizes spending by payee and compares payee totals with the average payee total over the past six months.
Income and Expense by Category	Summarizes income and spending by category.
Income and Expense by Payee	Summarizes income and spending by payee.
Current Budget	Summarizes income and expense categories and compares actual category totals for the year to budgeted category amounts. This report includes only transactions that you record in your bank, cash, and credit card accounts. (For this report to work, of course, you need to have a budget set up.)
Historical Budget	Summarizes income and expense categories and compares monthly actual category totals to monthly budgeted category amounts. This report includes only transactions that you record in your bank, cash, and credit card accounts. (For this report to work, you need to have a budget set up.)

Table 7-6	Quicken Tax Reports
Report	*Description*
Capital Gains	Lists all the realized gains on individual investments you hold. (A *capital gain* occurs when an investment is worth more than you paid for it. When you sell the investment, you realize the gain.)
Schedule A-Itemized Deductions	Lists and summarizes transactions that probably belong on your Schedule A tax form as itemized deductions: mortgage interest, property taxes, charitable contributions, and so on.
Schedule B-Interest and Dividends	Lists and summarizes interest and dividend income transactions that need to be reported on your Schedule B tax form.
Schedule D-Capital Gains and Losses	Lists and summarizes capital gain and loss transactions that need to be reported on your Schedule D tax form.
Tax Schedule	Lists all transactions you've entered as tax-related and subtotals them by line item.
Tax Summary	Lists all transactions you've described as falling into tax-related categories.

Table 7-7	Quicken Rental Property Reports
Report	*Description*
Cash Flow	Summarizes rental property cash income and cash expenses for a specified time period.
Cash Flow Comparison	Compares rental property category totals from two periods.
Schedule E-Supplemental Income and Loss	Displays profit and loss data by property, which is what you need to complete the Schedule E tax form.
Tax Schedule	Shows all the individual transactions for each rental property income amount and deduction amount reported on your Schedule E tax form.

Table 7-8	Quicken Business Reports
Report	**Description**
Accounts Payable	Summarizes the vendor bills you've recorded but not yet paid.
Accounts Receivable	Summarizes unpaid customer invoices.
Balance Sheet	Reports on account balances at a point in time. If you've set up all your business assets and liabilities in Quicken, this account-balances report works as a business balance sheet.
Cash Flow	Summarizes the money flowing into and out of business accounts by income and expense categories and by account transfers.
Cash Flow Comparison	Compares cash flows by category totals from two periods.
Missing Checks	Lists all the business checks you've written and flags any gaps in the check-number sequence.
Payroll	Summarizes transactions that use payroll in the category name.
Profit and Loss Comparison	Compares one period's income and expense with a previous period's income and expense.
Profit and Loss Statement	Summarizes a business's revenues and expenses for a particular period of time.
Project/Job by Business Tag	Shows income and expenses by business tag.
Project/Job by Project	Shows income and expenses by job or project.
Schedule C-Profit or Loss from Business	Displays profit and loss data by business, which is what you need to complete the Schedule C tax form(s).
Tax Schedule	Shows all the individual transactions for each business income amount and deduction amount reported on your Schedule C tax form.

Finding the report you want

Okay, if you've read or even skimmed the reports I describe in Tables 7-1 through 7-8, you're probably a little overwhelmed. Quicken produces a bunch of reports. How do you know which one provides the answers you want? What are you supposed to do? Sift your way through three dozen of these babies?

Fortunately, the answer is no. Quicken also provides something called EasyAnswer reports. In effect, EasyAnswer reports let you identify the question that you want a report to answer. After you identify the question, Quicken produces the appropriate report. Here's how this all works:

1. **Choose the Reports⇨EasyAnswer command.**

 The Reports and Graphs Center command appears on the Reports menu.

2. **Select the EasyAnswer report category in the Reports and Graphs window.**

3. **Indicate your question.**

 To tell Quicken what your question is, click one of the questions and then use the drop-down list boxes that accompany each question to further refine your question. The "Where did I spend my money during the period . . . ?" question, for example, lets you pick the period of time you're asking about: Last Year, Last Month, Current Year, Month to Date, and so on.

4. **Click Show Report.**

 Quicken produces a report that answers your questions. If you ask, "Where did I spend my money last year?", Quicken produces a Cash Flow report that summarizes the previous year's income and expenses by category.

Going to the printing dog-and-pony show

You can do some neat things with the reports you create. I won't spend a bunch of time talking about these things, but I do want to give you a quick rundown of some of the most valuable tricks.

Got a question about a number? Just zoom it

If you don't understand where a number in a report came from, point to it with the mouse. When you point to numbers, Quicken changes the mouse pointer to a magnifying glass marked with a + symbol. Double-click the mouse, and Quicken displays a list of all the transactions that make up that number.

This feature, known as QuickZoom, is extremely handy for understanding the figures that appear on your reports. If you printed a report that summarized spending by payee and then had a question about the payments made to Movies Galore, the cable company, you could double-click the Movies Galore number in the Spending by Payee report, for example. Quicken would display the report, like the one shown in Figure 7-5.

Ah, yes. Two cable TV bills. And you're not even buying the premium channels package. Yikes.

See a problem? Fix it

You can sometimes fix erroneous report data right in a report window. If you select a report transaction and Quicken enables the Edit button (upper-left corner of the report window), you can click that button to display an Edit menu. The menu lists editing commands you can use to delete the selected transaction or to change the category, payee, or memo information.

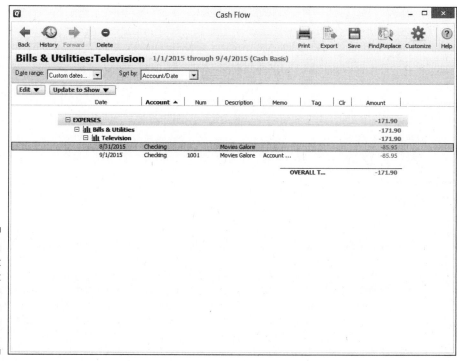

Figure 7-5:
The report you get after drilling down deep into the data.

Got a question about register transactions? Use a mini-report

If you're looking at the Quicken register, and you select either the Payee or Category field, Quicken adds a mini-report button to the end of the field. (The actual mini-report button looks like a small piece of paper.) If you click the mini-report button, Quicken creates a small report that summarizes the transactions falling into the same category or transactions with the same payee, as shown in Figure 7-6.

If you click the Show Report button, which appears in the mini-report window, Quicken creates a transaction report for the same information shown in the mini-report.

Figure 7-6: The mini-report report.

Sharing report data with spreadsheets

If you use Microsoft Excel, you can export the report to the spreadsheet program. Just click the Export This Report to One of the Formats button and then select the Report to Excel Compatible Format option. Quicken displays a dialog box that you use to name and locate a tab-delimited text file. (Any spreadsheet program worth its salt can open a tab-delimited text file.) You may need to use this feature if you want to use a spreadsheet to analyze the report data.

You can also copy the stuff that appears in a report window to the clipboard. Just click the Export button and choose the Copy Report to Clipboard command. Then, to use the copied report, start your spreadsheet (or other) program and choose Edit⇨Paste to paste the stuff from the clipboard. This process really isn't very hard, so go ahead and try it.

Sharing report data in PDF files

You can create a PDF version of the report. To do this, click the Export button and select the Export to PDF Format option. Quicken displays a dialog box that you use to name and locate the PDF file it will momentarily create. A *PDF file* of the report is just an electronic version of the report.

Editing and rearranging reports

You may notice that when Quicken displays the report window, it also displays rows of buttons, including Delete, Export, Back, Forward, History, Print, Save, Find/Replace, and Customize (refer to Figure 7-2 earlier in this chapter). Also appearing are the Date Range and the Subtotal By (or, context-depending, Column) drop-down list boxes. Earlier in the chapter, in "Printing the facts, and nothing but the facts," I talk about what the Date Range drop-down list box does. So in the interest of fair play, in this section, I briefly discuss what the other buttons do. (Not all these buttons are available in every report document window, and sometimes Quicken uses different names to refer to them. I don't know why, really. Maybe it's just to keep you guessing.)

You really don't need to worry about these other buttons. Read the discussion that follows only if you're feeling comfortable, relaxed, and truly mellow. Okay?

Back, Forward, and History

The Back and Forward buttons let you move back and forth between open report windows. The History button displays a list of the windows you've displayed; you can choose a previously displayed window by clicking it in the list.

Delete

The Delete button deletes the current report from the report list. You can use this button to, in effect, undo any changes you've made to a report and return to the default report specifications.

Export

I talk about this option in the "Sharing report data with spreadsheets" and "Sharing report data in PDF files" sections, earlier in this chapter. Look there if you have questions.

Sort

The Sort button displays a list of sorting options that you can use for arranging information in the report. Enough said.

Save

Say you get into this customization thing. If you do, you should know that you can save your customized reports by clicking the Save button. When you click Save, Quicken displays the Save Report dialog box, shown in Figure 7-7. Mostly, Quicken displays this dialog box so that you can give your creation a name. You also use this dialog box to indicate the financial activity center in which Quicken should save your report.

Figure 7-7:
The Save
Report
dialog box.

By the way, after you create a saved report, you can reproduce it by selecting the report from the My Saved Reports section of the Reports & Graphs Center.

Find/Replace

The Find/Replace button displays the Find and Replace dialog box (not shown), which you can use to locate or change transaction information, as I describe in Chapter 4.

Customize

The Customize button displays the Customize [Report] dialog box, where [Report] names the report you're fiddling with. The dialog box, which I discuss in more detail later in the chapter, lets you change the appearance and information presented in a report.

Date Range

I briefly mention the Date Range box earlier in this chapter, but here, I provide a slightly more detailed description. The Date Range text box displays a drop-down list that you can use to specify what time period you want listed in your report: the current month, last year, the current quarter to date, and so on.

Making your preferences known

In this chapter, I describe using the Reports-menu commands to produce reports. You can, however, also choose the Reports➪Reports & Graphs Center command to display a window that you use to see examples of and then produce reports.

I think the Reports menu approach is easiest, but the Reports & Graphs Center window provides one rather useful tool: the Preferences link (which appears in the top right of the window). When you click this link, Quicken displays a Preferences dialog box with a bunch of boxes and buttons that let you change the way

that Quicken initially generates reports. In other words, you use the Preferences link to specify the default report settings.

If I were a really great writer — the Stephen King of computer books, for example — I might be able to whip up a riveting discussion of how the Preferences link and dialog box work. I'm going to do both you and my publisher a favor, however, by making a suggestion: Just play with these option settings if you're interested. You'll find it more fun and a better learning experience.

Column subtotaling

The Column drop-down list box displays a list that enables you to tell Quicken you want to subtotal amounts by some criterion, as shown in Figure 7-8. Just select the criterion. Note that sometimes, Column is replaced by Subtotal By.

Figure 7-8:
The Column drop-down list box.

Charts Only Look Tricky

I love charts. I know that sounds goofy. But data graphics open up wonderful opportunities for communicating, and Quicken charts are really easy to use.

In fact, many times, Quicken adds a small chart to a report window. Take a look at Figure 7-9, for example, to see what I mean. You can also display just a chart, however.

To produce just a Quicken chart, first produce the report you want and then click the Show Graph button that appears in the report window. That's it. Easy as rolling off a log.

Note: Not all reports provide data that can be plotted in a graph. Accordingly, you won't see a Show Graph button in every report window.

Figure 7-9 shows a picture of a pie chart of spending data, but you'll have much more fun looking at your own data in a picture. By the way, you can drill down through a chart to see a report that describes the data being plotted (see "Got a question about a number? Just zoom it" earlier in this chapter).

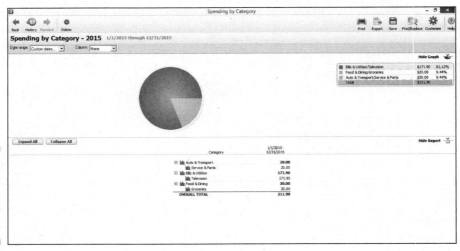

Figure 7-9:
The Spending By Category graph.

You can memorize customized graphs the same way you memorize customized reports. Just click the Save button at the top of the graph window. Then, when Quicken prompts you, give the graph a name. To reuse the graph later, select the graph from the My Saved Reports section of the Reports & Graphs Center.

Customizing Your Reports

If you want to extract some financial info tidbit, you can usually get what you want from one of the reports listed on the Reports menu, especially if you use the EasyAnswer feature to find the right report!

I should tell you something else, though: Quicken is remarkably sophisticated in its reporting. You can customize any report you see on the Reports menu.

To customize these reports, click the Customize button (available when a report window is displayed) to get to the nuts and bolts of your selected report.

I'm not going to describe the customization process in massive detail. I feel kind of bad about this omission, because there are probably a few people out there who, late one night, will decide that they want to know how to filter, sort, and customize. Of course, there are also people who will decide late some night that they want to know how to replace the transmission on a 1971 Triumph Spitfire, and I'm not describing that here, either.

But I do want to share a handful of (I hope) helpful hints.

Let me start by pointing out that the Display tab of the Customize Cash Flow dialog box (see Figure 7-10 for one example of this dialog box) provides text boxes you can use to name your report, pick what row and column headings get used, and specify how much detail appears on the report. You can, for example, indicate that you do or you don't want to see cents, or that you want Quicken to calculate and show percentages.

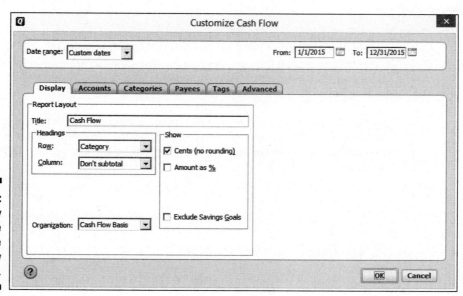

Figure 7-10:
The Display tab of the Customize Cash Flow dialog box.

The Accounts tab of the Customize dialog box (not shown) displays a list of the Quicken accounts you've set up, along with boxes and buttons you can use to specify which accounts' transactions and details you want to include in your report. You can use these options, for example, to tell Quicken that you want to see only transactions from your business checking account.

The Categories tab (see Figure 7-11), the Payees tab and the Tags tab display lists of your categories payees and tags so you can, for example, exclude a particular category or include only a selected set of payees or tags.

Figure 7-11:
The
Categories
tab of the
Customize
Cash Flow
dialog box.

Finally, the Advanced tab provides a bunch of other buttons and boxes you can use to fine-tune how a report looks. You can use Advanced-tab options to look at only cleared transactions, uncleared transactions, or tax-related transactions, for example.

Quicken doesn't provide the same customization options for every report. But in all cases, you can make lots of changes to your reports — which means you probably can customize your way to the perfect report for your situation.

Chapter 8

A Matter of Balance

I want to start this chapter with an important point: Balancing a bank account in Quicken is easy and quick.

I'm not just trying to get you pumped up about an otherwise painfully boring topic. I don't think balancing a bank account is any more exciting than you do. (At the Nelson house, we never answer the "What should we do tonight?" question by saying, "Hey, let's balance an account!")

My point is this: Because bank account balancing can be tedious and boring, use Quicken to speed up the drudgery.

Selecting the Account You Want to Balance

You need to tell Quicken which account you want to reconcile, or *balance*. But this step is easy. Just click the account in the Accounts bar. When you do, Quicken displays the register view for the account (as shown in Figure 8-1).

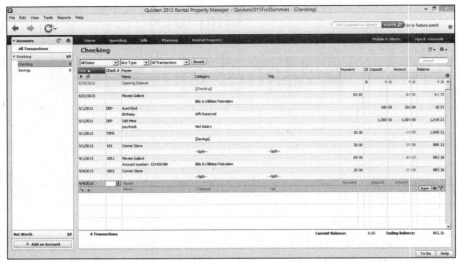

Figure 8-1:
The register
view for an
account.

Balancing a Bank Account

Trust me when I say that balancing a bank account is remarkably easy. In fact,
I'll go so far as to say that if you have any problems, they'll stem from . . . well,
sloppy record keeping that preceded your use of Quicken.

Telling Quicken, "Hey, man, I want to balance this account"

To tell Quicken that you want to balance, or reconcile, your account records
with the bank's records, click the Actions button and then choose the Reconcile
command. Quicken displays the Reconcile Details dialog box, shown in
Figure 8-2.

Figure 8-2:
The
Reconcile
Details
dialog box.

Giving Quicken the bank's information

As you probably know, in a reconciliation, you compare your records of a bank account with the bank's records of the same account. You should be able to explain any difference between the two accounts — usually by pointing to checks that you've written but that haven't cleared. (Sometimes deposits fall into the same category; you've recorded and mailed a deposit, but the bank hasn't yet credited your account.)

The first step, then, is to supply the bank's account information to Quicken. This information comes from your monthly statement. Give Quicken the figures it needs as follows:

1. **Verify the opening balance.**

 Quicken displays a figure in the Opening Balance text box. If this figure isn't correct, replace it with the correct figure. To do so, move the cursor to the text box and type over the given figure. (If you're reconciling your account for the first time, Quicken gets this opening-balance figure from

your starting account balance. If you've reconciled before, Quicken uses the Ending Balance that you specified the last time you reconciled.)

2. **Enter the ending balance.**

 Move the cursor to the Ending Balance text box and type the *ending,* or closing, balance shown on your bank statement.

3. **Provide the statement's ending balance date.**

 Move the cursor to the New Statement Ending Date text box and type the ending date for the statement you're using to reconcile.

4. **Enter the bank's service charge.**

 If your bank statement shows a service charge, and you haven't already entered it, move the cursor to the Service Charge text box and type the amount.

5. **Type a transaction date for the service-charge transaction.**

 Quicken supplies its best guess for the date. If you're reconciling for the first time, Quicken uses the current system date from your computer's clock. If you've reconciled the account before, Quicken picks a date one month after the last time you reconciled the account. If the date Quicken picks isn't correct, type the correct date.

 You can adjust a date one day at a time by using either the + or – key.

6. **Assign the bank's service charge to a category.**

 Quicken helps you out by displaying the Bank Charge category in the first Category text box — the one below the Service Charge text box. If you want to use a different category, click the down arrow in the Category text box to open the Category drop-down list box; then select a category by scrolling down the list and pressing Enter.

7. **Enter the account's interest income.**

 If the account earned interest for the month, and you haven't already entered this figure, type the amount in the Interest Earned text box.

8. **Enter a transaction date for the interest income transaction.**

 You already know how to enter dates. I won't bore you by explaining it again (but see Step 5 if you're having trouble).

9. **Assign the interest to a category.**

 Type an appropriate income category for any interest — perhaps something like, er, **Interest Inc**.

10. **Tell Quicken that the bank statement is complete.**

 To do so, just click OK. Quicken displays the reconcile window, which I describe in the next section.

Explaining the difference between your records and the bank's records

Next, Quicken compares your register's account balance with the bank statement's ending account balance. Then it builds a list of checks and deposits that your register shows but that haven't yet *cleared* (haven't been recorded by the bank). Figure 8-3 shows the Reconcile: Checking window that Quicken displays to provide you this information.

Figure 8-3: The Reconcile: Checking window.

As Figure 8-3 shows, the Reconcile: Checking window is basically just two lists: one of account withdrawals and one of account deposits. The window also displays some extra information at the bottom: the Cleared Balance (which is your account balance including only those transactions that you or Quicken have marked as cleared), the Statement Ending balance, and the Difference between these two figures.

Marking cleared checks and deposits

You need to tell Quicken which deposits and checks have cleared at the bank. (Refer to your bank statement for this information.) To do so, follow these steps:

1. **Identify the first deposit that has cleared.**

 You know how to do so, I'm sure. Just leaf through the bank statement and find the first deposit listed.

2. **Mark the first cleared deposit as cleared.**

 Scroll through the transactions listed in the right column of the Reconcile: Checking window (refer to Figure 8-3 earlier in this chapter), find the deposit, and then mark it as cleared by clicking it. Quicken places a check mark in front of the deposit and updates the cleared statement balance.

3. **Record any cleared but missing deposits.**

 If you can't find a deposit, you haven't entered it in the Quicken register yet. I can only guess why you haven't entered it. Maybe you just forgot. In any event, return to the Quicken register by clicking the Edit button and then enter the deposit in the register in the usual way — but type **c** (for *cleared)* in the Clr column. This mark identifies the deposit as one that's already cleared at the bank. To return to the Reconcile: Checking window, click the Return to Reconcile button.

4. **Repeat Steps 1–3 for all deposits listed on the bank statement.**

5. **Identify the first check or other withdrawal that has cleared.**

 No sweat, right? Just find the first check or withdrawal listed on the bank statement.

6. **Mark the first cleared check or other withdrawal as cleared.**

 Scroll through the transactions listed in the left column of the Reconcile: Checking window, find the first check, and select it to mark it as having cleared the bank. Quicken inserts a check mark to label this transaction as cleared and updates the Cleared Balance.

7. **Record any missing but cleared checks or withdrawals.**

 If you can't find a check or withdrawal — guess what? — you haven't entered it in the Quicken register yet. Display the Quicken register by clicking the Edit button. Then enter the check or withdrawal in the register. Be sure to type **c** (for *cleared)* in the Clr column to identify this check or withdrawal as one that's already cleared the bank. To return to the Reconcile: Checking window, click the Return to Reconcile button.

8. **Repeat Steps 5–7 for withdrawals listed on the bank statement.**

By the way, these steps don't take very long. It takes me about two minutes to reconcile my account each month. And I'm not joking or exaggerating. By two minutes, I really mean two minutes.

Making sure that the difference equals zero

After you mark all the cleared checks and deposits, the difference between the cleared balance for the account and the bank statement's ending balance should equal zero. Notice that I said *should*, not *will*. Figure 8-4 shows a Reconcile: Checking window in which everything is hunky-dory, and life is grand.

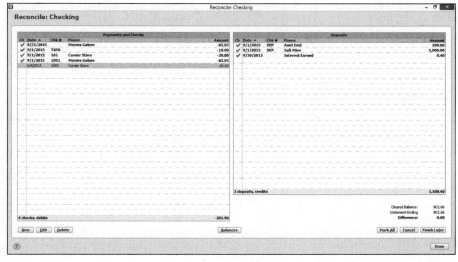

Figure 8-4:
The Reconcile: Checking window showing a zero balance.

If the difference does equal zero, you're done. Just click the Done button to tell Quicken that you're done. Quicken displays a congratulatory message telling you how proud it is of you; then it asks whether you want to print a Reconciliation report.

As part of the finishing-up process, Quicken changes all the cs to Rs. There's no great magic in this transformation. Quicken makes the changes to identify the transactions that have already been reconciled.

TIP

Can't decide whether to print the Reconciliation report? Unless you're a business bookkeeper or an accountant reconciling a bank account for someone else — your employer or a client, for example — you don't need to print the Reconciliation report. All printing does is prove that you reconciled the account. (Basically, this proof is the reason you should print the report if you

are a bookkeeper or an accountant; the person for whom you're reconciling the account will know that you did your job and will have a piece of paper to come back to later if he or she has questions.)

If the difference doesn't equal zero, you have a problem. If you click Done, Quicken displays a message box that provides some cursory explanations as to why your account doesn't balance. Then, if you indicate that you want to soldier on anyway, Quicken displays the Adjust Balance dialog box (shown in Figure 8-5). This dialog box tells you, in effect, that you can force the two amounts to agree by clicking the Adjust button.

Figure 8-5:
The Adjust
Balance
dialog box.

Forcing the two amounts to agree isn't a very good idea. To do so, Quicken adds a cleared and reconciled transaction equal to the difference. (I talk about this transaction in the upcoming section "Ten Things You Should Do If Your Account Doesn't Balance.")

If you want to reconcile later without saving your unfinished work, click Cancel in the Reconcile: Checking window and then click Yes when Quicken asks you whether you really want to quit without saving your work. The next time you click the Reconcile button, you'll have to start over from scratch.

If you can't get your account to reconcile but want to save your work, click the Finish Later button. Quicken leaves your reconciliation work basically half done. The transactions that you marked as cleared still show c in the Clr field, and you still have an unexplainable difference between the bank statement and your register.

Either way, postponing a reconciliation and not choosing to adjust the bank account balance is usually the best approach because it enables you to locate and correct problems. (I give you some ideas about how to do so in the next section.) Then you can restart the reconciliation and finish your work. (You restart a reconciliation in the same way that you originate one.)

Ten Things You Should Do If Your Account Doesn't Balance

I have some suggestions for reconciling an account that's causing you problems. If you're sitting in front of your computer wringing your hands, try the following tips.

Make sure that you're working with the right account

Sounds dumb, doesn't it? If you have a bunch of bank accounts, however, ending up in the wrong account is pretty darned easy. So go ahead and confirm, for example, that you're trying to reconcile your checking account at Mammoth International Bank by using the Mammoth International checking account statement.

Look for transactions that the bank has recorded but you haven't

Go through your bank statement to make sure that you've recorded every transaction that your bank has recorded. Cash-machine withdrawals, special fees or service charges (such as for checks or your safety deposit box), automatic withdrawals, direct deposits, and so on are easily overlooked.

If the difference is positive — that is, the bank thinks you have less money than you think you should — you may be missing a withdrawal transaction. If the difference is negative, you may be missing a deposit transaction.

Look for reversed transactions

Here's a tricky one. If you accidentally enter a transaction backward — enter a deposit as a withdrawal or a withdrawal as a deposit — your account won't balance, and the error can be difficult to find. The Reconcile: Checking window

shows all the correct transactions, but a transaction amount appears to be positive when it should be negative or negative when it should be positive. The check you wrote to Mrs. Travis for your son's piano lessons appears as a positive number (a deposit) instead of a negative number (a check), for example.

Look for a transaction that's equal to half the difference

One handy way to find a transaction that you entered backward — *if* you have only one — is to look for a transaction that's equal to half the irreconcilable difference. If the difference is $200, for example, you may have entered a $100 deposit as a withdrawal or a $100 withdrawal as a deposit.

I don't want to beat a dead horse, but the sign (that is, positive or negative) of the difference should help you find the problem. If the difference is positive — the bank thinks you have less money than your register indicates — you may have mistakenly entered a withdrawal as a deposit. If the difference is negative — the bank thinks you have more money than your register says — you may be missing a deposit transaction.

Look for a transaction that's equal to the difference

While I'm on the subject of explaining the difference by looking at individual transactions, let me make an obvious point: If the difference between the bank's records and yours equals one of the transactions listed in your register, you may have incorrectly marked the transaction as cleared or incorrectly left the transaction marked as uncleared.

I don't know. Maybe that was too obvious.

Check for transposed numbers

Transposed numbers occur when you flip-flop two digits in a number — enter $45.89 as $48.59, for example.

These turkeys always cause accountants and bookkeepers headaches. If you look at the numbers, detecting an error is often difficult because the digits are the same. When you're comparing a check amount of $45.89 in your register with a check for $48.59 shown on your bank statement, both check amounts show the same digits: 4, 5, 8, and 9. They just show them in different orders.

Transposed numbers are tough to find, but here's a trick you can try. Divide the difference shown in the Reconcile: Checking window by nine. If the result is an even number of dollars or cents, you may have a transposed number somewhere.

Have someone else look over your work

This idea may seem pretty obvious, but I'm amazed at how often a second pair of eyes can find something that you've been overlooking.

If you're using Quicken at home, ask your spouse. If you're using Quicken at work, ask the owner or one of your co-workers (preferably that one person who always seems to have way too much free time).

Look out for multiple errors

By the way, if you find an error by using this laundry list and still can't balance your account, you should start checking at the top of the list again. You may discover — after you find a transposed number — that you entered another transaction backward, or incorrectly cleared or uncleared a transaction.

Try again next month (and maybe the month after that)

If the difference isn't huge in relation to the size of your bank account, you may want to wait until next month and attempt to reconcile your account again.

Before my carefree attitude puts you in a panic, consider the following example. You reconcile your account in January, and the difference is $24.02. You reconcile the account in February, and the difference is $24.02. Then you reconcile the account in March, and — surprise, surprise — the difference is still $24.02.

What's going on here? Well, your starting account balance was probably off by $24.02. (The more months you try to reconcile your account and find that you're always mysteriously $24.02 off, the more likely it is that this type of error is to blame.)

After the second or third month, I think it's pretty reasonable to tell Quicken that it should enter an adjusting transaction for $24.02 so that your account balances. (In my opinion, this is the only circumstance that merits your adjusting an account to match the bank's figure.)

By the way, if you've successfully reconciled your account with Quicken before, your work may not be at fault. The mistake could be (drumroll, please) the bank's! And in this case, you should do something else. . . .

Get in your car, drive to the bank, and beg for help

As an alternative to the preceding idea, which supposes that the bank's statement is correct and that your records are incorrect, I propose this idea: Ask the folks at the bank to help you reconcile the account. (Check to see whether they charge for this service first, of course.) Hint that you think that the mistake is probably theirs. Smile a great deal. And one other thing: Be sure to ask about whatever product they're currently advertising in the lobby. (This behavior encourages them to think that you're interested in that 180-month certificate of deposit, and they'll be extra nice to you.)

In general, the bank's record keeping is usually pretty darned good. I've never had a problem as a business-banking client or as an individual. (I've also been lucky enough to deal with big, well-run banks.)

Nevertheless, your bank may have made a mistake, so ask the people there to help you. (*Note:* Be sure to have them explain any transactions that you discover only by seeing them on your bank statement.)

Chapter 9

Housekeeping for Quicken

. .

. .

*O*kay, you don't have to worry about chasing dust bunnies in Quicken, but you do have to take care of little housekeeping tasks. This chapter describes these chores and how to do them right, with minimal hassle.

Backing Up Is Hard to Do

You should back up the files that Quicken uses to store your financial records. But you need to know how to back up before you can back up.

Backing up the quick-and-dirty way

You're busy. You don't have time to fool around. You just want to do a passable job backing up files. Sound like your situation? Then follow these steps:

1. **Insert a writable CD into the appropriate drive or a flash drive into a USB port.**

 You can back up to any disc or storage device you can write to, such as a writable CD or flash drive. You need to know only which letters your computer uses to label its drives. If you don't, consult the documentation that came with your computer.

2. **Verify that the file you want to back up is active.**

 Expand the Accounts bar (if necessary) and then make sure that it displays one of the accounts in the file you want to back up. (If you don't remember setting up multiple files, don't worry. You probably have only one file — the usual case.)

3. **Start the backup operation by choosing File⇨Backup and Restore⇨Backup Quicken File.**

 Quicken displays the Quicken Backup dialog box, shown in Figure 9-1.

Figure 9-1:
The Quicken Backup dialog box.

4. **Identify the backup drive.**

 Select the Back Up on My Computer option button. Then verify that the disk letter shown in the text box is the one you want to use for backing up. If it isn't, click the Change button. When Quicken displays the Enter Backup File Name dialog box, shown in Figure 9-2, select the correct disk.

 You can use any removable media, including a flash drive, a recordable CD, or even an external hard disk.

5. **Click OK.**

Figure 9-2:
The Enter
Backup
File Name
dialog box.

You see a message onscreen that says, "Aye, Cap'n, I'm working just as fast as I can" (or something to that effect). Then you see a message that says the backup is complete. Don't worry. You'll never see a message that says, "She's starting to break up, Cap'n. She can't take warp 9 much longer." You see a warning message if the file you want to back up is too large. In this case, you need to shrink the file, use a different disk, or use multiple disks.

As Figure 9-1 indicates, you can also back up Quicken online. When you select the Use Quicken Online Backup option button and click Back Up Now, Quicken explains the service and gets you started. Just so you know, an online backup gets stored on Intuit's computers — Intuit makes Quicken — rather than on your computer's disks. Online backup works the same basic way as local backup, except you need an Internet connection, and the online backup service costs money. The service costs $9.99 to $149.99 a year at the time I'm writing this book, depending on the level of service you choose. I'm as cheap as the next guy, but I think the online backup option is truly something to consider. The prices seem cheap relative to the value of your data, especially if you're using Quicken for a small business. And one other thing: Often, you can sign up for a free 30-day trial to verify that the service works the way you want.

Deciding when to back up

Sure, I can give you some tricky, technical examples of fancy backup strategies, but they have no point here. You want to know the basics, right? So here's what I do to back up my files. I back up every month after I reconcile. Then I stick the flash drive in my briefcase, so if something terrible happens at home, I don't lose both my computer and the backup with the data.

I admit that my strategy has a few problems, however. Because I'm backing up only once per month, for example, I may have to re-enter as much as a month's worth of data if the computer crashes toward the end of the month. In my case, I wouldn't lose all that much work. But if you have really heavy transaction volumes — if you write hundreds of checks per month, for example — you may want to back up more frequently than monthly, such as once weekly. If you use the same disk or set of disks to back up your Quicken file, Quicken warns you before it replaces the old file with the new one. You can go ahead and let Quicken do this as long as you're sure that you won't want to access the old file anymore.

A second problem with my strategy is only remotely possible but still worth mentioning. If something bad does happen to the Quicken files stored on my computer's hard drive *and* the files stored on the backup disc, I'm up the proverbial creek without a paddle. I should also note that a removable disc may be more likely to fail or get lost than a hard drive is. If this worst-case scenario actually occurs, I need to start over from scratch from the beginning of the year. To prevent this scenario from happening, some people — those who are religiously careful — make more than one backup copy of their Quicken files.

By the way, Quicken periodically prompts you to back up when you try to exit. (You see a message that basically says, "Friend, backing up is a darn good idea.") You can, of course, choose to ignore this message. Or you can take Quicken's advice and do the backup thing as describe earlier in this chapter, in the section "Backing up the quick-and-dirty way."

You know what else? Here's a secret feature of Quicken: Quicken adds a folder called Backup to the Documents directory, and it sticks a backup copy of your files in this folder every few days. You can find out more on this feature later in this chapter, in the section "Losing your Quicken data when you haven't backed up."

Losing your Quicken data after you've backed up

What happens if you lose all your Quicken data? First of all, I encourage you to feel smug. Get a cup of coffee. Lean back in your chair. Gloat for a couple of minutes. You, my friend, will have no problem.

After you've gloated sufficiently, carefully do the following to reinstate your Quicken data on the computer:

1. **Get your backup disk.**

 Find the backup disk you created, and carefully insert it or plug it in. (If you can't find the backup disk, forget what I said about feeling smug; stop gloating and skip to the next section.)

2. **Start Quicken.**

 You already know how to do this, right? By the way, if the disaster that caused you to lose your data also trashed other parts of your computer, you may need to reinstall Quicken. Shoot. I suppose it's possible that you may even need to reinstall Windows.

3. **Choose File⇨Backup and Restore⇨Restore from Backup File.**

 Quicken displays the Restore from Backup File dialog box (not shown), which lets you restore from one of Quicken's automatic backup copies, from a backup copy you made by choosing the File⇨Backup and Restore⇨Backup Quicken File command, or from an online backup. To restore by using one of the automatic backup copies of the Quicken data file that Quicken secretly (and previously) made, simply select the automatic backup copy you want to use. Quicken automatically restores the file for you — and you get to skip to Step 6.

 Alternatively, you can click the Restore from your Backup button and then click the Browse button. Quicken looks at the selected folder or disk and displays a list of the files stored there, as shown in Figure 9-3. If your computer has another disk in it, and this other disk has the backup copy of the file, use the Look In drop-down list box to select the other drive.

 If you want to restore from an online backup copy of the Quicken data file, select the Restore from Online Backup button.

Figure 9-3:
The Restore
Quicken File
dialog box.

4. **Select the file you want to restore and then click OK.**

 Use the arrow keys or the mouse to select the file that you want to restore.

 If the file you select is the one Quicken used last, the program displays a message asking whether it's okay to *overwrite,* or replace, the file with the one stored on the disk.

 When you restore a file, you replace the current, in-memory version of the file with the backup version stored on the disk. Don't restore a file for fun. Don't restore a file for entertainment. Restore a file only if the current version is trashed and you want to start over by using the version stored on the backup disk.

5. **Click Restore Backup.**

 Quicken replaces the file it's currently using with the one from the backup disk. When it finishes, Quicken displays a message telling you that it has restored the file. You're almost done.

6. **Update the account registers as necessary.**

 Using the register windows for each of the accounts in a file, re-enter each of the transactions you recorded since you created the backup. Be sure that you update your accounts because you've almost certainly entered transactions since the last time you backed up.

Just to be on the safe side, you should back up the file after you complete this process. Using a new flash drive is probably a good idea, too. I've heard that lightning never strikes the same place twice, but I'm not sure that the old saying is true. If you have hard-drive problems or another recurring problem, whatever fouled up your file this time may rear its ugly head again — and soon.

Losing your Quicken data when you haven't backed up

What do you do if you haven't backed up your files in a while and you lose all the data in your Quicken files? Okay. Stay calm. All may not be lost.

First, you can try restoring the files from the semisecret Quicken backup directory. To do so, you follow the file-restoration steps I cover in the preceding section, with one minor exception: After you choose the Restore from Backup command, look at the list of automatic (semisecret) backup files that Quicken has squirreled away on your computer.

Select the newest automatic backup file and then click OK. Quicken uses that file to restore the current file. As I allude to earlier in this chapter, grabbing one of these secret backup copies of the Quicken data file may just work. And if it does, you should feel very lucky. Very lucky indeed.

Okay. Suppose that you've tried the approach described in the preceding paragraph, and it didn't work. What next? You have to re-enter all the transactions for the entire year. Yeah, I know. It's a bummer. This method isn't quick, and it isn't pretty, but it works.

If you have copies of the registers, of course, you can use these copies as your information sources to re-enter the information in your files. If you don't have copies of the registers, you need to use your bank statements and any other paper financial records you have.

If, for some unfortunate reason, the only copy you have of your Quicken data seems to have become corrupted, you can have Quicken try to rebuild the file. To do so, choose File⇨File Operations⇨Validate and Repair, and enter the name of the file you want rebuilt in the File Name text box. You typically do this, however, only when so instructed by Quicken or Intuit technical support people.

Working with Files, Files, and More Files

As part of setting up Quicken, you create what Quicken calls a *file:* a place where Quicken stores all your accounts (bank accounts, credit card accounts, investment accounts, and so on).

You can have more than one Quicken file at any time. Most people won't want to do this. But you can (for example) use different files to keep your personal financial records separate from business financial records.

Using multiple files does have two drawbacks, however. First, you can't easily record, in one fell swoop, account transfer transactions between accounts in different files. You need to record the transaction twice — once in the *source account,* the file where the transaction originates, and again in the *destination account,* the file to which you're transferring the transaction.

A second drawback with using multiple files is that Quicken only syncs the data from a single Quicken file with a mobile device like your smartphone.

Setting up a new file

To set up a new file so that you can create accounts in it, follow these steps:

1. Choose File⇨New.

Quicken displays the Create New File: Dude, Are You Sure? dialog box, shown in Figure 9-4.

Figure 9-4:
The Create
New File
dialog box.

2. **Select the New Quicken File option button and then click OK or press Enter.**

 Quicken displays the Create Quicken File dialog box, shown in Figure 9-5.

3. **Enter a name for the Quicken file.**

 Position the cursor in the File Name text box and type some meaningful combination of letters and numbers. You don't need to enter a file extension because Quicken supplies the correct file extension — .qdf — for you.

4. **Choose an appropriate file location.**

 Tell Quicken where you want to store the Quicken data files, using the Save In drop-down list box at the top of the dialog box.

5. **(Optional) Sync the new file with the Quicken Cloud.**

 If prompted, provide your Intuit ID so Quicken can sync the new file with any mobile device you've indicated that you want to use. (Refer to Chapter 1 for more information about the Intuit ID and the Quicken Cloud.)

6. **Add an account.**

 When Quicken displays the Add Account dialog box (shown in Figure 9-6) so you can add at least one starter account to the new file, click the hyperlink that references the type of account you want, and then follow the by-now-familiar onscreen prompts to add the account.

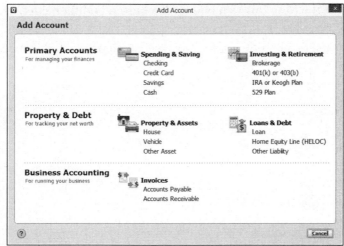

Figure 9-6:
The Add
Account
dialog box
lets you add
that first
account to a
new file.

7. Run Setup.

After you complete adding a new account (or possibly two), you see the Home tab. Click its Get Started button to finish setting up the new account.

Flip-flopping between files

You can work with only one file at a time. So after you create a second file, you need to know how to flip-flop between your files. If you're recording business stuff, for example, you want to be using the business file. What do you do, though, if a transaction comes in that's clearly meant for your personal file and you want to enter it there immediately? Flip-flopping allows you to get from one file to another in no time.

Flip-flopping is easy. Follow these steps:

1. Choose File⇨Open.

Quicken displays the Open Quicken File dialog box (see Figure 9-7).

2. Select the folder that contains the Quicken file, pick the file you want from the File Name drop-down list box, and then click OK.

Bingo. You're in the new file.

Figure 9-7:
The Open
Quicken File
dialog box.

If you really want to switch to another file with lightning speed, you can choose the name of the other file directly from the bottom of the File menu, where Quicken lists the last four files you used.

When files get too big for their own good

You can enter a large number of transactions in a Quicken file; in fact, you can record tens of thousands of transactions in a single account or file. Wowsers!

In spite of these huge numbers, I can think of some good reasons to work with smaller files if you can. For one, working with files of a manageable size means that you can back them up more easily and more quickly. Also, fewer transactions mean that Quicken runs faster because more memory is available for Windows. (Windows likes lots of memory — the same way that some people like lots of ice cream.)

Note: Oh, jeepers. My technical editor wants me to remind you that there are good reasons to work with large files when you can. And, of course, he's right. Having several years' worth of data at your fingertips, for example, is handy. With several years' worth of data, you can easily get answers to all sorts of questions: how much money wealthy relatives have given you over the years, how much cable television has gone up in price, and so on.

If your files have gotten too big for their own good, you can knock them down to size by creating a new file that contains only the current year's transactions.

You end up with a copy of the big file that you won't use anymore and a smaller, shrunken file with just the current year's transactions. Working with a smaller file probably means that Quicken will run faster. (The memory thing comes into play again.) And smaller files should make backing up easier because you can probably keep your files small enough to fit on just about any storage device.

Call me a Nervous Nellie — or a Nervous Nelson — but because shrinking a file involves wholesale change, I'd really feel more comfortable helping you through this process if you first backed up the file you're about to shrink. I don't think that you need to be anxious about anything, but just in case something does go wrong during the shrinking process, I know that you want to have a backup copy of the file to fall back on.

To shrink a Quicken file, follow these steps:

1. **Choose File⇨File Operations⇨Year-End Copy.**

 Quicken displays a portrait of Barry Nelson, the first actor to portray James Bond.

 No, not really — I just wanted to see whether you were awake. Actually, Quicken displays the Create a Year End Copy dialog box, shown in Figure 9-8.

Figure 9-8:
The Create
a Year
End Copy
dialog box.

2. Describe what you want in the current data file.

Your next step in creating a year-end copy is describing what information you want in the current data file, which is the Quicken file that you'll continue to work with. As the Create a Year End Copy dialog box suggests, you have two choices. The Do Nothing choice leaves the Quicken data file alone. The I Only Want Transctions In My Current Data Starting With This Date choice creates a copy of the Quicken data file by using only balances and transactions after a specified date. To shrink the current Quicken file, you predictably use the Do Something (please!) option by selecting the appropriate option button and then specifying the cutoff date.

When you *archive,* you make a copy of the Quicken data file, but (typically) just through the end of the preceding year. You continue to work with the big, everything-is-still-there data file. Why archive? So that you can have a copy of the Quicken data file as it existed at a particular point in time. You might archive the Quicken data file on CD and store the archive file with your tax return, for example. By doing this, you'll be sure of always being able to take a later look at the Quicken data file that explained your tax deductions.

3. Confirm the name in the Give the Archive File a Name and Location text box.

You can actually ignore the filename and folder location information that Quicken enters in the Give the Archive File a Name and Location text box. If you really must have it your way, however, you do have the option of replacing what Quicken suggests with another name. You can also click the Browse button and choose another folder location by using the dialog box that Quicken displays.

4. Specify a starting date.

Using the Specify Starting Date text box, type a cutoff date. (Nowadays, the folks at Quicken are calling this text box This Archive Data File Will Contain Transactions Up to and Including, but you guessed that, didn't you?) Quicken deletes from the current file all cleared transactions with dates that fall before the cutoff date.

This file is the one you work with and want to shrink.

I chose 1/1/2015 as the cutoff date in Figure 9-8 so that I could create a new file for all 2015 and later transactions. (**Note:** Quicken doesn't delete uncleared transactions, and it doesn't delete investment transactions.)

5. Click OK.

Quicken creates an old-transactions "Old File" with the filename discussed in Step 3. If you told it to, Quicken also deletes all the old

transactions from the current file so that your current file contains only the transactions that are dated after the cutoff date.

Then Quicken displays the dialog box shown in Figure 9-9, which tells you that the file was successfully copied.

Figure 9-9:
The File
Archived
dialog box.

6. **Do one of the following and then click OK:**

- Select the Current File option button if you want to use the current file you've just shrunk.

- Select the Archive File option button if you want to use the old-transactions file.

If you want to see the old-transactions, or archive, file again, you can select it in the Open dialog box (accessed by choosing File➪Open). You should *not* enter any new transactions in the old-transactions file, how-ever, because these new transactions will change the old file's ending account balance without changing the current file's beginning account balance.

Using and Abusing Passwords

I have mixed feelings about Quicken passwords. Theoretically, they let you lock up your Quicken data so that your rebellious teenagers (if you're using Quicken at home) or the night janitors (if you're using Quicken in a business) can't come in and print checks, process automatic payments, and just gener-ally mess things up.

Using passwords sounds pretty good, of course. But before you set up a pass-word and then start relying on it to protect your information, let me remind you that a Quicken password only prevents someone from accessing your data *with*

Quicken. Using a password doesn't prevent someone from fooling around with your computer itself. If the night janitors — or, heaven forbid, your teenagers — are nefarious types, they can erase your files with Windows or scramble them with another program, such as a spreadsheet or word-processing program. And they may even be able to get in and manipulate the data with another checkbook or accounting program.

Passwords come with one other little annoying problem, too: Darn it, you have to remember them.

For these reasons, I think that passwords are best left to computer systems that use them on a global basis to control access to all programs and to computer systems that can track all users (you, your teenagers, the night janitors, and anyone else) by name. Your PC doesn't fall into this category.

Setting up a file password

You still want a password? Okay. With much trepidation, I give you the following steps for setting up a password for a Quicken file:

1. **Select the file you want to protect with a password.**

 If the file you want to password-protect is not the active file, choose File⇨Open, double-click the file you want or select it in the Open dialog box, and click OK.

2. **Choose File⇨Set Password for This Data File.**

 Quicken displays the Quicken File Password dialog box, shown in Figure 9-10.

Figure 9-10:
The Quicken File Password dialog box.

3. **Enter the password in the New Password text box.**

 You can use up to 16 characters. Quicken differentiates between lowercase and uppercase characters, by the way, so Washington, wASHINGTON, and WASHINGTON are all different from its point of view. Also, Quicken doesn't display the actual characters you type; it displays asterisks instead. If you type **Dog**, for example, it displays <u>***</u>. (Passwords require strict secrecy, you see.)

4. **Enter the password you want to use again — this time, in the Confirm Password text box — and then click OK.**

 Congratulations! You're done.

Assigning a password to a file doesn't prevent you from doing anything with the file that you'd normally do. But the next time you try to use this file — after you start Quicken or when you try to select the file by choosing the File⇨Open command — Quicken will ask you for the file's password. You need to supply the password to gain access to the file.

So what are transaction passwords?

If you choose File⇨Set Password for This Data File, you create a file password that a Quicken user needs to provide before he or she gets access to the Quicken data. In general, you use such a password, called a *file password,* to protect the access into a Quicken file.

You can also set a *transaction password* by choosing File⇨Set Password to Modify Transactions. A transaction password works a little differently from a file password. With a transaction password, the user has to enter the transaction password if he or she tries to enter a transaction that's dated before a specified date. You specify the date, called the *cutoff date,* when you set up the transaction password.

My guess is that you'd use a transaction password when you want to lock the preceding year's records. In other words, if you don't want people to intentionally or accidentally change last year's transactions — because that would mean that they're screwing around with things like your records of tax deductions you've claimed on a return — you use a transaction password.

Transaction passwords are okay, I guess. But I'm going to go out on a limb here and suggest something: You can create and safely store backup copies of the Quicken file for last year or last month. Or you can keep the idiots from fooling around with your Quicken files. Jeepers, if somebody can't understand an instruction such as "Use the current date," do you really want them mucking about in your books?

Changing a file password

After you set up a file password, you're not stuck with it forever. You can change the password or remove it by choosing File⇨Set Password for This Data File.

If you've already set up a password, however, Quicken doesn't display the Quicken File Password dialog box (refer to Figure 9-10 earlier in this chapter). Instead, Quicken displays a mutated Quicken File Password dialog box that asks for the password you're now using and the new password you want to use in the future (as shown in Figure 9-11). Type the current password in the Old Password text box and the new password in both the New Password and the Confirm Password text boxes. Then press Enter or click OK. From now on, you need to use the new password to gain access to the file. If you don't want to use a password anymore, just leave the New Password and Confirm Password text boxes blank.

And a final tip for you concerning Quicken passwords: If you lose your password, the Quicken technical support ninjas provide a tool you can use to retrieve your password-protected file. (To locate this tool, visit `http://quicken.intuit.com/support`. Select your version of Quicken and then search on the keywords *Quicken Password Removal Tool*.)

Figure 9-11: Change your password here.

Quicken File Password

Old Password:

New Password:

Confirm Password:

Secure passwords are typically longer than six characters, should include a combination of letters and numbers, and should not contain obvious words such as your name.

Note: To remove old password, leave new and Confirm fields blank. Also note that passwords are case sensitive.

OK Cancel

Sanitizing a File

One other File menu command deserves quick mention; the File⇨Sanitize command.

When you choose this command, Quicken displays a dialog box you use to start a process during which you create a copy of your Quicken file — but a copy that's had quite a bit of your personal information removed from it: file passwords, financial institution log in credentials, obviously personal information from accounts and transactions. (You might use such a file, for example, to share financial information from your accountant during tax time.)

Chapter 10

Compound Interest Magic and Other Mysteries

*T*he Planning Tab's Planning Tools button provides several nifty little calculators (most of which are dialog boxes). I strongly encourage you to use these tools. At the very least, the calculators should make your work easier. And if you invest a little time, you should gain some enormously valuable perspectives on your financial affairs.

What's more, the most recent versions of some flavors of Quicken include a handful of more powerful financial planning wizards that I want you to know about. I won't walk you through the steps to using these wizards. But I do want to preview them in the same way that a restaurant critic tells you what you should and shouldn't order at some nice restaurant. You know what I mean. ("Darling, you absolutely must try the *foie gras,* but do stay away from the chocolate mousse. It's abominable. . . .")

Noodling Around with Your Investments

My favorite Quicken calculator is the Investment Savings Calculator. I guess I just like to forecast portfolio future values and similar stuff.

Using the Investment Savings Calculator

Suppose that you want to know how much you'll accumulate if you save $5,000 per year for 35 years in a stock mutual fund that you anticipate will earn 10 percent annually. Use the Investment Savings Calculator to estimate how much you should ultimately accumulate. To use it, follow these steps:

1. **Display the Savings Calculator.**

 Click the Planning tab to display its buttons. Click the Planning Tools button to display its list of calculators, and choose the Savings Calculator. Quicken displays the Savings Calculator dialog box. (See Figure 10-1.) Note that if the Planning tab isn't available, you can tell Quicken you want to see it by choosing View➪Tabs to Show➪Planning.

Figure 10-1:
The Savings Calculator dialog box.

2. **Enter what you've accumulated as your starting savings balance.**

 Move the cursor to the Starting Savings Balance text box and then type the amount of your current investments. If this amount is zero, for example, type **0**.

3. **Enter the annual yield that you expect your investments to earn.**

 Move the cursor to the Annual Yield text box and type the percentage. If you plan to invest in the stock market and expect your savings to match the market's long-term return of about 10 percent, for example, type **10**. (Don't type **.10**.)

4. **Indicate how long you plan to let your investments earn income.**

 Use the Save For text box to indicate how many time periods (years, months or whatever) you'll save. Then use the Save For drop-down list box to select the time period appropriate to your investment planning. (Usually, you'll select Years, as Figure 10-1 shows.) For example, if you select Years in the drop-down list box and you plan to let your investments grow for 35 years, you type **35**.

5. **Enter the anticipated inflation rate.**

 Move the cursor to the Inflation Rate text box and type the inflation rate. By the way, over the past century or so, the inflation rate averaged just over 3 percent.

6. **Enter the amount you plan to add to your investments every period.**

 Move the cursor to the Regular Contribution text box and type the amount you plan to add. Figure 10-1 shows how to calculate an individual retirement account's (IRA's) future value, assuming a $5,000 annual contribution.

7. **Indicate whether you plan to increase your annual contribution as a result of inflation.**

 Select the Increase Based on Inflation Rate check box if you plan to annually increase — by the annual inflation rate — the amount you add to your investment portfolio. Don't select the check box if you don't want to inflate the payments.

8. **After you enter all the information, click Calculate.**

 The Ending Savings Balance field shows how much you'll accumulate in present-day, uninflated dollars: $481,587.80. Hmmm. Sweet.

If you want to know the amount you'll accumulate in future-day, inflated dollars, deselect the Show in Today's $ check box.

To get more information on the annual deposits, balances, and so on, click the View Schedule button, which appears at the bottom of the Investment Savings Calculator dialog box. Quicken whips up a quick little report showing the annual deposits and ending balance for each year you plan to add into the savings. Try it. You may like it.

Trying to become a millionaire

So you want to be a millionaire someday.

To find out how to realize this childhood dream, use the Calculate option buttons, which appear in the Savings Calculator dialog box. (Refer to Figure 10-1.) With these option buttons, you click the financial variable (Ending Savings Balance, Regular Contribution, or Starting Savings Balance)

you want to calculate. For example, to determine the annual amount you need to contribute to your investment so that your portfolio reaches $1,000,000, here's what you do:

1. **Select the Regular Contribution option button.**

2. **Select the Inflate Contributions check box.**

3. **Enter all the other input variables.**

 Remember to set the Ending Savings Balance text box to 1000000. (The Ending Savings Balance field becomes a text box after you select the Regular Contribution option.)

 The Investment Savings Calculator computes how much you need to save annually to hit your $1,000,000 target.

Starting from scratch, it'll take 35 years of roughly $2,800-per-year payments to reach $1,000,000.00, as shown in Figure 10-2. (All those zeros look rather nice, don't they?) Note that this calculation assumes a 10 percent annual yield and that you adjust your contributions for inflation.

Figure 10-2:
The secret to your success: $2,800 per year for 35 years.

A timing assumption you should know

The Savings Calculator assumes that you'll add to your portfolio at the end of the period — what financial planners call an *ordinary annuity.*

"Jeepers, creepers," you say. "This seems too darn good to be true, Steve."

Well, unfortunately, the calculation is a little misleading. With 3 percent inflation, your million bucks will be worth *only* $355,383.59 in current-day dollars. (To confirm this present value calculation, select the Ending Savings Balance option button and then the Show in Today's $ check box.)

One of my pet ideas is that it really is possible for most people to become millionaires. There are just three tricks to doing so. First, make sure that you use tax-advantaged investments such as 401(k) plans and IRAs. Second, invest this money in a very low-cost, super-diversified mutual fund, such as the Vanguard Target Retirement 2050 fund, to make sure that over time, your returns average out to the average. Third, use Quicken and your computer to make smarter financial decisions; by doing this, you can rather easily free up an extra $50, $100, or even $200 per month. I talk about this subject in Chapter 18.

The Often-Unbearable Burden of Debt

To help you better manage your debts, Quicken provides a neat Loan Calculator that computes loan payments and balances.

Using the Loan Calculator to figure payments

Suppose that one afternoon, you're wondering what the mortgage payment is on one of those monstrous houses: tens of thousands of square feet, acres of grounds, cottages for the domestic help, and so on. You get the picture — something that's a really vulgar display of wealth.

To calculate what you would pay on a 30-year, $5,000,000 mortgage if the money costs 5 percent, use the Loan Calculator:

1. **Display the Loan Calculator.**

 Click the Planning tab. Click the Planning Tools button to display Quicken's list of financial calculator tools. Then choose the Loan Calculator. Quicken displays the Loan Calculator dialog box. (Figure 10-3 shows a picture of this handy tool.)

Figure 10-3:
The Loan Calculator shows that you can't afford that huge mansion.

2. **Enter the loan amount.**

 Move the cursor to the Loan Amount text box and type the amount of the loan. (If you're checking the lifestyle of the ostentatious and vulgar, type **5,000,000**.)

3. **Enter the annual interest rate.**

 Move the cursor to the Annual Interest Rate text box and type the interest rate percent. If a loan charges 5 percent interest, for example, type **5**.

4. **Enter the number of years you want to take to repay the loan.**

 Move the cursor to the Number of Years text box and type the number of years you plan to make payments.

5. **Indicate how many loan payments you plan to make per year.**

 Move the cursor to the Periods per Year text box and type the number of loan payments you plan to make per year. If you want to make monthly payments, for example, type **12**.

6. **Indicate how frequently the lender will calculate, or *compound,* interest.**

 Move the cursor to the Compounding Period text box and select the interest compounding period. If a loan uses monthly compounding, for example, select Monthly. (By the way, just so you know, most loans use compounding periods equal to the payment period. Some don't. But most do.)

7. **Click Calculate or move the selection cursor.**

 Quicken calculates the loan payment and displays the amount in the Payment field.

Hey, wait: $26,841.08. That doesn't seem so bad, does it? I mean, you could almost make an annual — oh, never mind. That's a monthly payment, isn't it? Yikes! I guess if you have to ask how much the mortgage payment is, you really can't afford it.

To get more information on the loan payments, interest and principal portions of payments, and outstanding loan balances, click the View Schedule button, which appears on the face of the Loan Calculator dialog box. Quicken whips up a quick loan amortization schedule showing all this stuff.

Calculating loan balances

To calculate the loan principal amount, select the Loan Amount option button in the Calculate section of the Loan Calculator dialog box. Then enter all the other variables.

For example, those $26,841.08-per-month payments for the monster mansion seem a little ridiculous. So calculate how much you can borrow if you make $1,000-per-month payments over 30 years and the annual interest rate is 4.25 percent:

1. **Select the Loan Amount option button.**

2. **Type** 4.25 **in the Annual Interest Rate text box.**

3. **Type** 30 **in the Number of Years text box.**

4. **Type** 12 **in the Periods per Year text box.**

5. **Type** 1000 **in the Payment per Period text box.**

6. **Click the Calculate button or move the selection cursor.**

 The Loan Calculator computes a loan amount of $203,276.87, as shown in Figure 10-4.

Figure 10-4:
The Loan
Calculator
dialog box.

The Refinance Calculator

You won't read about the Refinance Calculator here — but not because I'm lazy. Believe it or not, I enjoy writing about things that help you make better financial decisions. The Refinance Calculator merely calculates the difference in mortgage payments if you make new, lower payments; then it tells you how long it would take the savings from these lower payments to pay back the refinancing costs you incur.

For example, if you save $50 per month because you refinance, and it costs $500 to refinance, the Refinance Calculator tells you that it would take ten months of $50-per-month savings to recoup your $500.

You know what? Although you may want to know how long it would take to recoup the refinance costs, that information doesn't tell you whether refinancing is a good idea. Deciding whether to refinance is very, very complicated. You can't just look at your next few payments, as the Refinance Calculator does. You also need to look at the total interest you would pay with the old mortgage and the new mortgage.

I can't think of any good reason to use the Refinance Calculator; it just doesn't do what it purports to do.

So that I don't leave you hanging, however, let me give you two general rules to help you make smarter refinancing decisions:

- ✔ First, if you want to save interest costs, don't use refinancing as a way to stretch out your borrowing. That is, if you refinance, make sure that you make payments large enough to pay off the new mortgage by the same time you would have paid off the old mortgage. In other words, if you have 23 years left on your old mortgage, don't go out and get a 30-year mortgage. Find a lender who will let you pay off the new mortgage in 23 years by making extra principal payments each month.

- ✔ Here's a second trick, if you can find a willing lender. Ask the lender to calculate the annual percentage rate (APR) on the new mortgage, assuming that you'll pay off the mortgage by the same time you would have paid off the old mortgage. (An APR includes all the loan's costs — interest, points, miscellaneous fees, and so on — and calculates an implicit interest rate.) If the APR on the new loan is lower than the current loan's interest rate, refinancing would probably save you money.

Let me issue one caveat: When you base your refinancing decision on the comparison between the new loan's APR and the current loan's interest rate, you assume that you'll live in your current house until the mortgage is paid.

I hope this information helps. As I said, mortgage-refinancing decisions are tough if you truly want to save money.

The Retirement Calculator

I think that this section is the most important one in this book. No joke. Your financial future is much too consequential to go for easy laughs or cheap shots.

The dilemma in a nutshell

By the time the thirtysomething and fortysomething crowd reaches retirement, Social Security coverage almost certainly will be scaled back at least in some manner and for at least some recipients.

The truth about Social Security

Although the Social Security Administration (SSA) used to regularly send out benefit statements that estimated your future benefits, it no longer does that. Nevertheless, the SSA website, www.ssa.gov, does provide two useful items for thinking rationally about your possible future benefits: the benefits estimator and the Trustees' Annual Report. Let me explain.

You can use the SSA benefits estimator at www.ssa.gov/estimator to get to a web page that steps you through the process for calculating a pretty darn good estimate of your future benefits. And this information is great for planning your retirement.

The Trustees report (which is usually pretty easy to locate if you poke around a bit or search Bing or Google for the phrase *"Social Security Board of Trustees annual report"*) gives you good objective data on the health of the system and the effects of our politicians all bickering about this stuff. For example, the Annual Report typically alerts the public to the risk that if Congress does nothing, there will only be money to cover *x* percent of your benefits at some point a few decades in the future. For example, the statement may have said something along the lines of "Blah, blah, blah, and if Congress does nothing to fix the funding challenges faced by the nation's aging workers, in 2035 the trust fund will be depleted, and Social Security tax receipts will be only enough to pay three-quarters of the retirees' and other recipients' benefits. . . ." Okay, that's a bummer. I know.

But think about the worst-case scenario. If Congress really does nothing, the SSA Trustees now tell us through the Annual Report by what amount our benefits will be cut. The 2013 annual report, for example, suggests that the trust fund runs out of money in roughly 20 years, and, at that point, benefits will have to be cut back to 77 percent of their current levels. For example, someone who would have gotten $1,000 per month will get only $770. Okay, that's not good. But as long as you're not depending solely on Social Security, it isn't quite a financial meltdown, either. You can save just a bit more money yourself and more than make up the difference. To give you an idea about the relative challenge of this personal solution, with 20 years of work left, you need to save about $100 a month to make up the difference. If you're not currently taking advantage of an employer-provided pension fund with a match, most of this money can come from your employer and through tax savings.

But the problem isn't just Social Security. Most employer-provided pension plans are *defined contribution plans,* which add specific amounts to your pension (such as 2 percent of your salary), rather than *defined benefit plans,* which promise specific pension amounts (such as $1,000 per month). As a result, although you know that someone will throw a few grand into your account every so often, you don't know how much you'll have when you retire.

So what does all this mean? In a nutshell, you need to think about your retirement now. Fortunately, the Quicken Retirement Calculator can help you.

More about timing

The Retirement Calculator assumes that you or your employer will add to your retirement savings at the end of the year — what financial planners call an *ordinary annuity*. If you or your employer adds to your retirement savings at the beginning of the year, you earn an extra year of interest. As a result, your after-tax income will be more than Quicken shows.

Retirement planning calculations

Imagine that you decide to jump into your employer's 401(k) thing (a type of profit-sharing plan) and that it allows you to plop $6,000 into a retirement account that you think will earn about 9 percent annually.

Fortunately, you don't need to be a rocket scientist to figure this stuff out. You can just use the Retirement Calculator:

1. **Display the Retirement Calculator.**

 Click the Planning tab. Click the Planning Tools button. Choose the Retirement command. Quicken displays the Retirement Calculator dialog box, shown in Figure 10-5.

2. **Enter your current age.**

 Move the cursor to the Current Age text box and type a number. You're on your own here, but let me suggest that this is a time to be honest.

3. **Enter your retirement age.**

 Move the cursor to the Retirement Age text box and type a number. Again, this is purely a personal matter. (Figure 10-5 shows this age as 65, but you should retire when you want.)

4. **Enter the age to which you want to continue withdrawals.**

 Move the cursor to the Withdrawal Until Age field and type a number. I don't want to beat around the bush here. This number is how old you think you'll be when you die. I don't like the idea any better than you do. Let me say, though, that ideally you want to run out of steam — there, that's a safe metaphor — before you run out of money. So go ahead and make this age something pretty old — like 95.

5. **Enter what you've already saved as your current savings.**

 Move the cursor to the Current Savings text box and type your current retirement savings: for example, if you have some IRA money or you've accumulated a balance in an employer-sponsored 401(k) account. Don't worry if you don't have anything saved — most people don't.

6. **Enter the annual yield that you expect your retirement savings to earn.**

 Move the cursor to the Annual Yield text box and type the percent. In the little example shown in Figure 10-5, I say the annual yield is 9 percent. This is, I'll remind you, slightly less than the average return that the stock market produces over long periods of time.

 You can use the long-term return the stock market delivers as your expected yield if you're taking a do-it-yourself approach, investing in a diversified portfolio of stocks (such as through mutual funds), and you're really watching your investment expenses — such as would be the case if you're using low-cost index funds to keep costs low. If you're working with a financial planner that charges you, say, 1 percent a year, obviously, your return will be 1 percent less in effect. Also, if you're investing some portion of your money into lower-risk investments like bonds, that approach (although perhaps very prudent) will slightly reduce your annual yield.

7. **Enter the anticipated inflation rate.**

 Move the cursor to the Inflation Rate text box and type the inflation rate. By the way, in recent history, the inflation rate has averaged just above 3 percent. (Refer to Figure 10-5.) I use 4 percent in Figure 10-5 to be just a bit more conservative.

8. **Enter the annual amount added to your retirement savings.**

 Move the cursor to the Annual Contribution text box and type the amount that you or your employer will add to your retirement savings at the end of each year. In the example, I say that I plan to add $6,000. (Refer to Figure 10-5.)

9. **Enter any other income you'll receive — such as Social Security.**

 Move the cursor to the Other Retirement Income (SSI, and so forth) text box and type a value. (Figure 10-5 shows $24,000.) Note that this income is in current-day, or uninflated, dollars. By the way, you can visit the SSA website at www.ssa.gov and use its Estimate Your Retirement Benefits link to get a good working estimate of your future retirement benefits. For more information about this, refer to "The truth about Social Security" sidebar.

10. **Indicate whether you plan to save retirement money in a tax-sheltered investment.**

 Select the Tax Sheltered Investment option button if your retirement savings earn untaxed money. Select the Non-Sheltered Investment option button if the money is taxed. *Tax-sheltered investments* are such things as IRAs, annuities, and employer-sponsored 401(k)s and 403(b)s. (A *403(b)* is kind of a profit-sharing plan for a nonprofit agency.)

Retirement Calculator	×

Retirement Calculator

Calculate: ⊙ Annual retirement income
 ○ Annual contribution
 ○ Current savings

Current age: `40`

Retirement age: `65`

Withdrawal until age: `95`

Current savings: `0.00`

Annual yield: `9.000%`

Inflation Rate: `4.000%`

Annual contribution: `6,000.00`

☐ Increase based on inflation rate

Other retirement income: `24,000.00` per year
(Social Security, etc.)

Annual retirement income after taxes: 33,838.07

☑ Show in today's $
(no inflation adjustment)

Tax Assumptions: Retirement tax rate: `15.000%`

⊙ Tax sheltered investment
○ Non-sheltered investment - Current tax rate: `28.000%`

[Calculate] [View Schedule]

(?) [Done]

Figure 10-5:
The
Retirement
Calculator
dialog box.

As a practical matter, tax-sheltered investments are the only way to ride. By deferring income taxes on your earnings, you earn interest on the money you otherwise would have paid as income tax.

11. Enter your current marginal tax rate, if needed.

If you're investing in taxable stuff, move the cursor to the Current Tax Rate text box. Then type the combined federal and state income tax rate that you pay on your last dollars of income.

12. Enter your anticipated retirement tax rate.

Move the cursor to the Retirement Tax Rate text box, and then . . . hey, wait a minute. Who knows what the rates will be next year, let alone when you retire? I think that you should type **0**, but remember that Annual Retirement Income after Taxes is really your pretax income (just as your current salary is really your pretax income).

13. Indicate whether the annual additions will increase.

Select the Increase Based on Inflation Rate check box if the additions will increase annually by the inflation rate (because your salary and 401(k) contributions will presumably inflate if there's inflation).

14. After you enter all the information, click Calculate and take a peek at the Annual Retirement Income After Taxes field.

Figure 10-5, for example, shows $33,838.07. Not bad, really. If you want to see the after-tax income in future-day, inflated dollars, deselect the Show in Today's $ check box but leave the Increase Based on Inflation Rate check box selected.

To get more information on the annual deposits, balances, income, and so on, click the View Schedule button, which appears on the face of the Retirement Calculator dialog box. Quicken whips up a quick little report showing the annual deposits, income, and ending retirement account balances for each year you plan to add to and withdraw from your retirement savings.

If you're now bummed out about retirement

First, don't feel depressed. At least you know *now* if your golden years seem a little tarnished. After all, you acquired Quicken to help you sort out your finances. Now you can use Quicken and your newly gained knowledge to help improve your financial lot.

Basically, retirement planning depends on just three things:

✓ The number of years that the retirement savings will accrue interest

✓ The *real yield* (that is, adjusted for inflation) you earn — in other words, the annual yield minus the predicted inflation

✓ The yearly payments

Anything you do to increase one of these variables increases your retirement income.

If you invest, for example, in something that delivers higher real yields, such as the stock market, you should see a big difference. (Of course, you usually bear more risk.) Or if you wait an extra year or two to retire, you wind up making more annual payments and earning more interest. Finally, if you boost the yearly payments (for example, by participating in an employer-sponsored 401(k) or 403(b) plan, where your employer matches a portion of your contribution), you'll see a huge change.

Noodle around with the variables. See what happens. You may be surprised.

Retirement roulette

Use the Calculate option buttons in the Retirement Calculator (refer to Figure 10-5) to determine a retirement income variable. You can calculate current savings, annual contribution, or, as I describe earlier in the section "Retirement planning calculations," the annual after-tax income.

To calculate the yearly payment required to produce a specific level of retirement income, for example, select the Annual Contribution option button. Then enter all the other variables — including the desired after-tax income — and click Calculate. The Retirement Calculator figures how much you need to save to hit your target retirement income.

Cost of College

Ouch. I have a couple of daughters, so I know how you feel. Man, oh, man, do I know how you feel.

The College Calculator

Suppose that you have a child who may attend college in ten years, and you haven't started to save yet. If the local university costs $20,000 per year and you can earn 5 percent annually, how much should you save?

The College Calculator works like the Retirement Calculator:

1. **Display the College Calculator.**

 Click the Planning tab. Click the Planning Tools button. Choose the College Calculator command. Quicken displays the College Calculator dialog box, shown in Figure 10-6.

2. **Enter the annual college costs.**

 Move the cursor to the Annual College Costs text box. Then type the current annual costs at a school Junior may attend. Figure 10-6 shows this amount as $20,000.

3. **Enter the number of years until enrollment.**

 Move the cursor to the Years Until Enrollment text box and type a number. For example, if Junior will start college in ten years, type **10**.

4. **Enter the number of years enrolled.**

 Move the cursor to the Number of Years Enrolled text box and type a number. Assuming that Junior doesn't fool around, type **4** or **5**.

5. **Enter the amount of the current college savings.**

 Move the cursor to the Current College Savings field and type an amount. Figure 10-6 shows this amount as $20,000. Perhaps Grandpa has really come through for little Junior on this.

6. **Enter the annual yield that you expect the college savings to earn.**

 Move the cursor to the Annual Yield text box and type the percent. Figure 10-6 shows the yield as 5 percent.

7. **Enter the inflation rate anticipated in college tuition.**

 Move the cursor to the Inflation text box and type the inflation rate percent. Figure 10-6 shows this rate as 4 percent.

8. **Indicate whether you plan to increase your annual contribution as a result of inflation.**

 Select the Adjust Based on Inflation Rate check box if you plan to annually increase — by the annual inflation rate — the amount you save. Figure 10-6 shows this check box selected.

9. **After you enter all the information, click Calculate or move the selection cursor.**

 The Annual Contribution field shows how much you need to save each year until the child graduates from college.

Just to beat this thing to death, Figure 10-6 shows that the lucky student will attend five years at a college that currently costs $20,000 per year and that you expect to earn 9 percent annually and anticipate 4 percent annual inflation. Given these cold hard facts, you need to start saving $4,120.67 every year.

Because I'm a CPA, I want to offer you a quick tax-planning tip. If you do embark on a serious college savings program for a child or grandchild, take a look at the Sec. 529 college savings plans that are offered by most banks, brokers, and mutual fund companies. With a Sec. 529 plan, neither you nor the future college student gets taxed on the interest the college savings earn as long as the money is ultimately used for college expenses.

To get more information on the annual deposits, tuition, and balance, click the Schedule button, which appears on the face of the College Calculator dialog box. Quicken whips up a quick little report showing the annual deposits, tuition, and ending college savings account balances for each year you add to, and Junior withdraws from, the college savings money.

If you're now bummed out about college costs

Look at the positive side: You now understand the size of the problem and the solution.

College planning depends on four things:

- ✔ College costs
- ✔ The number of years that the savings earn interest
- ✔ The *real yield* (that is, adjusted for inflation) you earn — in other words, the annual yield minus the predicted inflation
- ✔ The yearly payments

I don't mean to sound like a simpleton, but you can ease the burden of paying for a college education in four basic ways:

- ✔ Reduce the years spent in school.
- ✔ Reduce the annual costs (by finding a less-expensive school).
- ✔ Invest in things that deliver higher yields.
- ✔ Boost the yearly payments.

You should consider especially the first two factors: years in school and annual costs because out-of-the-box thinking in these areas can pay off handsomely. Some high schools, for example, pay for students to attend

community college — which means that these students get up to two years of college paid for by the local school district. High school advanced placement classes may have the same effect. And note that college costs vary widely. I think the best deal that I've seen is the not-for-profit, online Western Governors University (www.wgu.edu), which costs roughly $6,000 per year to attend. Note that students who get their high schools to pay for community college classes and then go to a school like Western Governors for two years pay maybe $12,000 for their college education.

Use the Calculate option buttons (refer to Figure 10-6) to compute a specific financial variable. Select the variable you want to calculate and then input the other values. The College Calculator computes the flagged variable.

Finding a less-expensive school isn't necessarily the same thing as looking for the cheapest tuition fees. Another huge factor these days is whether a program takes four years or five years to complete. A cheap-tuition school that requires five years may be more expensive than, say, a good private school that gets a student out — and working — in four years.

Planning for Taxes

Quicken also comes with a very powerful, very useful Tax Planner. The Tax Planner helps you make a precise estimate of the taxes that you'll owe. To use the Tax Planner, take the following steps:

1. **Display the Tax Planner.**

 Click the Planning tab. Click the Tax Tools button. Choose the Tax Planner command. Quicken displays the Tax Planner window.

 Note: Quicken may display a dialog box that asks whether you want to learn how TurboTax can help with year-round tax planning. Click No if you see this message. You have my help.

 To move past any introductory information, click the Year, Status, or Scenario links shown in the upper-left corner of the Tax Planner window. (See Figure 10-7.)

2. **Verify the tax year and filing status.**

 You want to start by verifying that the big picture assumptions that the Tax Planner makes are correct. Accordingly, make sure tax year and filing status look right. By the way, the initial guesses that Quicken makes probably are correct. Quicken can guess the year by looking at your computer's clock. It can usually determine your filing status based on information that you supply when you set up Quicken. But if one of these bits of information is wrong, use the Tax Year and Filing Status drop-down list boxes to specify the right year and filing status (married, single, and so on).

Figure 10-7:
The Tax
Planner
window
showing
your
planning
options.

If you don't know your filing status, look at last year's tax return.

Note: From the Tax Planner Options, text boxes you can also choose a *Scenario,* which is just a set of income tax inputs. You may have only one Scenario, or you may have several Scenarios based on different guesses about your income and deductions.

3. **Enter the wages and salaries that you and your lovely or handsome spouse expect.**

 Click the Wages link on the left. Then, when Quicken displays the Wages text boxes, type your wages and, if you're married, those of your spouse. Quicken totals your wages and then makes a first rough calculation of the amount you'll owe in taxes. Of course, Quicken needs to collect some more data before this number is accurate, so don't freak out yet.

 You can move to the next set of input text boxes by clicking the Next link and to the previous window of input text boxes by clicking the Previous link. The Next and Previous links appear near the bottom of the Tax Planner window. (You may have to scroll down to see them on your computer.)

4. **Enter the other income you'll have from interest, dividends, capital gains, and so on.**

 To record the other income that you need to pay taxes on, click the Interest/Dividend Inc, Business Income, Capital Gains, and Other Income links and provide the information that Quicken requests. Some of these numbers are pretty easy to guess. Some of them aren't. You can also look at last year's tax return or at the year-to-date information you've already collected by using Quicken.

5. **Identify any adjustments to your gross income.**

 Click the Adjustments link; then, using the Adjustments to Income text boxes, identify or estimate any adjustments to gross income that you'll have. Most people make only one adjustment — contributions to a deductible IRA. Self-employed individuals, however, also typically have several other adjustments, including one-half of their self-employment tax (which Quicken automatically calculates and enters), a portion of any health insurance paid, and Keogh and Simplified Employee Pension (SEP) contributions.

6. **Estimate your itemized deductions.**

 Click the Deductions link and then use the Standard and Itemized Deductions text boxes to estimate your deductions for expenses, such as state and local taxes, mortgage interest, and charitable contributions. Alternatively, if you'll probably or possibly use the standard deduction, carefully check any of the boxes that Quicken uses to determine which standard deduction you should use.

7. **Tell Quicken how many personal exemptions you'll claim.**

 Click the Exemptions link and then specify the number of dependents you'll claim on your return. The basic rule is that you get one exemption for every person in your family (you, your spouse if you're filing jointly, and your kids) as long as they live in your house. I should mention, however, that things become tricky if you have shirttail relatives (your Aunt Enid, for example) living at your house, if your kids live away from home or are married, or if some of the kids in the house have divorced parents. If you have questions because one of these situations sounds vaguely familiar, get the IRS preparation instructions and read the part about who is and is not a dependent.

8. **Indicate whether you owe any other taxes or have tax credits you can use to reduce your taxes.**

 Click the Other Tax, Credits link and then use the Other Taxes & Credits text boxes to describe any of the federal taxes you'll pay in addition to the usual federal income tax. The other taxes, by the way, typically include just two taxes: self-employment tax (which is the tax that self-employed people pay in place of Social Security and Medicare tax) and,

in special cases, the alternative minimum tax. A bunch of tax credits exists. You can very possibly look at your previous years' returns to see if they apply (typically) in your situation.

9. **Enter any estimated taxes you've paid or any federal income taxes your employer has withheld from your paycheck.**

 Click the Withholding link and use the Withholding text boxes to record how much money you've paid through withholding. Then click the Tax Payments link and use the Estimated Tax Payments text boxes to record how much you've paid in estimated tax payments and to guess how much you'll pay in the coming months.

10. **Return to the Tax Planner Summary and review the Quicken program's calculations.**

 After you complete the preceding steps, click the Tax Planner Summary link and review the calculations that Quicken makes. Quicken estimates the total tax you'll pay (which is useful and interesting in itself), the estimated refund or payment you'll have to make, and one other particularly useful bit of information — your marginal income tax rate (which Quicken labels *Marginal Rate*). If you want to print a copy of the Tax Planner's information and calculations, click Print (in the upper-right corner of the window).

Knowing your marginal income tax rate enables you to make more precise investment calculations. For example, the Retirement Calculator — described earlier in the chapter in the section cleverly titled "The Retirement Calculator" — uses your marginal income tax rate to make more precise calculations. You can also use the marginal income tax rate to calculate the after-tax return that taxable investments deliver. Simply multiply the taxable return by the factor (1 − marginal tax rate).

The Other Planning Tools

In the preceding pages of this chapter, I talk about the personal financial planning tools that are most useful. Before I wrap up my discussion, let me quickly mention that Quicken provides some other interesting and, for some people, useful tax and financial planning tools.

For example, the Projected Balances command, which appears on the Planning Tools menu, projects bank account balances using withdrawals and deposits that Quicken can guess about because you've set up bill or income reminders. (I talk about reminder transactions in Chapter 12.)

If you open the Tax Tools menu, you'll notice Deduction Finder, Itemized Deduction Finder, Capital Gains Estimator, Tax Withholding Estimator, Online Tax Tools, and TurboTax commands. These calculation tools walk you through specific tax accounting and planning projects — and may be helpful to some taxpayers.

At the top of the Planning window, Quicken provides links to other planning tools, too: Debt Reduction, Lifetime Planner, and Savings Goals. Click these links to begin walking through the steps for working your way out from under your debts, planning for retirement or saving for some future expenditure. For what it's worth, in my opinion, most people won't be interested in taking the time to use these planning wizards. But if you're really serious or worried or compulsive about one of these topics, it just may be worth your time to explore a bit.

Part III
Home Finances

Add Security to Quicken

Enter symbol or name for this new security

Ticker Symbol: IBM **Look Up...**

Name:
(If ticker symbol is unknown)

Note: Entering a symbol will allow Quicken to download security information such as asset classes and historical prices.

☑ Include this security on my watch list

Cancel **Next**

To find out how to simplify your taxes by carefully structuring your investments across taxable and tax-deferred accounts, visit www.dummies.com/extras/quicken2015.

In this part . . .

- ✔ Expand your use of Quicken to monitor credit cards, debit cards, cash accounts, and even online accounts such as PayPal so you know about all your cash flows.

- ✔ Track your borrowing for items such as vehicles and real estate to manage your debts and minimize interest costs.

- ✔ Minimize your tax burden by appropriately managing your tax-deferred investments in IRAs, 401(k)s, and similar investment accounts.

- ✔ Improve your investment performance by keeping better records of investment profits and losses, returns, and asset allocations.

Chapter 11

Credit Cards, Petty Cash, and PayPal

*Y*ou can use Quicken to track your credit cards and even the cash in your pocket in much the same way that you use Quicken to keep a checkbook. Tracking these items uses a nearly identical process — with a few wrinkles.

First, however, I need to discuss whether you should even bother.

Tracking a Credit Card

If you do carry a credit card balance — and about 50 percent of people do — you can set up a credit card account and use it for tracking credit card purchases. If you just need to keep track of how much you charge during the month (even if you're going to pay the balance in full), you must also set up a credit card account and use it. I should make one other point: To track

not just what you charge (by using spending categories), but also *where* you charge it (by using the Payee field), you must set up a credit card account and use it.

Note: If you use a credit card account in a small-business or rental-property situation, you should set up a credit card account and use it because credit card charges should be deducted on your tax return in the same year as the charge occurs.

I don't use Quicken to track my credit card purchases because I pay my credit card balance in full every month. (Don't feel bad if you don't; it's like a natural law that CPAs like me must do this.) Therefore, I don't have an open credit card balance to track. What's more, when I pay the monthly credit card bill, I can easily use the Split Transaction window to describe my spending categories: $3.53 on food for lunch, $52.64 for car repair, and $217.54 for books (my personal weakness). If you're in the same boat — meaning that you use a credit card but you don't carry a balance — you don't need anything special to track your credit card purchases. And of course, you don't need to use Quicken to tell you your account balance because it's always zeroed-out at the end of the month.

Setting Up a Credit Card Account

If you want to track credit card spending and balances with Quicken, you must set up a special credit card account. (By comparison, you use bank accounts to track other things, such as the money that flows into and out of a checking account.)

Adding a credit card account

To set up a credit card account, you follow roughly the same steps as you do to set up a bank account. Here's what you do:

1. **Display the Quicken home page.**

 You can do this by clicking the Home tab. Figure 11-1 shows the Quicken home page.

2. **Click the Add an Account button.**

 The Add an Account button appears in the lower-left corner, by the way. (I mention this because the button is a little hard to spot.) Quicken displays the Add Account dialog box (see Figure 11-2).

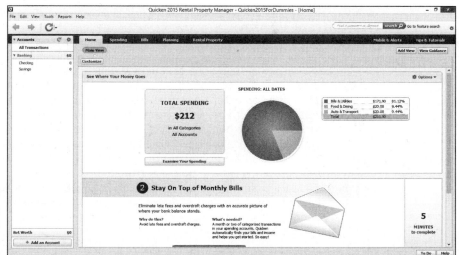

Figure 11-1:
The Quicken
home page.

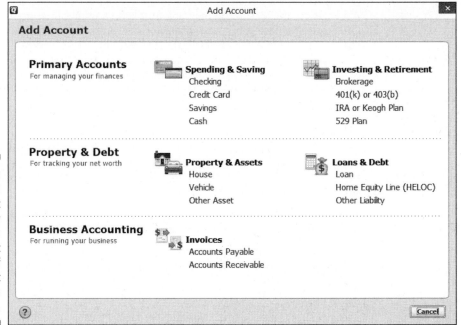

Figure 11-2:
The Add
Account
window
allows you
to select
the type of
account
you want to
set up.

3. **Click the Credit Card option link to tell Quicken you're setting up a credit card account.**

4. **Identify the financial institution.**

 Quicken displays a dialog box that asks for the name of the credit card issuer. The first "identify your financial institution" dialog box, shown in Figure 11-3, lets you enter the issuer name or part of the name in a text box or lets you select your bank from Quicken's list of popular banks. After you identify the bank issuing the credit card, Quicken prompts you to provide your online username and password. If you don't want Quicken to make online connections to your bank, you can click the Advanced Setup link (at the bottom of the dialog box) to indicate that you don't want to identify your credit card issuer. When Quicken displays the dialog box that asks whether you want to download transactions or manually enter them, select the I Want to Enter My Transactions Manually option button and click Next.

5. **Name the account and then click Next.**

 When Quicken displays the dialog box that asks you to give a name to the credit card account (not shown here), move the cursor to the Account Name/Nickname text box and type a name. In some flavors of Quicken, this dialog box also supplies option buttons you can use to indicate what you use the credit card for: Personal Transactions, Business Transactions, and Rental Property Transactions. After you click Next, Quicken displays the Add Credit Card Account dialog box that lets you provide the account balance on a specific date, as shown in Figure 11-4.

6. **Enter the date on which you'll start keeping records for the credit card account.**

 You probably should choose the date of your last statement, as Quicken suggests. Move the cursor to the Statement Ending Date text box and type the date in *MM/DD/YYYY* format. August 31, 2015, for example, should be entered as **8/31/2015**.

7. **Enter the balance you owed at the end of the last credit card billing period after making your payment; then click Next.**

 Move the cursor to the Statement Ending Balance text box and type the balance value by using the number keys. After you click Next, Quicken displays a message stating that account setup is complete.

8. **Click Finish.**

 Quicken finally gets the message and redisplays the Quicken home page (refer to Figure 11-1 earlier in this chapter).

Figure 11-3:
This Add Credit Card Account dialog box asks for your financial institution.

Figure 11-4:
This dialog box lets you provide the account balance on a specific date.

Note: As you complete credit card account setup, Quicken may also display a message that urges you to sign up for your credit card company's online banking services. For now, ignore this message. If you want to sign up later, just tell your bank, and it'll help you get set up.

Selecting a credit card account so that you can use it

To tell Quicken that you want to work with an account, you use the Accounts bar. Just click the credit card account's name.

You can also use the Accounts List window to get to the new credit card account — or to any other account, too. To get to the Accounts List window again, choose Tools⇨Accounts List and then select the account you want to work with.

After you select the account you want, Quicken displays the register for that account so that you can begin recording transactions (which I describe in the next section).

Entering Credit Card Transactions

After you select a credit card account, Quicken displays a special version of the register, as shown in Figure 11-5.

Figure 11-5:
The credit card version of the Quicken register.

Touring the credit card register

The credit card register works like the regular register that you use for a bank account. You enter transactions in the rows of the register. After you record a charge, Quicken updates the credit card balance and the remaining credit limit (if you entered the optional credit limit information when you set up the account).

You can use the same techniques and commands as you do for your regular ol' bank account register. I talk about these in earlier chapters, so I won't regurgitate those discussions here.

Recording a credit card charge

Recording a credit card charge is similar to recording a check or bank account withdrawal. For the sake of illustration, suppose that you charge $30.57 for dinner at your favorite Mexican restaurant. Here's how you record this charge:

1. **Enter the charge date.**

 Move the cursor to the Date field (if it isn't already there) and type the date, using *MM/DD* format. You'd enter August 1, 2015, as **8/1**, for example. You usually don't have to type the year because Quicken retrieves the current year number from the little clock inside your computer. Or, if you want, get crazy: Click the box at the end of the field that remotely resembles a calendar, and Quicken displays a pop-up calendar from which you can select the appropriate month and day (see Chapter 4 for more information).

 Don't bother with the Ref field (if you see it). Quicken optionally supplies this field so that you can record the credit card reference number — a bit of data that's usually about 20 characters long. You, my friend, have better things to do with your time. Just skip the field.

2. **Record the name of the business you paid with a credit card.**

 Move the cursor to the Payee field and type the name of the person or business you paid. If the restaurant is Florentia's Cantina, for example, type **Florentia's Cantina** in the Payee field.

3. **(Optional) Enter a memo description.**

 Move the cursor to the Memo field and type the specific reason you're charging the item, such as a special date with your spouse or an important

business meeting. The Memo field — just so you know — appears only when the register display is set to Two-Line Display mode.

4. **Enter the category.**

Move the cursor to the Category field, open the drop-down list box, and select the appropriate category. You may categorize a restaurant charge as Food & Dining:Restaurants, for example, if you're using Quicken's suggested categories and subcategories.

5. **(Optional) Tag the description.**

If you're using tags to classify the data even more granularly, move the cursor to the Tag field and select the tag you want to use for the transaction. If you're like "Tags, what the heck?!", turn back to the very end of Chapter 2 and look through the last few paragraphs.

6. **Enter the charge amount.**

Move the cursor to the Charge field and type the total charge amount — **30.57** in this example. Don't type a dollar sign, but do type the period to indicate the decimal place and cents.

7. **Record the charge, and click the Save button.**

Quicken beeps, calculates both the new credit card balance and the remaining credit limit, and then moves the cursor to the next slot in the register.

Figure 11-6 shows the charge at Florentia's. Good food and reasonable prices — you can't ask for much more than that.

Figure 11-6:
The charge at Florentia's Cantina.

Changing charges you've already entered

Press the arrow keys or click the mouse to highlight the charge that you want to change. Press Tab and Shift+Tab or the mouse to move the cursor to the field that contains the misinformation you want to fix. Then you can fix the entry and record the transaction by clicking the Save button. That's easy enough, isn't it?

Paying credit card bills

If you're tracking the credit card account balance with a credit card account like the one I'm describing here, Quicken provides two ways for you to pay a credit card bill.

Note: If you're not using a credit card account in Quicken, you record the check you send to pay a credit card bill in the same way you record any other check. And that means you don't have to read anything I'm about to say.

A most bodacious way to pay a credit card bill

This method is pretty simple, so don't blink.

Look at your credit card statement. Decide how much you want to pay. Select the bank account on which you'll write the check. Then write the check and record it in the bank account register — but as a transfer to the credit card account.

You're done. If you have questions, take a peek at the selected check transaction shown in Figure 11-7. It pays $30.57 of the credit card balance. The only trick — if you want to call it that — is that the credit card account is specified as the account to which the money is transferred. (You can see the other account by right-clicking the transaction and choosing Go to Transfer from the contextual menu, or you can click the other account's QuickTab, of course.)

If you could look at the credit card account register now — of course, you can't because you're not sitting in front of my computer — you would see that this check reduces the credit card balance by $30.57.

Figure 11-7:
A check transaction that pays a credit card balance.

A less bodacious way to pay a credit card bill

You can also tell Quicken that you want to pay some portion of the credit card bill as part of reconciling the credit card's account balance. What happens is that after you reconcile the credit card account, Quicken asks (or may ask) whether you want to make a payment. If you say you do, Quicken prompts you to describe the payment.

I think that this method is slightly more difficult. But if you want to reconcile your credit card account, think about using this second method. If you're reconciling a credit card statement and paying some portion of the credit card balance at the same time, you may find this method more convenient. Who knows?

I describe how to reconcile a credit card account in the very next section.

Reconciling That Crazy Account

You know that trick in which you compare your checking account records with your bank's records of your checking account? The one in which you calculate the difference between what you think is your account balance and what the bank thinks is your balance? And this difference is supposed to equal the total of the transactions floating around out there in the system? You can use this same trick on your credit card account.

To reconcile a credit card account, first get your credit card statement. Next, display the credit card account in a transaction list window.

What the nasty credit card company says

To tell Quicken what that nasty credit card company says, follow these steps and put on some music if you can't seem to get the rhythm thing right:

1. **Click the Account Actions button in the transaction list window and choose the Reconcile command.**

 Quicken displays the Reconcile: Credit Card dialog box, as shown in Figure 11-8.

Figure 11-8: The Reconcile: Credit Card dialog box.

2. **Enter the charges and cash advances that your statement shows.**

 Move the cursor to the Charges, Cash Advances text box and then type the number.

3. **Enter the payment and credits that your statement shows.**

 You know the drill: Move the cursor to the Payments, Credits text box and type the number.

4. **Enter the new balance shown on the credit card statement.**

 Now, I bet this is a surprise. Go ahead and type the figure in the Ending Balance text box — even if you just can't believe you charged that much.

5. **Enter the ending statement date.**

 I don't know why Quicken is now collecting this piece of information. For more than ten years, Quicken has been able to reconcile your credit card account (and any other account) without this snidbit of data.

6. **Enter the monthly interest charge by using the Finance Charges text box.**

 Pause for a moment of silence here if this topic makes you sad, sad, sad.

7. **Assign the monthly interest to the appropriate spending category, such as Interest Exp.**

 Move the cursor to the Category text box and type the category name. (Are you getting bored yet? I know: Move and type . . . move and type . . . all I ever seem to say is "Move and type.")

 You can click the little down arrow at the end of the text box to see a list of categories.

8. **Click OK.**

 Quicken displays the Reconcile: Credit Card window (see Figure 11-9). Use this window to tell Quicken which credit card charges and payments appear on your statement. (This step is akin to looking at a bank statement and noting which checks and deposits have cleared the bank.)

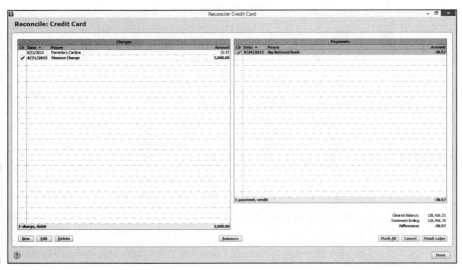

Figure 11-9:
The
Reconcile:
Credit Card
window.

Ouch! Did I really spend that much?

After you give Quicken an overview of your credit card situation, you can note which charges have cleared and which charges haven't.

If you're comfortable whipping through a bank reconciliation, you can probably do this reconciliation with your eyes closed. If you need some help, leave your eyes open so that you can read these steps:

1. **Find the first charge listed on the credit card statement.**

2. **Mark the charge as cleared.**

 Charges are listed in the left list box. If you charged a bunch of stuff, scroll through the transactions listed in the Charges window until you find the charge. After you see a charge that appears on your credit card statement, click it. Or select the charge by using the arrow keys and then press the spacebar. Quicken adds the check-mark symbol in front of the list entry in the Clr column to mark this charge as cleared and then updates the cleared statement balance.

3. **Enter any missing charges.**

 If you can't find a charge, you probably didn't enter it in the Quicken register yet. Open the credit card account register by clicking its tab and then enter the charge in the register in the usual way — except enter **c** (the letter *c*) in the Clr column by clicking the Clr field. By doing so, you identify the charge as one that's already cleared. When you finish, click the Return to Reconcile button to return to the Reconcile: Credit Card window.

4. **Repeat Steps 1–3 for charges listed on the credit card statement.**

 Or until you're blue in the face.

5. **Find the first payment or credit listed on the credit card statement.**

 Any payments and credits appear in the right list box.

6. **Mark the payment or credit as cleared.**

 Scroll through the transactions listed in the Payments window until you find the first payment or credit and then select it. Or select the credit and then press the spacebar. Quicken adds the check-mark symbol in front of the list entry to mark the payment or credit as cleared and then updates the cleared statement balance.

7. **Enter any missing payments or credits.**

 If you can't find the payment or credit — you probably know what I'm going to say — you haven't entered it in the Quicken register yet. Open the credit card account register by clicking its tab and then enter the

payment or credit in the register in the usual way, but put **ac** in the Clr column. When you finish, click the Return to Reconcile button to return to the Reconcile: Credit Card window.

8. **Repeat Steps 5–7 for payments or credits listed on the credit card statement.**

If you record a transaction wrong, do this

As you're looking through the credit card statement, you may discover that you incorrectly recorded a transaction. If this happens, display the credit card register so that you can make the necessary fixes.

Oh, that explains the difference

After you mark all the cleared charges and payments, the difference between the cleared balance for the credit card and the statement's ending balance should be zero.

Figure 11-10 shows how this looks. By the way, reconciling with fictitious data is darned easy.

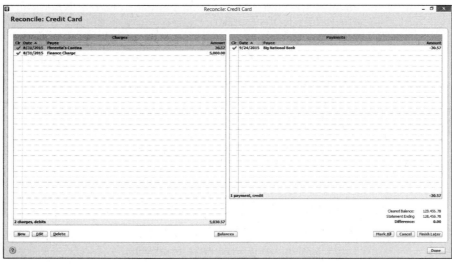

Figure 11-10: When the difference between the cleared balance and the statement is zero, the reconciliation is complete.

If you're ready to finish

If the difference does equal zero, you're cool. You're golden. You're done. (Sort of makes you sound like fried chicken, doesn't it?)

All you need to do is click Done to tell Quicken that you're done. Quicken asks you whether you want to make a credit card payment. Jump ahead to the "Paying the bill as part of the reconciliation" section for help doing just that.

If the difference doesn't equal zero, you have a problem. If you clicked Done in spite of the problem, Quicken displays a message that has some cursory explanation of why your account doesn't balance. This message also tells you that you can force the two amounts to agree by pressing Enter.

Forcing the two amounts to agree isn't a very good idea, though. To make the balances agree, Quicken adds a cleared transaction equal to the difference. (Quicken asks for a category if you choose the adjustment route.)

Despite the ease of making adjustments, you should still correct the error responsible for the difference.

Chapter 8 provides some ideas for trying to figure out why a bank account that should balance doesn't. You can apply the same list of tips to credit card reconciliations if you're in a bad way.

If you want to postpone the inevitable

You can postpone reconciling the account by clicking the Finish Later button. When you click this button, you abandon your reconciliation work. Transactions that you mark as cleared still show c in the Clr text box. You still have an inexplicable difference between the credit card statement and your register. Even so, postponing a reconciliation is usually better than forcing the cleared balance to equal the credit card statement balance. By postponing a reconciliation, you can (ideally) find the problem or problems and fix them. Then you can restart the reconciliation and finish your work. (You restart a credit card reconciliation in the same way that you originally started one.)

When you finish, Quicken redisplays the Transactions tab. You may notice that when you mark credit card transactions as cleared, Quicken puts c in the Clr column of the credit card register. When you finish reconciling the credit card account, Quicken changes all these cs to Rs. None of what Quicken does here is magical. Quicken just makes this change to identify the transactions that have already been through the reconciliation process. (The c shows that a transaction has been marked as cleared. The R shows that a transaction has been reconciled.)

Paying the bill as part of the reconciliation

After you finish reconciling the credit card account, Quicken does two things:

✔ If some of the stuff in the credit card register doesn't agree with the credit card statement, Quicken displays a message box to alert you to these, er, discrepancies. Then it suggests that you let it bring your records into agreement with the statement (see Figure 11-11). To synchronize your records with the credit card statement, verify that Quicken is using a reasonable expense category to categorize the discrepancy and then click Adjust.

Figure 11-11:
The Adjust
Register to
Agree with
Statement
dialog box.

> Adjust Register to Agree with Statement
>
> **Adjust Register to Agree with Statement**
>
> To make your register match your statement, Quicken will make the following adjustments.
>
> Missing charges adjustment **30.57**
>
> Category (optional)
>
> (?) **Adjust** **Cancel**

✔ Quicken does a second thing after you finish reconciling a credit card account: It asks whether you want to pay the bill. Figure 11-12 shows the Make Credit Card Payment dialog box, which is the tool that Quicken uses to collect the necessary data. You simply identify the bank account on which you want to write the check and indicate whether you'll use a printed check or a handwritten check. Then Quicken records a check that pays the credit card balance into the register. You can edit, print, and do whatever else you want to do with this check in the usual way.

Figure 11-12:
The Make
Credit Card
Payment
dialog box.

The Online Banking Hoopla

As I briefly mention in Chapter 6, Quicken supports online banking. If you have your credit card with a credit card company — probably a bank — that's set up to handle Quicken online banking, you can grab your credit card statement directly from the company. If you have a checking account at the bank that issued the credit card, you can also pay your credit card bill simply by transferring money from your checking account to your credit card. (This feature is actually pretty slick, I have to say.)

The big hoopla concerning this feature — at least as it relates to credit cards — is that you don't have to enter the credit card transactions in a register. Rather, you retrieve them by using an Internet connection.

Should you even bother?

Is the online-banking-with-a-credit-card-thing a feature that you should look into? Does it really save you time? Is it a good deal? Inquiring minds want to know, so I'll tell you what I think. (I should point out that what I'm about to say next is just my humble opinion.)

I think that when you consider the time savings, online banking in general is well worth the fee you probably have to pay for the service. You'll probably pay only a few dollars a month. (What you pay depends on the bank issuing the credit card.)

Something bothers me about the whole deal, however: You really just receive an electronic version of your statement, which means (at least from my perspective) that you're more likely not to see erroneous transactions. And reconciling your bank statement against. . .well, your bank statement isn't going to make a whole heck of a lot of sense. (Golly, gee, Batman — the charge to Edna's Pet School appears on both statements, too!)

How to use Online Account Access with your credit card

Okay, so you've listened to my side of the story, but you still want to use the Quicken Online Account Access feature with your credit card — and your bank is one that provides this service. "What next?" you're wondering.

Here's the answer: You set up online credit card accounts the same way you set up online bank accounts. ***Note:*** For more information about the Quicken Online Account Access feature, see Chapter 6.

Petty Cash and Mad Money

You can track petty cash in your business as well as the petty cash in your wallet by using a special Quicken cash account. To track the cash, you must set up a cash account and then enter the increases and decreases in the cash account's register. Sure, this stuff isn't exactly rocket science, but shoot, I thought I'd just go over it quickly to show you how easy it really is. Okay?

Adding a cash account

To set up a cash account — an account for "pocket money"– you follow roughly the same steps as you do for setting up a bank account. Because you've probably already set up a bank account, you can move quickly through the following steps to set up a cash account:

1. **Display the Quicken home page.**

 Click the Home tab, and Quicken displays the Quicken home page (refer to Figure 11-1). You remember this puppy.

2. **Click the Add an Account button to set up a new account.**

 The Add an Account button appears in the lower-left corner of the window. Quicken, of course, is no fool, so it displays the Add Account dialog box.

3. **Set up a cash account.**

 You can guess how to do this, can't you? You indicate that you want to set up a cash account and then simply step through Quicken's questions about the account you want to set up. You need to give the account a name, such as *cash* or *pocket money*. And you need to provide a starting balance value using the faithful, familiar Add Account dialog box, as shown in Figure 11-13.

4. **Click Next and then click Done.**

 When you finish describing the cash account, click Done. Quicken displays the new cash account in a register window.

Figure 11-13:
The final Quicken Add Cash Account dialog box used for cash accounts.

Tracking cash inflows and outflows

After you set up a cash account, you can use it to track the cash you receive and spend in the same way that you track the deposits and checks for a bank account.

To record your cash inflows and outflows, use the QuickTab for the account, which should appear on the Accounts bar. Figure 11-14 shows the cash-account version of the register. Until you start entering transactions, only the first opening balance transaction shows.

To record the amount of money you spend, fill in the Date, Payee, and Spend fields. To record the amount of money you receive, fill in the Date, Payee, and Receive fields. To track the reasons that you're receiving and spending the cash, use the Memo and Category fields.

Figure 11-14:
The cash-
account
version of
the register.

Recording checks you cash instead of deposit

By the way, you don't necessarily need to set up a cash account if you like to spend cash (rather than, say, write checks or charge on a credit card). If you just cash a check and you do have a bank account set up, you can record the transaction in another way that may be simpler: Just use the Split Transaction window to show both the income category (Salary, for example, for an individual) and how you're going to use the money.

If you cash a $1,000 check, for example, and plan to use the $1,000 for spending money, you may show a positive $1,000 in the Net Salary category and a negative $1,000 in the Entertainment:Amusement spending category. Figure 11-15 shows this trick.

Note that the transaction shown in Figure 11-15 produces a transaction that equals zero. This is correct. Cashing a check that you never deposited doesn't affect your checking account balance. But by filling out the Split Transaction window, as shown in Figure 11-15, you do end up recording both the $1,000 of income and the $1,000 of expense.

Don't worry. I won't ask why you're carrying around $1,000 in cash.

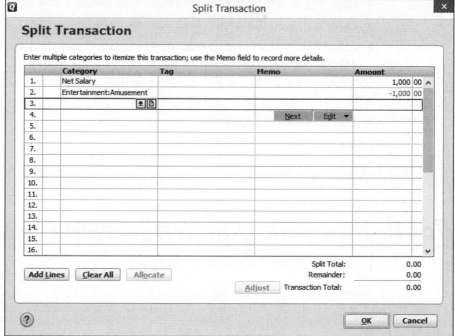

Figure 11-15:
A zero-
amount
transaction
is one handy
trick.

Updating cash balances

You can update a register's cash balance to reflect what you actually have in petty cash, your wallet, under the mattress, in the cookie jar, or wherever else you keep your cash by following these steps:

1. **Display the cash account register.**

2. **Click the Actions button and choose Update Balance.**

 Quicken displays the Update Balance dialog box, as shown in Figure 11-16.

Figure 11-16:
The Update
Balance dia-
log box.

3. **Enter the actual cash balance in the New Balance text box.**

4. **Enter a date in the Adjustment Date text box.**

5. **Choose the category that you want to update from the Category for Adjustment drop-down list box.**

 After you click the arrow to the right of the drop-down list box, you get a list of all the categories you've set up.

6. **When you finish, click OK.**

 Quicken updates the cash account's balance.

And that, my friend, is that.

PayPal Can Be Quicken's Friend

One final point before I end this discussion.

If you use PayPal, you can and should use Quicken to track the money flowing into and out of your PayPal account. Fortunately, tracking a PayPal account with Quicken is pretty dang easy.

To track PayPal using Quicken, you just want to remember these three points:

✓ A PayPal account is really just another bank account, albeit a special sort of bank account. Accordingly, you want to set up a Quicken PayPal account in the same way that you set up any other Quicken bank account. (Refer to Chapter 2 for additional information about setting up a bank account.)

✓ If you use your credit card to pay money into the PayPal account, you're actually transferring money from your credit card account to your PayPal account. To record this transfer, you record a credit card charge in your credit card register (similar to the charge made to Florentia's Cantina shown in Figure 11-6 earlier in this chapter). Rather than use a Quicken category, however, you specify the PayPal account.

✓ You should reconcile your PayPal account just like you do any other bank account or credit card account. During this reconciliation, be sure to record any PayPal charges.

And one final snidbit for people who really want to push the envelope: PayPal allows you to download your transaction history into a QIF file, which you can then import into Quicken by choosing the File⇨File Import⇨QIF File command. You may want to refer to both Quicken's and PayPal's online Help for more information.

Chapter 12

Other People's Money

A while back, a popular financial self-help writer used to argue that one of the secrets to financial success is using other people's money: the bank's, the mortgage company's, the credit people's, your brother-in-law's. . . . You get the idea.

Me? I'm not so sure that using other people's money is the key to financial success. Borrowing other people's money can turn into a nightmare.

Quicken can help you here. No, the folks at Intuit won't make your loan payments for you. But in a way, they do something even better: They provide you a tool to monitor the money you owe other people and the costs of your debts.

Should You Bother to Track Your Debts?

I think that tracking your debts — car loans, mortgages, student loans, and so on — is a good idea when lenders fail to tell you the amount that you're paying in annual interest or the amount you owe after each and every payment.

If your lenders are doing a good job of keeping you informed, I don't think that using Quicken for this purpose makes much sense. Heck, it's their money. They can do the work, right?

Let me make one more observation. If lenders have half a clue, they send you a United States 1098 tax form at the end of every year. The number shown on that form equals your tax deduction if the interest stems from a mortgage, business, or investment loan. Note that personal interest expenses aren't deductible anymore, so you shouldn't track them unless you really want to be mean to yourself.

How Do You Get Started?

To track other people's money with Quicken, you must set up a *liability account.* Setting up one of these babies is easy. Just remember that you must set up a liability account for every loan or debt you want to track: one account for your mortgage, another for your car loan, still another for your student loan, and so on.

Setting up a liability account for an amortized loan

An *amortized loan* is one on which you make regular, equal payments. Over time, the principal portion of each payment pays off, or *amortizes,* the loan principal. If you borrowed money to purchase a house, a car, a Winnebago, or anything else that's really expensive and that you pay off over several years, chances are good that your loan is of the amortizing variety.

Setting up a loan account requires a few dozen steps, but none of the steps is difficult, and none takes that much time to complete. As long as you have your loan information handy — the loan amount, interest rate, balance, and so on — setting up this type of account is a snap.

Here's the recipe for setting up a liability account:

1. **Click the Add an Account button.**

 The Add an Account button appears in the lower-left corner of the Accounts bar.

2. **Tell Quicken you want to set up a loan account.**

 When Quicken displays the Add Account dialog box, choose Loan⇨ Manual Account Setup. Quicken displays the Loan Details dialog box (see Figure 12-1).

Figure 12-1:
The Loan
Details dia-
log box.

3. **Name and (optionally) classify the loan account.**

 Use the Name of This Loan in Quicken text box to give the loan a name. And please be clever here. Then consider using the Loan Type drop-down list box to classify the loan by selecting a loan type (such as auto loan, consumer loan, or commercial loan) from the list.

4. **Enter the date that you borrowed the money in the Opening Date text box; or, if your loan has a grace period (like the one for a student loan), enter the date when your loan enters the repayment period.**

 Quicken needs to know this date so it can calculate the interest that the loan started to accrue when you borrowed the money. The program suggests the current system date as the Opening Date, but this is probably wrong.

5. **Enter the original loan balance.**

 Enter the original loan amount in the Original Balance text box. You can get this amount, if you're unsure, from the original loan documents.

6. **Specify the interest rate.**

 Enter the loan's interest rate in the Current Interest Rate text box. The loan interest rate, by the way, isn't the same thing as the *APR,* or annual percentage rate. You want to enter the actual interest rate used to calculate your payments. Enter the interest rate as a decimal amount. Don't type 7⅝, for example; instead, type **7.625**. You should be able to get this rate from the lender or the prospective lender.

7. **Enter the loan term (in years) in the Original Length text box.**

 If you set up a 30-year mortgage, for example, type **30**. You may have to perform one tiny trick when entering this figure. If you set up a loan that includes a balloon payment, enter the number of years over which the loan will be fully paid — not the number of years used for calculating the loan payment. Loan payments may be calculated based on a 30-year term, but the loan may require a balloon payment at the end of 7 years. In that case, type **7** in the Original Length text box.

8. **Indicate how often the bank calculates loan interest.**

 Use the Compounding Period text box to specify how often the bank calculates interest on the loan. The interest-compounding period usually equals the payment period.

9. **Describe how often you make a loan payment by using the Payment Schedule drop-down list box.**

 If you make regular monthly payments, for example, select Monthly from the Payment Schedule drop-down list box. If you can't find an entry in the Payment Schedule drop-down list box that describes how often you make payments, select the Other Period list entry and then type the number of payments you make each year in the Payments Per Year text box. (Note that the Payments Per Year text box doesn't appear unless you select Other Period.)

10. **Enter the current balance if you've made any payments.**

 If you've already made payments on the loan, specify how much you still owe on the loan after making the last payment by using the Current Balance text box. If you don't know the current balance, call the lender and ask for it. If you haven't made any payments yet, skip to Step 11.

11. **Correct the calculated payment amount (if necessary).**

 After you enter the loan information discussed in the preceding steps, Quicken calculates the loan payment, using the loan balance, term, and interest rate you entered. In most cases, the calculated payment Quicken gives you should be correct. But if the calculated payment is wrong — say, because of a rounding error or because your loan includes a balloon payment — enter the correct loan principal and interest amount in the Monthly Payment text box.

 You can tell Quicken to recalculate the payment or current balance amount by using some new bit of loan information you enter. Just click the field you want to update and then click the Recalculate button.

12. **Click Next.**

 Confirm that the Quicken calculations make sense and then click Next. Quicken displays the second Loan Details dialog box (shown in Figure 12-2).

13. Verify the principal and interest payment calculated by the program.

If it's wrong, you can keep going, but let me point out a minor (yet annoying) problem. You probably entered one of the loan calculation inputs incorrectly, such as the loan balance, loan term, or the interest rate. Fortunately, these errors are only minor bummers. Later in this chapter (in the "Fixing loan stuff" section), I describe how to start over.

14. (Optional) Indicate any amounts you pay besides principal and interest.

If your lender requires you to add a little extra to the payment — such as for insurance, say, or for property taxes — enter that amount in the Other text box. If you want, you can also enter an extra principal payment in the Extra Principal Paid Monthly text box.

If you want to set up a loan payment so that it includes an extra chunk of principal payment, you can enter either the extra amount in the Extra Principal Paid Monthly text box. Or you can select the Total Determines Extra Principal option button. When you select the option button, Quicken turns the Total Payment field into a text box. In that text box, enter the total payment you can afford to make, including any extra principal.

15. Set up a loan reminder.

To help you remember your loan payments — hey, nobody likes late payment fees — Quicken at this point displays a message box (not shown here) that informs you that it added a loan reminder message

to the account so you don't forget. You can also use this message box to tell Quicken that it can actually enter the loan payment transaction for you; just select the check box labeled "Automatically Enter The Transaction Into The Register" and specify how many days before the due date the transaction should be entered. You can also fine-tune the way the reminder and data entry work by using the Loan Payment Reminder dialog box (see Figure 12-3) which automatically appears. To tweak your reminder and transaction data entry, enter the lender name in the Pay To text box and the next payment date in the Due Next On text box, and then select the bank account you'll use to make the payment from the From Account drop-down list box.

Figure 12-3:
The Loan
Payment
Reminder
dialog box.

16. Describe the transaction splits.

If you've read Chapter 4, you may remember (from the section on splitting transactions) that Quicken allows you to split transactions into multiple categories. Good. That trick works for loan payments, too, as you may not be surprised to hear. If you want to split a loan payment, click the Split link in the Loan Payment Reminder dialog box and then click the Split button in the little message box that Quicken displays. Quicken displays the Split Transaction dialog box (see Figure 12-4), which you can use to describe any additional amounts the lender requires you to pay. In the case of a mortgage, for example, you may be required to pay property taxes or private mortgage insurance. After you enter the information, click Adjust and then click OK twice. Quicken calculates the full payment and redisplays the Loan Payment Reminder dialog box (refer to Figure 12-3).

17. Tag or add a memo description to the loan payment transaction.

If you click the Tag or Memo link on the Loan Payment Reminder dialog box, Quicken displays a little message box you can use to add a tag or memo. I talk a little bit about how tags and memo descriptions work in Chapter 4. (See, for example, the section on recording checks.) But let me also point out here that if you're using Quicken to track rental property, you want to tag the loan transaction by using the tag specific to a particular rental property. (See Chapter 16 for more information about using Quicken for rentals.)

18. (Optional) Fine-tune the way the reminder works.

If you want, you can click the Optional Settings link to get to other links that let you specify things like how many days in advance you want to be reminded. How these optional reminder settings work requires no lengthy explanation from me. If you're interested, just click around a bit and do a little experimenting.

19. Click Done twice.

Quicken adds the new loan payment to your financial records, along with the payment details and any reminder message settings you set up.

Figure 12-4: The Split Transaction dialog box.

Fixing loan stuff

Nobody's perfect, right? You may have made a tiny little mistake in setting up either the loan or the loan payment. This mistake doesn't need to be a major financial or personal crisis, however. Just display the loan account window's Loan Details tab by clicking the account name in the Accounts bar and then clicking the Loan Details tab (see Figure 12-5).

Figure 12-5:
The Loan
Details tab.

The Loan Details tab provides lots of interesting loan-related information, so take a couple of minutes to look it over. At the top of the tab, for example, Quicken tells you about the loan's terms, including the original balance, the origination date, the term, any balloon payment, the interest rate, and the compounding period. In the bottom part of the tab, Quicken displays a line chart that plots the paydown of the loan principal.

Changing loan terms

To edit most bits of the loan information, click the Edit Terms button. Quicken displays the Loan Details dialog box, as shown in Figure 12-6. This version of the Loan Details dialog box works just like the nearly identical Loan Details dialog box you used to originally describe the loan. (See Figure 12-1.) You can change any loan term by editing the contents of its text box. (If you have questions about what the different loan terms mean or their effect, refer to the preceding section.)

Hey, can I mention one other thing about the loan account window shown in Figure 12-5? See that tab labeled Payment Details? If you click the Payment Details tab, Quicken displays a pie chart that shows how loan payments break down into principal, interest, and (if applicable) other components. (Figure 12-7 shows the dialog box.) If you click the Edit Payment Details button, which appears just under the pie chart, Quicken displays another version of the "second" Loan Details dialog box originally shown in Figure 12-2. The second Loan Details dialog box lets you make changes in the loan payment breakdown. The Payment Details tab also shows a little register-style list of recent payments. You may want to take a minute to experiment with this tab, too. The information provided is pretty neat.

Working with interest rate changes

If you need to change the loan interest rate regularly, say because you've borrowed money on an adjustable- or variable-rate loan, you can click the loan account window's Interest Rate edit link. (This link appears in the upper-right corner of the loan account window.) When you click this link, Quicken displays the Loan Interest Rate dialog box (shown in Figure 12-8). This dialog box has a very simple purpose: It lists the interest rates you entered for a loan and the dates when these interest rates were used in loan calculations. For an adjustable-rate loan, click the arrowhead button next to the Adjustable-Rate Loans label to expand the dialog box so that it looks like the one shown in Figure 12-8.

Figure 12-7:
The
Payment
Details
dialog box.

Figure 12-8:
The Loan
Interest
Rate
dialog box.

If you want to record new interest rates — because you have a variable-rate loan and the interest rate changes, for example — display the Loan Interest Rate dialog box and then follow these steps:

1. **Indicate that you want to record a new interest rate.**

 Click the Add New Rate button in the Loan Interest Rate dialog box. Quicken displays the Variable Interest Rate dialog box, shown in Figure 12-9.

Figure 12-9: Changing a loan's interest rate.

2. **Provide the effective date of the interest rate change.**

 Use the Effective Date text box to indicate when the new interest rate becomes effective. You can either type a date or open the drop-down list box and select a date from the calendar.

3. **Give the new interest rate.**

 Type the new interest rate in the Interest Rate text box. When you move the selection cursor to a new box, Quicken refigures the loan payment and sticks the new loan payment figure in the Regular Payment text box.

4. **Click OK.**

Removing loans

You can delete (remove) loans you no longer need or shouldn't have added in the first place. Here are the steps:

1. **Display the loan account window by clicking the loan name on the Accounts bar.**

 Quicken displays the loan account window and either the Loan Details or Payment Details tab.

2. **Choose the Actions menu's Edit Account command.**

 Quicken displays the Account Details dialog box (see Figure 12-10).

Account Details

| General | Display Options |

| Account Name | Loan | | Financial Institution | |
| Description | | | Account Number | |

Account Type: Loan

Interest Rate	5	%		Contact Name		
Linked Asset Account	(none)			Phone		
Loan Type	Loan			Home page	*Bank Web page*	Go
			Activity page	*Activity Web page*	Go	
			Other page	*Other Web page*	Go	

Comments

? Delete Account OK Cancel

Figure 12-10: You can use the Account Details dialog box to remove a loan account.

3. **Delete the loan account by clicking the Delete Account button.**

4. **When Quicken asks you to confirm your deletion, type the word "Yes" into the Type Yes To Confirm text box**

You'd probably remove only a loan account that you previously added as an experiment or a loan account that you added incorrectly and need to restart from scratch. You probably wouldn't want to remove a loan account you've paid off, because you may want information about the loan later on.

Delivering a Pound of Flesh (Also Known as Making a Payment)

After you set up a liability account, you're ready to hand over a pound of your flesh — that is, make a payment. Before you say that this phrase is just some sort of populist bull-dweeble, I want to remind you that this metaphor comes from Shakespeare's *The Merchant of Venice,* in which a loan is guaranteed by a pound of human flesh. Furthermore, I want to point out that with this allusion, I've been able to incorporate both violence and high culture into a computer how-to book. Sweet.

Recording the payment

After you set up the loan and the loan payment, you're ready to record the payment.

To record the payment, follow these steps:

1. **Display the loan account.**

 Click the loan account on the Accounts bar and then click the Payment Details tab.

2. **Choose the Enter Loan Payment command.**

 Click the Actions button (the button in the upper-right corner of the screen that shows that little gear) and then choose the Enter Loan Payment command from the menu that Quicken displays. Quicken displays the Enter Expense Transaction dialog box (see Figure 12-11).

3. **Verify the loan payment details.**

 Quicken should have filled out the Enter Expense Transaction dialog box correctly. But this is your money, after all, so be careful. Make sure that the right information appears.

4. **Click Enter Transaction.**

 Quicken enters the loan payment in the liability register and bank account register. If you want to print and mail a paper check, you can do that in the way I describe in Chapter 5.

Handling mortgage escrow accounts

I should talk about one minor, mortgage recordkeeping annoyance: mortgage escrow accounts.

If you have a mortgage, you know the basic procedure. Although your mortgage payment may be $536.82 per month, your friendly mortgage company (while insisting that it trusts you completely) makes you pay an extra $125 per month for property taxes and other such things. In other words, even though you're paying only $536.82 per month in principal and interest, your monthly payment to the mortgage company is, according to this example, $661.82 ($536.82 + $125).

The mortgage company, as you probably know, saves this money for you in an *escrow* account or a set of escrow accounts. A couple of times yearly, the mortgage company pays your property taxes; a time or two per year, it pays your homeowner's insurance. If you have private mortgage insurance, it may pay this fee every month as well. And so it goes.

The question, then, is how do you treat this stuff? As with most things, you can take the easy way (which is rough, dirty, and unshaven) or the hard way (which is precise, sophisticated, and cumbersome).

You can choose whichever method you want. It's your life.

The rough, dirty, and unshaven method

Suppose that you do pay an extra $125 per month. You can treat this extra $125 as another expense category, such as Tax:Property or Other Housing or Property Expenses. (I'm just making up these categories. If you can think of better ones, use your own.)

Nice. Easy. No fuss. These words and phrases pop into my head when I think about the rough, dirty, and unshaven method of mortgage escrow recordkeeping. Figure 12-12 shows a sample Split Transaction window filled out this way. If the Split Transaction window seems like too much fuss, mosey on over to Chapter 4, where I give you the rundown on using it.

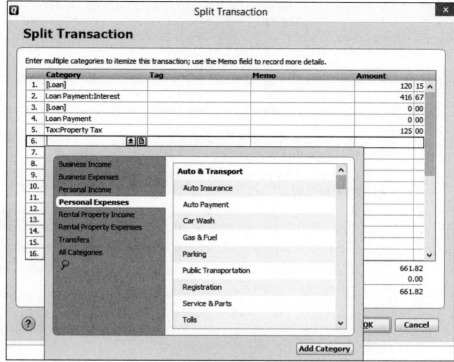

Figure 12-12:
A mortgage
payment
with an
escrow
account
treated as
an expense.

I use the rough, dirty, and unshaven method. Let me make a confession, though. This approach doesn't tell you how much moolah you have stashed away in your escrow accounts. It also doesn't tell you how much you really spend in the way of homeowner's insurance, what you're entitled to claim as a property tax deduction, or how much the bank is bleeding you for private mortgage insurance.

To get these figures, you have to peruse the monthly and annual mortgage account statements — that is, if you get them. Or you have to call the mortgage lender and rattle a cage or two.

Still, with all its shortcomings, I like the easy-to-use, rough, dirty, unshaven method.

The precise, sophisticated, and cumbersome approach

You say you can't live with the uncertainty, the stress, the not knowing? Then I have another approach just for you.

You can set up an *asset account* for each escrow account for which the mortgage company collects money.

You set up an asset account the way you set up a checking account. And, in fact, you should think of escrow accounts essentially as special checking accounts in which your lender deposits money collected from you so that it can pay your property taxes and insurance.

Because I explain this "setting up a checking account" process in Chapter 1, I cover it quickly here. You set up an asset account with its starting balance equal to the current escrow account balance. To do so, follow these steps:

1. **Display the Quicken home page or some other Quicken tab that shows the Accounts bar along the left edge of the window.**

2. **Click the Add an Account button to indicate that you want to create a new account.**

3. **As you step through the seemingly interminable account setup process, identify the account as an asset account and give it a name.**

4. **Tell Quicken how much money is in the account as of a specific date.**

 If you've set up an account or two in your time, this process should take you about 40 seconds.

After you set up your asset account and record its current balance, you're ready to cruise. Record payments in the escrow as account transfers whenever you record the actual loan payment.

You need to do one other thing: When you set up an escrow account, you must record the payments that the bank makes from your escrow account to the county assessor (for property taxes) and to the insurance company (for things such as homeowner's and private mortgage insurance). You don't know when these payments are really made, so watch your monthly mortgage account statements.

When the mortgage company disburses money from the escrow account to pay your first property tax assessment, for example, you need to record a decrease equal to the payment for property taxes and then categorize the transaction as a property tax expense. This process isn't tricky in terms of mechanics. The account increases after every loan payment and decreases after a disbursement.

Basically, the Asset Account register mirrors the Checking Account register. The only difference is that the Checking Account register's Payment and Deposit fields are relabeled as the Decrease and Increase fields in an Asset Account register. To get to this account's register, click its name on the Accounts bar.

This second approach doesn't seem like all that much work, does it? And if you use this approach, you can track escrow balances and escrow spending precisely. You can, for example, pull your property tax deduction right from Quicken. (Jeepers, maybe I should try the sophisticated approach next year.)

Your Principal-Interest Breakdown Won't Be Right

Not to bum you out, but your principal-interest breakdown is often wrong. You may calculate interest expense as $416.67 when your bank calculates it as $416.69. A few pennies here, a few pennies there, and pretty soon your account balance and interest expense tallies are a few pennies off.

So you can't change the world

You can try calling the bank, telling whomever you talk to what a bozo he (or she) is, and then demanding that someone there correct your balance. (If this approach works for you, let me know.)

Or (and this method is really more practical) you can adjust your records to agree with the bank's records. Here's how:

1. **Display the register for the liability.**

 To get to this account's register, you just click the account name on the Accounts bar and then click the Payment tab.

2. **Click the Account Actions button and choose the Update Balance command from the resulting menu.**

 (Go ahead. Tap your keys very hard if you're angry that the bank won't adjust its records.) Quicken displays the Update Balance dialog box, shown in Figure 12-13.

Figure 12-13: The Update Balance dialog box.

3. **Enter the correct account balance (that is, the one that the bank says is correct).**

 Type the correct figure in the New Balance text box. (The amount probably comes from the year-end or month-end loan statement.)

4. **Enter the last day of the month or year for which you're making the adjustment.**

 Enter a transaction date in the Adjustment Date text box. (You must use a transaction date that sticks the adjustment transaction — which fixes the principal-interest split — in the right month or year.)

5. **Record the adjustment.**

 When the Update Balance dialog box correctly describes the needed adjustment, click OK.

Slightly smarter adjustments

The Update Balance dialog box (shown in Figure 12-13) adjusts the loan balance to whatever value you indicate, but then it forgets to categorize this adjustment, instead calling the change a *balance adjustment*. That's okay, I guess. But if you want to be slightly smarter about this adjustment, you should adjust the interest expense category. Let me explain.

When you record loan payments, you split the loan payment between the interest expense category and a principal account transfer that reduces the liability. When the liability gets reduced either too much or not enough — as would be the case if you need to adjust the liability balance — you must fix the liability balance *and* the principal-interest split.

Suppose that over the course of a year, you record $0.17 too little interest expense — and, therefore, record $0.17 too much principal reduction, despite your best efforts to be accurate. You need to increase the liability account balance by $0.17 in this case, but you also need to increase the interest expense figure by $0.17.

If you want to be just a little bit more obsessive-compulsive than Quicken is, you can do so. Simply display the loan account register, select the adjustment transaction, and then use the appropriate interest expense category for Adjustment.

Automatic Payments

Quicken has a couple of nifty features — Scheduled Transactions and the Calendar — that can help you with automatic loan payments.

The Calendar and Scheduled Transactions features may be useful in other instances as well. A business, for example, may use the Scheduled Transactions and Calendar features to schedule and plan employee payroll checks, tax returns, and deposits. But I think that these features are most useful in the case of a loan, so I talk about them here.

Scheduling a bill reminder

If a payment occurs regularly — for a loan or some other regular bill, such as your cable TV service — you can tell Quicken to remind you about the payment, or you can set it up as a scheduled payment. When you do so, Quicken either reminds you or automatically records the payment for you, based on a schedule.

Follow these steps to set up such a reminder or scheduled transaction:

1. **Display the Calendar window.**

 To display the Quicken Calendar window, press Ctrl+K or choose the Tools⇨Calendar command. Either way, Quicken displays the Calendar window, shown in Figure 12-14. The figure shows a calendar for the current month and, optionally, a list of memorized payees.

Figure 12-14: The Calendar window.

 Note: If you can't see the list of transactions along the right edge of the Calendar window, click the Options button and then choose the Show Memorized Payees List command from the menu Quicken displays. By dragging payees' names from the list to the Calendar, you add transactions to the calendar one at a time, using previously recorded transactions.

2. **Display the first month for which you want to schedule the transaction.**

 Using the left- and right-arrow buttons, select the starting month for the reminder or scheduled transaction. You can also enter a date in the Go to Date box and click the Go button. Quicken displays the month you want to schedule a payment for inside the Calendar window.

3. **Click the Add Reminder button and choose Bill Reminder from the menu.**

 Quicken displays the first Add Bill Reminder dialog box (not shown), which you use to enter the payee name. You can also click the button at the right end of the Pay To box to drop down a list of previous payees and then select one.

4. **Click Next, and use the second Add Bill Reminder dialog box to describe the recurring payment.**

 You use the second Add a Bill Reminder dialog box (see Figure 12-15) to describe the recurring payment.

Figure 12-15:
The second
Add Bill
Reminder
dialog box.

5. **Verify that the Pay To and Amount Due fields are correct.**

 They probably are. But I have kind of a compulsive personality. Because I've been telling you to check all this other stuff, I thought I'd also suggest that you check these fields. Quicken uses the last payment amount to the payee as the suggested amount due, by the way.

6. **Check the payment-scheduling stuff.**

 Verify that the Due Next On text box and labeling show the correct date for the first payment. If Quicken doesn't show the current due date, click the button that shows a picture of a stubby little pencil to display a pop-up box with boxes that let you specify how often the payment should be made; which day of, say, the month the payment is due; and the date when payments should stop.

7. **Identify how the payment should be made.**

 Open the From Account drop-down list box and then select the appropriate account.

8. **Categorize, tag, and bag.**

 If you're scheduling a reminder for a transaction that you've already correctly recorded once, the Category, Tag, and Memo fields should show the correct information. You should still check them, however. You don't want to have Quicken copy some old error you made. (Note that the Tag field appears only if you've enabled the Show Tag Field option in the Register section of the Quicken Preferences window.) Quicken opens text boxes that let you make changes in the Category, Tag, and Memo fields when you click the Add Category, tag, or memo link in the Details field.

9. **Click Done.**

 Quicken adds the payee's transaction to the Calendar.

Note: When you schedule payments, you may implicitly break your budget. If you've set up a budget and scheduling a payment does "break" the budget, Quicken alerts you. Quicken also asks (in the nicest way possible) whether you want to update your budget. For more information about budgeting, refer to Chapter 3.

Scheduling income and transfer reminders

If you click the Add Reminder button, shown in the lower-left corner of the Calendar window (refer to Figure 12-14 earlier in this chapter), Quicken displays a menu of three commands: Bill Reminder, Income Reminder, and Transfer Reminder.

Although I describe in step-by-step detail only the Bill Reminder command (see the preceding paragraphs), you can use the Income Reminder and Transfer Reminder commands in the same basic way that you use the Bill Reminder command. The Income Reminder command lets you schedule reminders to record recurring income or deposit transactions such as from a regular payroll check. The Transfer Reminder command lets you schedule reminders to record recurring transfers such as mortgage payments from your checking account.

Another way to schedule transactions

Quicken allows you to automatically schedule the adding of transactions. To create these scheduled transactions, click the Manage Reminders button at the bottom of the Calendar window or choose Tools⇨Manage Bill & Income Reminders. Quicken displays the Bill and Income Reminders window (see Figure 12-16).

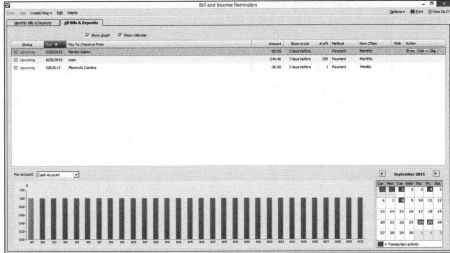

Figure 12-16:
The Bill and
Income
Reminders
window.

To create a scheduled transaction, click the Create New button and select the Bill Reminder, Income Reminder, or Transfer Reminder command from the resulting menu. After you choose the transaction you want to schedule, Quicken displays a dialog box (not shown here) that you use to describe an automatically scheduled transaction. you can automatically schedule any kind of transaction — loan payments, insurance premiums, child support, or whatever. (I'm describing automatically scheduled transactions in this chapter, though, because loan payments are among the most common ways to use this Quicken feature.) If you have questions about how bill, income, or transfer reminders work, refer to "Scheduling a bill reminder" earlier in this chapter. But know that income and transfer reminders work very, very similarly to bill reminders.

The Create New menu's Scheduled Transaction Group command deserves a bit more discussion, though, so let me briefly touch on that subject. If you choose Scheduled Transaction Group from the menu Quicken displays when you click the Create New button, Quicken displays the Create Transaction Group dialog box (see Figure 12-17).

A *scheduled transaction group* is a collection of transactions that you schedule together — such as all the bills you need to pay on the first of the month or out of your second paycheck.

Figure 12-17:
The Create
Transaction
Group
dialog box.

To create a scheduled transaction group, use the Create Transaction Group dialog box to name the group, pick the account from which you'll use funds, and then provide payment date and frequency information.

The Create Transaction Group dialog box provides a list of memorized transactions that you can use to indicate which transactions belong in the group. Check the box for each transaction you want to add.

Checking out the Calendar

The bar along the top of the Calendar (refer to Figure 12-14) provides some other tools that you may want to use. I'm not going to spend much time on them; you'll have more fun trying them out yourself than you would reading about them. Nevertheless, let me give you a bird's-eye view:

- ✔ The **Add Note** button lets you post a note on a calendar day. You use this feature to create reminder notes that will also appear in the Alerts area of the Cash Flow Center. You may want to post a note saying *Remember Wedding Anniversary* on the big day, for example. After you click this button, Quicken displays a dialog box in which you type the message. Then you click (in effect) Save My Butt. The program also marks the calendar day with a little yellow square — a miniature stick-on note. Click the square to read the message.

- ✔ The **Options** button displays a menu of commands that let you specify which transactions should appear in the Calendar, add an account balance graph in the Calendar window, and fiddle with the memorized transactions list. The transactions shown in that list box along the right edge of the Calendar window, by the way, are memorized transactions. (Chapter 4 briefly discusses memorized transactions.)

Chapter 13

Tracking Tax-Deferred Investments

. .

In This Chapter

▶ Knowing when to use Quicken investment record keeping

▶ Setting up a tax-deferred investment account

▶ Recording your initial investment

▶ Buying investments

▶ Recording profits

▶ Selling your investments

▶ Adjusting your share counts and price information

. .

*I*nvestment record keeping is something that more of us need to think about. More of us are investing as the population ages and we prepare for retirement. And the recent bouts of sheer craziness in the financial markets means that we probably all need to save more.

Fortunately, Quicken provides great tools for managing your investments, including your tax-deferred investments. And this chapter talks about those tools. But first, I should talk about whether you even need to do this.

Deciding to Use Investment Features

The Quicken investment record-keeping feature lets you do three important things:

✔ Track your interest and dividend income.

✔ Track real and potential capital gains and losses.

✔ Measure an investment's performance by calculating the annual return from an investment.

If you're a serious investor, these things probably sound worthwhile. But before you invest any time discovering how Quicken investment record keeping works, be sure that you need all this power.

Are your investments tax-deferred?

If your investments are *tax-deferred* — if, for example, you're using individual retirement accounts (IRAs), Simple IRAs, Roth accounts, or 401(k)s — you don't really need to track investment income and capital gains and losses. Tax-deferred investments have no effect on your personal income taxes in the United States. You get a tax deduction for the money you stick into IRAs, for example, and anything you take out is taxable. Or in the case of a Roth IRA or Roth 401(k), you don't get a deduction for amounts you stick into the account, but you also don't get taxed on amounts taken out of the account — which means that you don't need to closely account for Roth IRA investments, at least for tax accounting reasons.

With tax-deferred investments — such as deductible IRAs, 401(k)s, and Simple IRAs — you record all that you should need to know via your checking account. Checks earmarked for investment are categorized as *IRA Deductions*, for example, and investment account withdrawals deposited into your checking account are categorized as *IRA Distributions*. In other words, you don't need to set up special accounts for tracking your investments. Your bank accounts track everything you need to keep track of.

Note: For purposes of this chapter, 529 plans are also tax-deferred investments, but a 529 plan works a little differently. In a 529 plan, you save money for someone else's college costs — probably a child or grandchild. You don't get a tax deduction when you put money into the 529 plan, but the investment earnings are *not* taxed as they are realized. And later, when the plan beneficiary (again, probably your child or grandchild) withdraws money, the withdrawals aren't taxed as long as the money is used for college costs. In a sense, a 529 plan works like a Roth account — except that the money goes for college, not for retirement.

Are you a mutual fund fanatic?

I want to make a related point. If you're a fan of mutual funds, you don't need Quicken to measure the funds' annual returns. Fund managers provide these figures for you in quarterly and annual reports. Sometimes you also get personal performance data that's even more granular at the mutual fund's website. In sum, part of what you're paying the mutual fund manager for is record keeping and performance management.

Accordingly, if you're investing in mutual funds through a tax-deferred account, you probably *really* don't need to be going to the extra work of figuring out the Quicken investment recording stuff.

Some investors don't need Quicken

Let me give you an example of someone who doesn't need to use the Quicken program's investments feature: me. Once upon a time, I bought and sold common stocks, fooled around with a dozen or more mutual funds, and found out firsthand why junk bonds are called junk bonds. (Apparently, junk bonds are more risky, so they fluctuate wildly in value.) For the past couple of decades, and even though my investment account has grown steadily through compound interest and additional savings, I've simplified my financial affairs considerably.

I don't invest directly in stocks, bonds, or mutual funds these days; instead, I stick money almost entirely into an IRA. My investments don't produce appreciable taxable dividends or interest income; neither do they regularly produce taxable or tax-saving capital gains or losses. Money that I put into the IRA is tax-deductible. And money that I ultimately take out of the IRA will be taxable.

I'm also sticking with a handful of mutual funds, but I don't need to calculate the annual return; that's what mutual fund managers do. So I don't need to figure, for example, what my shares of Vanguard Total Stock Market Portfolio (my favorite mutual fund) delivered as an annual return when I include both the 1 percent dividend and the 8 percent price change.

Because I don't need to track investment income, track capital gains and losses, or calculate the progress of my investment portfolio, I don't need Quicken investment record keeping for my personal use.

Many investors do want Quicken

Many people — including mutual fund investors using tax-deferred investment options such as 401(k) plans, 403(b) plans, and individual retirement accounts — do want to track their investments with Quicken, of course, in spite of the laziness I'm trying to promote. Accordingly, I'm going to describe how to track tax-deferred accounts with Quicken.

Furthermore, if you have a taxable portfolio stuffed full of individual stocks and bonds, you're going to want to use Quicken to track your other taxable investment accounts anyway. And if you're going to go to that work, it's not much additional effort to track tax-deferred investments with Quicken, too.

How to pick a mutual fund

Would you mind terribly if I took a minute to provide a handful of tips about how to pick a mutual fund? I guess I'm thinking that maybe, just maybe, my observations might be useful to you. I'm not, after all, trying to earn a commission by selling you some financial product or service, so maybe I can be a bit more objective. I'm also rather overeducated (with a couple of master's degrees — one in finance and one in taxation). And I've been a CPA for, jeepers, 30 years; am a former registered investment advisor but am not trying to sell you investments; and, most interestingly, have seen countless real-life examples of people's investing successes and mistakes.

Here, then, are my tips:

✔ **Carefully watch your investment expenses, including both commissions and the mutual fund management fees.** Why? Despite what you may have been told, you almost never get extra investment returns by paying extra for investment advice or financial planning. And note that every bit of financial research — the kind that finance professors do — supports this statement. Usually, you want to pick the cheapest mutual fund alternative. Almost always, that's an index fund. One other note: Remember that paying a 2 percent fee on investments earning 8 percent means you're giving up 25 percent of your profit to the mutual fund or financial advisor. That's like a 25 percent tax!

✔ **Use tax-deferred investment accounts such as 401(k)s, 403(b)s, and IRAs for your investments.** Income taxes can be a huge drag on your investment returns. And over the decades that you'll be investing, minimizing your income taxes will add at least tens of thousands of dollars (and potentially hundreds of thousands of dollars) to your wealth.

✔ **To diversify, use an inexpensive index fund, one per investment category.** You can diversify by investing in one index fund that invests in the U.S. stock market, another index fund that invests in corporate bonds, another that invests in real estate investment trusts, and so on. Diversification reduces your investment risk.

✔ **Consider one of the new target retirement funds such as those offered by Vanguard, T. Rowe Price, and Fidelity.** With one of these babies, you don't worry about trying to diversify. You don't worry about asset allocation or rebalancing. You don't worry about adjusting your investment mix as you get older. You just pick a single fund that's tied to your retirement year. If you'll retire in 2035, you buy the target retirement that assumes you'll retire in 2035. That's it. That's the last investment decision you need to make.

✔ **For goodness' sake, don't trade, attempting to buy low and sell high.** Trading rarely works, and it's always expensive. Be a long-term investor who buys inexpensive mutual funds and holds them for the long term.

✔ **Invest some time and money in beefing up your investment knowledge.** You can do this by reading pretty much anything that Burton Malkiel or John Bogle has written. I particularly like and recommend Burton Malkiel's *A Random Walk Guide to Investing* (published by W. W. Norton & Company).

Tracking a Tax-Deferred Investment

If you need to track a tax-deferred investment, you need to know how to set up a tax-deferred account and then record your investment activities.

If you'll use Quicken to track any of your investments, you shouldn't skip this section. Understanding how tax-deferred investment works makes tracking taxable investments much, much easier for you.

Setting up a tax-deferred investment account

Setting up an investment account to track a tax-deferred investment account works the same way as setting up any other account:

1. **Click the Add an Account button at the bottom of the Accounts bar.**

 Quicken dutifully displays the first Quicken Add Account dialog box that you use to add a new Quicken account (see Figure 13-1). If you've read this book in order so far, you've likely seen this dialog box many times by now. It asks you to identify the type of account you want to add.

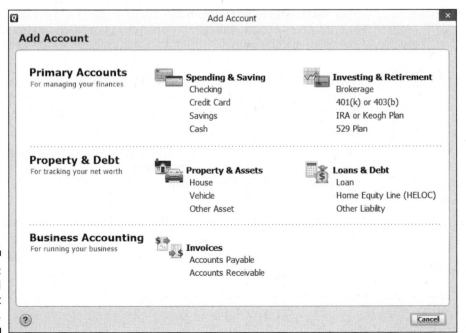

Figure 13-1:
The first Add Account dialog box.

2. **Identify the type of investments in the account.**

 You select the appropriate Investing & Retirement hyperlink to indicate that you're adding an investment account: Brokerage, 401(k) or 403(b), IRA or Keogh Plan, or 529 Plan. When you do, Quicken asks for the name of the financial institution you use.

 Just to quickly identify what these account types actually are, a *529 plan* is a college savings account that complies with Sec. 529 of the Internal Revenue Code. The *401(k)* and *403(b)* accounts are retirement accounts that comply with Sec. 401(k) and Sec. 403(b) of the Internal Revenue Code. The *IRA* or *Keogh* account type is for individual retirement accounts (IRA) and Keogh accounts (an old type of retirement savings account). The standard brokerage account option is the catch-all account type for investment accounts that *aren't* tax-favored retirement or college savings accounts. (I talk about this type of account in Chapter 14.)

3. **Identify the financial institution.**

 After you specify which type of investment account you're setting up, Quicken displays the second Add Account dialog box, which asks for the name of the bank or broker holding your investments. This dialog box lets you enter the bank or broker name or part of the name in a text box or lets you choose it from a list of popular banks. If you do identify the bank or financial institution, Quicken prompts you to provide the online username and password you use to access your account information electronically. Alternatively, click the Advanced Setup hyperlink at the bottom of the dialog box to indicate that you don't want to identify your bank or broker. Quicken ten displays another version of the second Add Account dialog box, which lets you click the I Want to Enter Transactions Manually button to indicate that you want to enter investment transactions manually.

 Note: Quicken really wants you to grab your transactions electronically from the bank or financial institution. But entering the transactions manually usually works well when you're just starting with Quicken.

4. **Click Next, name the investment, and then click Next again.**

 Quicken displays the third Add Account dialog box (shown in Figure 13-2). Move the cursor to the Account Name/Nickname text box and type a name for the account. If you're setting up an account to track an individual retirement account, you might type **IRA**.

 When you click Next, Quicken displays the fourth Add Account dialog box.

Add IRA / Keogh Account

Enter the name you'd like to use for this account in Quicken.
For example: "Alice's IRA" or "Ralph's Rollover IRA"

Account Name/Nickname IRA

? Cancel Back Next

Figure 13-2:
The third
Add
Account
dialog box.

5. **Provide the last statement date and then click Next.**

 The fourth Add Account dialog box (see Figure 13-3) asks for the date of
 the statement you're using to enter your investment information. This
 date is the starting date, in essence, for your investment record keeping
 with Quicken. Enter the date and then click Next.

6. **Describe the cash balance or money market balance (if any) associ-
 ated with the account and then click Next.**

 As you probably already know if you're investing through a broker, some
 investment accounts have a cash account associated with the main
 investment account. The cash in this account, of course, provides the
 money you use for additional investments. And when you receive cash
 from selling some investment or from some dividend, the money goes
 into this account.

 To describe this cash account, use the Cash and Money Market text
 boxes to give the opening balances. You can probably guess this, but
 at the risk of being redundant, the information that you provide to set
 up a cash account or money market fund mirrors the information you
 provide to set up a regular ol' checking account.

Figure 13-3:
The fourth
Add
Account
dialog box.

7. (Optional) Identify the account owner.

If you set up a 401(k) or 403(b) account, Quicken may prompt you to enter information about who owns the tax-deferred investment account: you or your spouse. Using the boxes and buttons available, try to answer these questions as best you can about whether an account is yours or your spouse's, whether the account relates to current or past employment, and so on. Don't worry too much about this, however; it's just icing on the cake. When you've answered the questions as best you can, click Next to display the sixth Add Account dialog box (see Figure 13-4).

8. Name the security, provide the ticker symbol, and then click Next.

This sixth dialog box does two things for you:

- It collects the investment's ticker symbol (if available) so that you can download share prices several times during the day and drive yourself half mad with anxiety. If you don't know the ticker symbol, click the Ticker Symbol Lookup button to display a Quicken web page that lets you find the ticker symbol.

- It asks you to name the security held in the investment account you're setting up, using the Security Name box. This won't make sense in some cases, such as when you're holding a single certificate of deposit in an IRA. But in other cases, such as when you've set up an IRA with a mutual fund company and invested in three mutual funds within the IRA, identifying the securities within the account separately makes sense.

When you click Next, Quicken displays the seventh Add Account dialog box, shown in Figure 13-5.

9. Provide a total shares count.

Enter the number of shares you hold of each security you identified in Step 8.

10. **Click Next.**

 Quicken displays a dialog box summarizing the investment that you've just entered. If something seems to be amiss, click the Back button to find the Add Account dialog box where you entered some incorrect bit of information. If everything seems okay, click Done. For some types of tax-deferred investment accounts, Quicken may also ask for additional information. If you set up an IRA account, for example, Quicken asks about the type of IRA you're setting up and whether the IRA belongs to you or to your spouse. Quicken may also ask about the possibility that you're setting up an account to track a single mutual fund. Answer any questions by clicking the Yes or No button as appropriate. When you're done answering all the questions, click Finish.

11. **Review the new (partially described) investment.**

 To check your work so far, click the Investing tab and its Portfolio button. Quicken displays the Portfolio window, which shows your new investment account and provides a bit of additional, investment-related information (see Figure 13-6).

Figure 13-6:
The Investing tab shows the newly set-up investment account.

Recording your initial investment

After you set up an investment account and describe the securities in the account, you can record an initial purchase of the investments.

You need to know the original price of those first shares, of course. So dig through that kitchen drawer where you stuff bank statements, financial records, and those kooky birthday cards from Aunt Enid.

When you find the proper paperwork that shows the number of shares you purchased and the price per share, here's what you do:

1. **Open the investment account, if it isn't already open.**

 Open the investment account by clicking the account name on the Accounts bar.

 If the Investing tab isn't shown, choose View⇨Tabs to Show⇨Investing.

2. **Tell Quicken that you want to enter cost basis data.**

 Click the Enter hyperlink in the Cost Basis column. If the Cost Basis column doesn't show the Enter Cost hyperlink, click the plus (+) symbol next to the Security Name you chose for the mutual fund. After you click the hyperlink, Quicken displays the Enter Missing Transactions dialog box, shown in Figure 13-7.

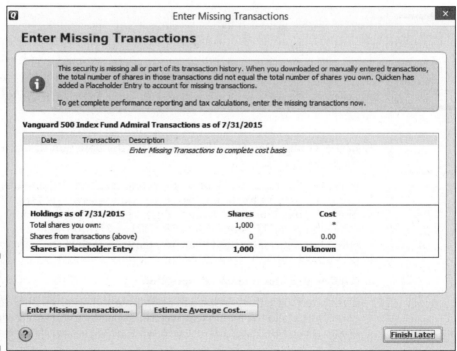

Figure 13-7:
The Enter Missing Transactions dialog box.

3. **Click the Enter Missing Transaction button.**

 Quicken displays the Buy – Shares Bought dialog box, shown in Figure 13-8.

Figure 13-8:
The Buy –
Shares
Bought
dialog box.

4. **In the Transaction Date text box, enter the date you first purchased the fund shares.**

 Move the cursor to the Transaction Date text box and enter the date by using *MM/DD/YYYY* format. ***Note:*** You don't have to enter a two-digit month or day number if a single digit makes sense. Enter July 18, 1998, for example, as **7/18/98** or July 18, 2008 as **7/18/08**. Quicken is smart enough to figure the right year. You may also select the date from the pop-up calendar.

5. **(Optional) Enter a memo description.**

 If you want to tie the purchase to a confirmation order number, for example, enter the data in the Memo text box. I suppose that you could use this text box to record anything: *Kilroy was here. Save the whales. Don't tread on me.*

6. **Indicate the size of your purchase.**

 To enter the total number of shares, move the cursor to the Number of Shares text box. (Fractional shares are okay.)

7. **Indicate what you paid per share.**

 With the cursor in the Price Paid text box, enter the amount you paid for the lot. After you supply Quicken the adjusted cost basis, it calculates the total cost.

8. **Record the initial purchase of mutual fund shares by clicking the Enter/Done button.**

 Quicken redisplays the Enter Missing Transactions dialog box (refer to Figure 13-7).

9. **(Optional) Repeat Steps 2–8, if necessary.**

 You need to repeat Steps 2–8 to record any other lots you purchased. If you own 1,000 shares of Vanguard 500 Index, but you accumulated these shares by buying shares ten times over the past ten years, you need to record ten separate lots. The last time through the steps, if you're setting up a tax-deferred investment account that you didn't really need to set up, you can ask yourself why you didn't listen to me when I said you don't need and therefore don't want to do this for tax-deferred investments.

After you describe each lot that makes up your holdings of the mutual fund investment, the Enter Missing Transactions dialog box shows that there aren't any placeholders for missing transactions because the Shares placeholder and the Cost placeholder should both equal zero (see Figure 13-9). You can click Done.

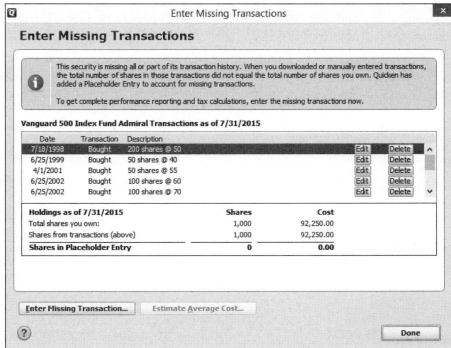

Figure 13-9:
The Enter Missing Transactions dialog box after one enters all the missing transactions.

> If you make a mistake entering a transaction, you can click the Edit or Delete button to the right of the transaction to change or remove the erroneous data.

Buying investments

As you buy additional investments — by contributing additional amounts to your retirement account or by reinvesting dividends and capital gain distributions — you record the transactions for the investment account.

By writing a check

If you buy shares by writing a check, display the investment window (by clicking the Investing tab and then clicking the investment account) and then record the purchase by following these steps:

1. **Click the Enter Transactions button.**

 Quicken displays the dialog box used to enter investment transactions.

2. **Select Buy – Shares Bought from the Enter Transaction drop-down list box.**

 Quicken displays the Buy – Shares Bought version of the investment transaction entry dialog box, shown in Figure 13-10.

Figure 13-10: The Buy – Shares Bought dialog box.

3. **Enter the purchase date in the Transaction Date text box.**

4. **(Optional) Enter a description in the Memo text box.**

5. **(Optional) Enter the bank account on which you'll write the check that pays for the shares.**

 If you're not purchasing shares using money available in a cash account connected to the investment account, select the account name from the Account drop-down list box.

6. **Indicate the size of your purchase by using the Number of Shares and the Price Paid text boxes.**

 Tell Quicken the size of your investment by entering the number of shares purchased and the price paid per share.

7. **Enter the commission or fee that you paid.**

 Move the cursor to the Commission text box and enter the commission or fee you paid to purchase the shares. (The amount shown in the Total Cost text box includes this figure.)

8. **Record the purchase.**

 Click the Enter/New button if you want to record the transaction and enter another new transaction, or click the Enter/Done button if you want to record just the single transaction. Quicken records your purchase of new shares. You're now a capitalist. Congratulations.

By reinvesting dividends, interest, or capital gains

When you reinvest your dividends, interest, or capital gains, you also must record your reinvestment transactions. Essentially, you're buying new shares with the dividend or capital gain proceeds you could have received. To record the reinvestment of investment profits, display the investment window (by clicking the Investing tab and then clicking the investment account) and then follow these steps:

1. **Click the Enter Transactions button.**

 Quicken displays the dialog box used to enter investments transactions.

2. **Select Reinvest – Income Reinvested from the Enter Transaction drop-down list box.**

 Quicken displays the Reinvest – Income Reinvested version of the investment transaction entry dialog box, shown in Figure 13-11.

Figure 13-11:
The
Reinvest –
Income
Reinvested
dialog box.

3. **Enter the purchase date (in this case, the reinvestment date) in the Transaction Date text box.**

4. **(Optional) Type a brief explanation of the transaction in the Memo text box.**

5. **Use the Amount and Shares columns to describe the reinvestment.**

 Take another look at Figure 13-11. No, really, go ahead. I'll wait. See those rows labeled Dividend, Interest, Short-Term Cap Gain Dist, Mid-Term Cap Gain Dist, and Long-Term Cap Gain Dist? And see the columns labeled Amount and Shares? Use these rows and columns to record the amounts of dividends, interest, and capital gains distributed to you by the mutual fund and to record the numbers of shares you purchase by reinvesting these amounts. If you receive $1,800 in dividends and use this amount to purchase 10 shares, you enter **1800** in the Dividend Amount box and **10** in the Dividend Shares text boxes, respectively.

6. **Record the reinvestment transaction.**

 Click the Enter/New button if you want to record the transaction and enter another new transaction, or click the Enter/Done button if you want to record just the single transaction.

Figure 13-11 shows $1,800 of dividends being reinvested in the mutual fund by buying 10 more shares.

Recording your profits

Perhaps regularly, you'll receive distributions directly from the investment account's investments but don't immediately reinvest them. Instead, you deposit these proceeds in the investment accounts' cash account or money market account.

To record these kinds of distributions, you follow a process very similar to the one I describe in the preceding section. To record an income transaction directly into the investment account, follow these steps:

1. **Click the Enter Transactions button.**

 If necessary, click the investment account to display the account's information in a register and then click the Enter Transactions button. Quicken displays the dialog box used to enter investment transactions.

2. **Select Inc – Income (Div, Int, Etc.) from the Enter Transaction drop-down list box.**

 Quicken displays the Inc – Income (Div, Int, Etc.) version of the investment transaction entry dialog box. The Inc – Income (Div, Int, Etc.) version of the investment transaction entry dialog box closely resembles the Reinvest – Income Reinvested dialog box, so I won't show it here.

3. **Enter the distribution date in the Transaction Date text box.**

4. **Use the Transfer Account drop-down list to identify the account into which you'll deposit the check that the mutual fund company sends you.**

5. **(Optional) Type a brief description of the distribution in the Memo text box.**

 Be creative. Type your wedding anniversary, the name of your dog, or even a piece of data related to the dividend or distribution.

6. **Indicate the dividend or capital gains distribution amount.**

 Enter the amount in the appropriate amount text box. A dividend, I hope you can guess, goes in the Dividend box; a short-term capital gain goes in the Short-Term Cap Gain Dist box, and so on.

7. **Record the dividend or distribution transaction.**

 When you click either the Enter/New or the Enter/Done button, you record the dividend. If you click the Enter/New button, Quicken leaves the dialog box open so that you can enter some other transactions.

Selling investments

Selling mutual fund shares works basically the same way as buying them, only in reverse. To record the sale of shares held in an investment account, perform the following actions:

1. **Click the Enter Transactions button.**

 Display the investment window by clicking the Investing Center button and then clicking the Enter Transactions button. Quicken displays the dialog box used to enter investment transactions.

2. **Select Sell – Shares Sold from the Enter Transaction drop-down list box.**

 Quicken displays the Sell – Shares Sold version of the investment transaction entry dialog box, shown in Figure 13-12.

Figure 13-12: The Sell – Shares Sold dialog box.

3. **Enter the sale's date in the Transaction Date text box.**

4. **(Optional) Type a brief description of the sale in the Memo text box.**

5. **Tell Quicken which shares you're selling.**

 If you're selling all your shares, select the Sell All Shares in This Account check box.

If you're not selling all your shares, click the Specify Lots button so Quicken that displays the Specify Lots Sold in This Transaction dialog box (see Figure 13-13). Then use the Shares to Sell column to indicate how many shares from each lot you're selling. Note that you can effect the capital gain you pay by picking shares with higher or lower original cost bases. Pick shares with a higher original cost, for example, that you reduce the capital gain and therefore the capital gain taxes.

Figure 13-13: The Specify Lots Sold in This Transaction dialog box.

The figure shows the "Specify Lots Sold in this Transaction" dialog box:

Sold 200 shares of Vanguard 500 Index Fund Admiral at 185 per share on

VFIAX — Specify the shares sold in this transaction.

Purchase date	Type	Holding Period	Purchase price	Available to Sell	Shares to sell	Gain/Loss
6/25/2002	Bought	Long Term	70	100	0	0.00
6/25/2003	Bought	Long Term	90	100	0	0.00
8/31/2004	Bought	Long Term	110	100	0	0.00
6/25/2005	Bought	Long Term	130	100	0	0.00
6/25/2005	Bought	Long Term	150	100	80	2,000.00
7/31/2006	Bought	Long Term	165	100	100	2,000.00
8/1/2015	Bought	ST to 8/2/2016	180	10	10	50.00
8/1/2015	ReinvDiv	ST to 8/2/2016	180	10	10	50.00
			Total	1,020	200	$4,900.00

Auto Select shares sold with these strategies:

First Shares In Minimum Gain
Last Shares In Maximum Gain

Reset selections

Total Shares to Sell: 200
Remaining to select: 0

OK Cancel

6. **Give Quicken the number of shares you're selling.**

 Use the Number of Shares box to specify the number of shares you're selling (if you didn't select the Sell All Shares check box in Step 5).

7. **Indicate the price per share that you received by using the Price Received text box.**

 With a little luck, your selling price is more than you paid.

8. **Enter the commission or fee you paid to sell the shares in the Commission text box.**

 Quicken calculates whatever you don't enter. If you tell Quicken how many dollars you sell (by using the Price Received text box), it calculates the number of shares you sell by dividing the total sales amount

by the price per share. If you tell Quicken how many shares you sell (by using the Number of Shares text box), it calculates the total sales amount by multiplying the number of shares by the price per share. I guess this feature is handy.

9. **Enter the bank account into which you're going to deposit the sale's proceeds.**

 Open the To drop-down list box and select the appropriate account. (Probably, you'll deposit the proceeds in the associated cash account.)

10. **Click one of the Enter buttons.**

 Quicken records your sale.

Correcting a mistake

If you make a mistake, don't worry; it's not a problem. You can edit an investment transaction. To edit a particular transaction, first display the account with the transactions. To do this, click the investment account on the Accounts bar. Quicken displays the investment transactions for the account (see Figure 13-14).

Figure 13-14: The Investment Transactions list.

To edit one of the transactions you see listed for the investment account, double-click the transaction. Quicken opens the dialog box you originally used to record the transaction (such as the one shown in Figure 13-15), and you use it to make your changes.

Figure 13-15:
The Edit
Sell –
Shares Sold
dialog box
appears
when you
indicate that
you want
to edit a
shares-sold
transaction.

(Edit Sell - Shares Sold dialog box)

Enter transaction: Sell - Shares Sold — Enter the sale of shares of a security (add the proceeds to my cash balance).

Sell - Shares Sold:

Transaction date: 8/1/2015 Security name: Vanguard 500 Index Fund Admiral

Account: IRA ☐ Sell all shares in this account

Memo: Number of shares: 200

 Price received: 185 per share

 Commission: 0.00

Record proceeds? [Specify Lots...]

◉ To this account's cash balance Total sale: 37,000.00

○ To:

[?] [Cancel] [Clear] [Enter/Done]

Working with slightly tricky investment transactions

I haven't described every possible investment transaction that you're likely to encounter in a typical tax-deferred investment account — although I *have* described nearly every one I've encountered in the past two or three decades. You should know, however, that Quicken lets you record three additional, common-to-tax-deferred-investment-account transactions by specifying several almost magical actions: shares out, stock split, and reminder transactions.

How do I remove shares from an account?

You can tell Quicken to remove shares from an account — without moving the money represented by the shares — to some other account. Why would you want to remove shares from an account by using a *shares-removed* transaction? I can think of two such situations:

✔ You erroneously added shares to the account with the shares-added transaction action, and now you need to remove them.

✔ You're using an investment account to record old investment activity, such as activity from last year.

The first instance is self-explanatory, because you're simply correcting an error that you made. In the second case, however, you don't want to transfer the proceeds of an investment sale to a cash account because the money from the sale was already recorded as a deposit at some point in the past.

You can record a shares-removed transaction directly in Quicken by clicking the Enter Transaction button and choosing Remove – Shares Removed from the Enter Transaction drop-down list box. Then fill in the rest of the fields in the dialog box the same way that you would for a regular ol' sell transaction. The only difference is that you won't give a transfer account for the sale proceeds — because there aren't any proceeds.

What? The stock split and then doubled?

Stock splits don't occur very often. When they do occur, however, the company issuing the shares in effect gives you a certain number of new shares (such as two) for each old share you own.

To record a stock split, you click the Enter Transactions button and select Stock Split from the Enter Transaction drop-down list box. When Quicken displays the Stock Split version of the dialog box used to enter investment transactions (see Figure 13-16), you indicate the ratio of new shares to old shares. For a two-for-one split, for example, you indicate that you get two new split shares for each old unsplit share. The whole process is pretty easy.

Figure 13-16: The Stock Split version of the investment transaction entry dialog box.

Stock Split				
Enter transaction:	Stock Split ▾	Enter a stock split or a reverse stock split.		
Stock Split:				
Transaction date:	6/25/2014	Security name:	Vanguard 500 Index Fund Admiral ±	
Account:	IRA ▾	New shares:	2	
		Old shares:	1	
Memo:		Price after split:	90 (optional)	
?	Cancel	Clear	Enter/New	Enter/Done

Quicken, will you remind me of something?

A *reminder* transaction is the electronic equivalent of a yellow stick-on note. If you put a reminder transaction in an investment account, Quicken gives you a reminder message on the reminder date. You can't goof up anything by trying out reminders, so if you're curious, enter a reminder transaction for tomorrow and see what happens.

You can post a reminder note by clicking the Enter Transaction button, selecting Reminder Transaction from the Enter Transaction drop-down list box, and filling in the dialog box that Quicken displays (see Figure 13-17).

Figure 13-17: The Reminder Transaction version of the investment transaction entry dialog box.

You may want to use reminder transactions to record due dates for contributions to retirement accounts or for required minimum distributions amounts or dates.

Reconciling an account

You reconcile a tax-deferred investment account the same basic way that you reconcile a bank account. The only real difference — and it doesn't affect reconciliation mechanics — is that you focus on investment shares and not on account balance dollars. To begin reconciling a tax-deferred investment account, display the Investing tab, click the Account Actions button, and choose the Reconcile command. If you have questions about what to do next, refer to Chapter 8; it describes how you reconcile a bank account, but the same procedures apply to both tax-deferred and regular investment accounts.

Trying reports

I just want to say one thing about Quicken reports as they relate to your investments, both tax-deferred and taxable: *The reports are available.* (For more information, see Chapter 7.)

Using menu commands and other stuff

For the most part, the commands and menus available for an investment account (no matter whether you're talking tax-deferred or taxable) are the same as those available for all the other accounts that Quicken supplies. I write about the commands that I think are most helpful to new users in the preceding chapters of this book. If you have a question about how the Void Transaction(s) command works, for example, refer to the index, which directs you to a specific discussion of that command.

Updating Securities Prices

You can collect current market prices and store this information with your accounts (both tax-deferred and taxable).

To update security prices automatically, just display the Investing tab and click the Portfolio button. Then, when Quicken displays the Portfolio tab (see Figure 13-18), click the Update button and choose the One Step Update command. Quicken grabs nearly current security prices from the Quicken website.

Figure 13-18:
The Portfolio view of the Investing tab, or window.

To update the market price for a security manually, you also need to display the Portfolio view of the Investing tab. When you've done that, just use the arrow keys or click the mouse to select the security. Then move the cursor to the Quote/Price text box and enter the current price.

When you use either the automatic or manual method of updating the pricing information, Quicken recalculates the Market Value field of the Portfolio tab as well as the Market Value figure at the bottom of the register window.

If you invest exclusively in tax-deferred investments, the information in this chapter should be all you need. If you also invest more actively in taxable accounts, you may want to turn to Chapter 14, which describes how you use a Quicken investment account to track a typical brokerage account.

I'm not going to go into more detail here about what all these extra bells and whistles do, however. If you're interested in this stuff, just take the time to explore these commands. You *will* gain some interesting insights into your financial investments.

The Investing tab

You can do more with the Investing tab (refer to Figure 13-18) than just update share prices or play peekaboo with your various investments.

For starters, the Investing tab lets you slice and dice portfolio information. The Show drop-down list box lets you customize how Quicken reports on your investment holdings. The Group By drop-down list box lets you group your investment accounts into categories (industries, sectors, asset classes, and so on). The As Of field lets you specify the date on which you want to see and set market prices and values. And the Customize button displays a dialog box that lets you add all sorts of information to the Investing tab — information that can give you all sorts of insights into how you're doing with your investing.

Interested in digging even deeper? No problem. Click the Performance or Allocations button to get additional information. The Performance button, for example, displays a screenful of information about the historical cost and market value of your investments. The Allocations button breaks down your investments into asset classes (big-company stocks, little-company stocks, bonds, and so forth).

The Update button displays a menu of commands you can use to keep your portfolio data current as well as get current and historical prices of securities. (Go ahead and experiment with the Update button's commands: You can't hurt anything.)

Chapter 14

Stocks and Bonds

● ●

In This Chapter

▶ Setting up a brokerage account

▶ Describing the securities in a brokerage account

▶ Transferring cash to and from a brokerage account

▶ Buying stocks and bonds from a brokerage account

▶ Recording income from securities held in a brokerage account

▶ Recording margin interest, miscellaneous income and expenses, and return of capital

▶ Updating securities prices

▶ Adjusting your brokerage cash balance and account shares

● ●

*A*fter you understand how Quicken handles tax-deferred investments, working with a regular taxable brokerage account (and the extra complexity that such an account typically includes) is a snap.

 If you haven't yet used Quicken for tax-deferred investment record keeping or read Chapter 13, I recommend that you at least skim Chapter 13. That chapter provides some useful information about the fundamentals of investment record keeping with Quicken.

Setting Up a Brokerage Account

Setting up a brokerage account is similar to setting up a regular tax-deferred account. Because I describe this process in painstaking detail in Chapter 13, I don't repeat the discussion here.

The one bit of information that I will note is this: During the investment account setup process, when Quicken asks you what kind of account you're setting up, specify that you're setting up a standard brokerage account.

Recording your initial share balances

If you've already read or skimmed Chapter 13 (which talks about using Quicken to track tax-deferred investments), you may remember a section titled "Recording your initial investment." That little section explains how to tell Quicken what you paid for the mutual fund shares, stock shares, and so forth, held in your tax-deferred investment account.

Okay. So here's the deal. Just as you need to describe your starting share balances when you set up a tax-deferred investment account, you need to describe your starting share balances when you set up a standard brokerage investment account. In other words, if you own three stocks in your brokerage account — IBM, GE, and Boeing — you need to describe how much you paid and when you purchased your IBM, GE, and Boeing shares.

Rather than copy that earlier discussion (I'd literally be copying and pasting material from Chapter 13), let me refer you to the "Recording your initial investment" section in Chapter 13. Go through the nine-step process described there for each stock you hold.

Working with brokerage accounts

Brokerage accounts work like tax-deferred accounts, which I describe in Chapter 13, except for a handful of minor differences.

Essentially, only three general differences exist between tax-deferred investment accounts and brokerage investment accounts:

- ✔ Brokerage accounts typically use more extensive security lists (whereas tax-deferred investment accounts don't).
- ✔ Brokerage accounts have cash accounts (whereas tax-deferred investments usually don't).
- ✔ Brokerage accounts let you record a handful of goofy transactions that tax-deferred investment accounts don't (because they don't make sense in the context of conventional tax-deferred investments).

I spend the next few paragraphs of this chapter describing features that are unique to brokerage accounts.

Setting up security lists

Typically, a brokerage account probably contains more than one type of *security.* You may have shares of Boeing, General Motors, or Google. You name it, and someone owns it.

Therefore, a brokerage account uses a list of securities — and you, as the investor, need to create and maintain the list of securities (stocks, bonds, and so on) that your account holds.

To do so, set up the brokerage account (as described in the first part of this chapter) and then complete the following steps:

1. **Choose the Security List command.**

 Display the Investing tab, click the Tools button, and choose the Security List command. Quicken displays the Security List window, shown in Figure 14-1. Note that any mutual funds you've already set up appear in the list as securities.

2. **Click the New Security button in the Security List window.**

 Quicken displays the first Add Security to Quicken dialog box, shown in Figure 14-2.

3. **Enter the stock symbol for the security in the Ticker Symbol text box.**

 If you don't know the symbol, make sure that you have the name of the security correct and then click the Look Up button to search for the ticker symbol at Quicken.com.

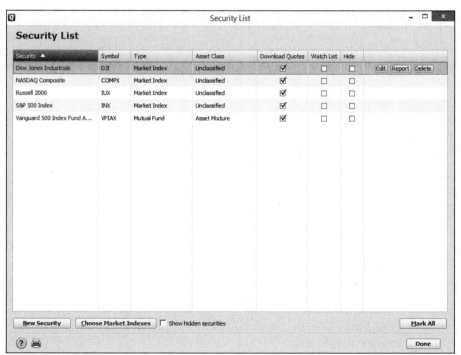

Figure 14-1:
The Security
List window.

Add Security to Quicken ×

Enter symbol or name for this new security

Ticker Symbol: [IBM] [Look Up...]

Name: []

(If ticker symbol is unknown)

Note: Entering a symbol will allow Quicken to download security information such as asset classes and historical prices.

☑ Include this security on my watch list

(?) [Cancel] [Next]

Figure 14-2:
The first Add Security to Quicken dialog box.

4. **Click Next to continue.**

 Quicken retrieves information about the stock whose ticker symbol you entered and displays it in another Add Security to Quicken dialog box.

5. **Click Done.**

 Quicken adds the security to the security list and redisplays the Security List window. If you have additional securities, you can add them by repeating Steps 2–4. Also, you can add securities on the fly while you're recording the purchase of a security for the first time. When you do this, Quicken starts this little "Oh, let's add another security to the list" process for you at Step 3.

 Before I quit this discussion of the security list, let me just make a couple of observations. See those buttons along the right top edge of the Security List window? (Go ahead and flip to Figure 14-1 for a peek.) You can use them to do useful stuff. Click Edit to change security information. Click the Report button to display a report of transactions for the security. Click the Delete button to remove the selected security from the list. Finally, use the Watch List and Hide check boxes to add a security to your watch list or to hide the selected security. Just thought you'd want to know.

Working with cash

One of the big differences between a brokerage account and a traditional tax-deferred investment account is that a cash management, or *money market,* account is always, always attached to the brokerage account — and is actively used.

When you initially set up a brokerage account, your money goes into this account. (The broker bought you a muffin and coffee in this meeting, remember?)

You purchase your first shares with the cash from this account. And when you sell shares, all cash proceeds go into this account.

Transferring cash to and from an account

Because you work with cash in a brokerage account, you need to know how to record the cash that flows into and out of the account.

To transfer cash to an account, follow these steps:

1. **Display the investment account's window.**

 You can do this in more than one way, as luck would have it, but one easy way is to click the investment account on the Accounts bar. The investment account window should look something like the one shown in Figure 14-3 (if you're lucky).

Figure 14-3: The Transaction List shows the activity within an investment account.

2. **Indicate that you're transferring money.**

 Click the Enter Transactions button. Quicken displays the dialog box shown in Figure 14-4. Choose Cash Transferred into Account from the Enter Transaction drop-down list box.

Figure 14-4:
The dialog
box used
to record
transfers
into an
account.

3. Record the transaction date, amount, and account.

To record the amount of a cash transfer, confirm the transaction date (shown in the Transaction Date text box), enter the dollar amount in the Amount to Transfer text box, and then specify the checking account supplying the cash in the Transfer Account drop-down list box. Then click the Enter/New or Enter/Done button. (If you click Enter/New, Quicken records the transaction but leaves the dialog box open so you can record some more transactions.)

To transfer cash from an account, follow these steps:

1. Display the investment account window.

2. Indicate that you're transferring money from an account.

Click the Enter Transactions button. Quicken displays the dialog box shown in Figure 14-5. Choose Cash Transferred out of Account from the Enter Transaction drop-down list box.

3. Record the transaction date, amount, and account.

To record the amount of a cash transfer, again confirm the transaction date (using the Transaction Date text box), enter the dollar amount in the Amount to Transfer text box, and specify the checking account receiving the cash in the Transfer Account drop-down list box. Then click either the Enter/New or Enter/Done button.

Figure 14-5:
The dialog
box used
to transfer
cash from a
brokerage
investment
account.

[Figure: Cash Transferred out of Account dialog box]

Enter transaction: [Cash Transferred out of Account ▼] Enter the transfer of cash out of this account.

Cash Transferred out of Account:

Transaction date: 6/25/2015

Account: Brokerage Amount to transfer: 2,000.00

Transfer account: Savings

Memo: Description:

(?) [Cancel] [Clear] [Enter/New] [Enter/Done]

Recording other cash-related transactions

The Enter Transaction drop-down list box supplies five other cash-related transactions: Write Check, Deposit, Withdraw, Online Payment, and Other Cash Transaction.

I could write up step-by-step instructions for recording these types of transactions. But you know what? You won't have any trouble working with these babies. When you choose one of these other transactions from the Enter Transaction drop-down list box, Quicken displays a dialog box that lets you collect and enter the same sorts of information you enter in the regular Quicken register.

All I want to do here, then, is point out to you that Quicken does provide these transaction types for its cash accounts.

Buying near and selling dear

Buying and selling securities in a brokerage account is very similar to buying and selling shares of a tax-deferred investment. You fill in the same fields in almost exactly the same way:

1. **Display the investment account window.**

2. **Click the Enter Transactions button.**

Mutual (fund) acquaintance

I don't want to get into the subject of load mutual funds versus no-load mutual funds — you pay a commission to buy load funds, and you don't pay a commission to buy no-load funds — but if you're interested in how these two types of funds work, flip open the *Wall Street Journal* and look for advertisements for no-load fund managers such as USAA, Vanguard, Scudder, and T. Rowe Price. Give them a call, and they'll tell you why they think that you should bypass the middleman: your financial advisor. Next, talk to a financial advisor, who will tell you why you *shouldn't* bypass the middleman. Then you make the decision.

What? You want *my* opinion? With much trepidation, I'll tell you: I always use no-load mutual funds because I'm a big fan of the do-it-your-self approach. You save substantial amounts in commissions and, typically, in annual maintenance fees. Quite honestly, if you can figure out how to use Quicken and are reading a chapter like this one, you have enough smarts to choose your own mutual funds (especially if you're willing to do a bit of research through reading). Try Andrew Tobias's classic, *The Only Investment Guide You'll Ever Need* (Harvest Books) or Burton Malkiel's *A Random Walk Guide to Investing* (W.W. Norton & Company). You can also visit the www.bogleheads.org website for some great information and advice. I also think that a good financial advisor — *good* is the operative word here — is well worth the commission fee if he or she helps you avoid expensive mistakes. It isn't necessarily easy to find a good financial advisor, however.

3. **When Quicken displays the dialog box, choose Buy – Shares Bought from the Enter Transaction drop-down list box.**

 Quicken, ever responsive to your needs, displays the Buy – Shares Bought dialog box (shown in Figure 14-6).

4. **When Quicken displays this dialog box, provide the transaction date and select the security from the Security Name drop-down list box.**

5. **Describe the purchase details.**

 Use the Number of Shares, Price Paid, and Commission text boxes to describe your purchase. (You can get this information from your order confirmation slip.)

6. **Click the Enter/New or Enter/Done button when you're finished.**

 Pretty simple, right?

Figure 14-6:
The Buy
– Shares
Bought dia-
log box.

Selling a security works the same basic way as buying a security:

1. **Display the investment account window and then click the Enter Transaction button.**

2. **When Quicken displays the dialog box, choose Sell – Shares Sold from the Enter Transaction drop-down list box.**

 Quicken displays the Sell – Shares Sold dialog box (shown in Figure 14-7).

3. **Use the Transaction Date list box to provide the sales date.**

4. **Use the Security Name drop-down list box to identify the stock, bond, or mutual fund you're selling.**

5. **Use the Number of Shares, Price Received, and Commission text boxes to describe your sale.**

6. **Select the option button To This Account's Cash Balance or the To option button to specify whether Quicken should adjust some bank-account balance for this transaction.**

7. **Click the Specify Lots button.**

 If you purchased share lots at different prices or at different times, you can click the Specify Lots button to open the Specify Lots for Investment dialog box, where you can pick and choose which lots to sell so that you can minimize the capital gains taxes you'll owe. (Good idea, huh?) A *lot* is simply a batch, or set, of shares that you purchase at one time. If you sell the most expensive lots, you reduce your capital gains and the taxes on those gains.

- *To pick an entire lot:* Double-click it. (You need to double-click the date field, by the way.)

- *To pick a portion of a lot:* Select it; then, in the Selected text box, type the number of shares from the lot you want to sell.

- *To clear your selections and start over:* Click the Reset button.

The Specify Lots for Investment dialog box also provides nifty command buttons for automating the process of selecting lots. If you click the Maximum Gain or the Minimum Gain button, Quicken picks lots for you in a way that produces the largest possible or smallest possible capital gain, respectively. Alternatively, you can click the First Shares In or the Last Shares In button to sell the oldest shares or newest shares first, respectively. This business about picking the lots you sell is rather arbitrary, of course. By letting Quicken pick lots, you can manipulate the capital gain you'll have and the capital gains taxes you'll pay. But it's all legal (as long as you specifically tell the brokerage company which lots you're selling) and honorable. And it can save you money because you can time your capital gains so that they occur when they'll cost you the least.

If you're someone who has large capital loss carryforwards — as many investors do after the brutal years of the previous decade — your capital loss carryforwards may totally wipe out any gains you have to recognize over the next few years (or decades; gulp). In this case, you may not get much benefit from fooling around with this specific identification business. Consult your tax advisor for details.

8. **Click the Enter/New or Enter/Done button.**

Figure 14-7:
The Sell –
Shares Sold
dialog box.

Recording dividends, capital gains, and other goodies

Taking care of this stuff is easy. Any time you receive investment income, click the Enter Transactions button and choose Inc – Income (Div, Int, Etc.) from the Enter Transaction drop-down list box. When Quicken displays the dialog box used to record income, use the Security Name drop-down list box to confirm the stock, bond, or mutual fund producing income. Then use the Dividend, Interest, Short-Term Cap Gain Dist, Mid-Term Cap Gain Dist, and Long-Term Cap Gain Dist text boxes to record the amount and type of income, as shown in Figure 14-8.

Figure 14-8:
The dialog box used to record income.

	Inc - Income (Div, Int, etc.)	✕

Enter transaction: | Inc - Income (Div, Int, etc.) ▼ | Enter the receipt of cash income (interest, dividends, or capital gains distributions) that you did NOT reinvest.

Inc - Income (Div, Int, etc.):

Transaction date: 8/6/2014

Account: Brokerage

Transfer account:

Memo:

Category for Miscellaneous:
Requires 'Misc' Amt

Security name: nternational Business Machines Corp ±

Dividend:

Interest:

Short-term cap gain dist:

Mid-term cap gain dist:

Long-term cap gain dist:

Miscellaneous:

Total proceeds: 0.00

(?) Cancel | Clear | Enter/New | Enter/Done

Note: You use the Transfer Account drop-down list box to identify the account into which income amounts are deposited when you don't use the investment account's regular cash account.

To record dividends, capital gains, and other income when you reinvest the money you receive, click the Enter Transaction button and choose Income Reinvested from the Enter Transaction drop-down list box. When Quicken displays the dialog box, describe the amounts received and how you've reinvested.

Recording other not-so-tricky transactions

Quicken lets you record all sorts of transactions in a brokerage account. You can do not only reminder and stock-split actions (which I describe in Chapter 13), but also a bunch of other things.

I briefly describe these other transactions here and explain how to record them because you're more likely to encounter them when you're working with a standard brokerage account.

Bonds . . . James Bonds . . .

If you invest in bonds, you know that a bond's price is actually quoted as a percentage of its face value. A bond that sells for $950 with a face value of $1,000, for example, is quoted as 95 because the $950 price is 95 percent of the $1,000 face value. Quicken, however, doesn't let you describe a bond's price as a percentage. You must enter the bond price as its price in dollars and cents.

Going for the gold

You can use Quicken to record precious-metal investments. Suppose that you're hoarding Krugerrands (1-ounce gold coins minted in South Africa). For this investment, the price is the price per Krugerrand, and the shares figure is actually the number of ounces (equal to the number of Krugerrands). Because Quicken doesn't supply price-per-ounce or number-of-ounces fields, you insert the information into the Price and Shares fields of the Investment list.

Recording margin interest expenses

To record margin interest expense, click the Enter Transactions button and select Margin Interest Expense from the Enter Transaction drop-down list box. When you do, Quicken displays the margin interest expense version of the investment transaction entry dialog box, which you use to describe the cost of your financial adventure. Only the most sophisticated investors should be using margin interest expense, anyway. If you're one of these financial cowboys or cowgirls, I assume that you're smart enough to figure out this stuff on your own.

Paying a miscellaneous expense

Sometimes you need to pay an expense. One rarely sees expenses occur for stock or bond investments. Expenses sometimes do arise, however, for real estate partnership interests (which can be treated like common stock shares) or precious-metal investments (which can also be treated like common stock shares).

If you need to pay a fee for account handling or for storing your stash of Krugerrands, for example, you can record such an expense by clicking the Enter Transaction button and then choosing Miscellaneous Expense from the Enter Transaction drop-down list box. When Quicken displays the dialog box, fill out the boxes in the miscellaneous expense version of the investment transaction entry dialog box.

Recording a return of capital

Ah, yes, the old *return of capital* trick. . . Sometimes the money you receive because you own a security isn't really income. Rather, it's a refund of part of the purchase price.

Consider this example. You buy a mortgage-backed security — such as a Ginnie Mae bond — for which the *mortgagee* (the person who borrowed the mortgage money) pays not only periodic interest, but also a portion of the mortgage principal.

Obviously, you shouldn't record the principal portion of the payment you receive as income. You must record this payment as a mortgage principal reduction or — in the parlance of investment record keeping — as a *return of capital.*

As another example, suppose that you invest in a limited partnership or real estate investment trust that begins liquidating. Some of the money that the investors receive in this case is really a return of their original investment, or a return of capital.

To record a return-of-capital action, click the Enter Transaction button. When Quicken displays the return-of-capital version of the investment transaction entry dialog box, choose Return of Capital from the Enter Transaction drop-down list box and describe the security that's returning capital.

Special investment transactions

Quicken also supplies some special investment transactions to record the receipt of stock options, exercise of stock options, and repricing of stock options. It also supplies investment transaction types for short-selling and investment transactions for dealing with corporate mergers, spinoffs, and reorganizations. To use these special investment transactions, you follow the same general approach described in the preceding sections.

More Quick Stuff about Brokerage Accounts

Let me tell you a couple of other quick things. You'll almost certainly find these tidbits helpful.

Monitoring and updating securities values

Regardless of whether you're working with a mutual fund account or with securities in a brokerage account, you can collect current market prices and store them with the Quicken account information.

To record the current market price for a security manually, click the Investing tab (so that your investments show up), and use the up- and down-arrow keys to select the security (or use the mouse to click the security's name). Then move the cursor to the Quote/Price field and enter the current price.

To grab current market prices automatically (electronically), click the Investing tab's Update button and choose the One Step Update command.

Adjusting errors

You can adjust the cash balance in a brokerage account and the shares balance in brokerage accounts if (for some reason) the figures are incorrect.

Oops, my brokerage cash balance is wrong

How you adjust the cash balance in a brokerage account depends on how you set up the account.

To adjust an investment account's cash balance, when the cash balance information isn't tracked in a separate linked cash account, click the investment account's name on the Accounts bar, click the Actions button, and choose Update Cash Balance from the resulting menu. When Quicken displays the Update Cash Balance dialog box, shown in Figure 14-9, specify the correct cash balance and the date as of when the figure you enter is correct.

Figure 14-9:
The Update
Cash
Balance
dialog box.

To adjust an investment account's cash balance (or *cash management account,* as some brokerage houses call it), click the account name on the Accounts bar, click the Actions button, and choose Reconcile from the resulting menu. You reconcile a brokerage cash account the same way that you reconcile a regular old checking account. For information about how to reconcile a checking account, refer to Chapter 8. That chapter describes how to reconcile a bank account, but reconciling a brokerage cash account works the same way.

Oops, my brokerage account shares balance is wrong

To adjust the shares balance for a security in a brokerage account, click the brokerage account on the Accounts bar, click the Actions button, and choose Update Share Balance from the resulting menu.

Quicken next displays the Adjust Share Balance dialog box, shown in Figure 14-10, where you specify the security, the correct number of shares, and the date for which you're entering the balance. Fill in the text boxes and then click either Enter/New or Enter/Done. Quicken adjusts the shares balance for the security you specified.

Figure 14-10:
The Adjust Share Balance dialog box.

A few words on the Investing tab's other tools

If you've read this whole chapter, you know that I mostly describe how you get information in the windows and dialog boxes of the Investing tab. But before I stop talking about the Investing tab, I want to give you a little more information on how you work with the tab's commands and buttons to monitor your investments.

The first thing to notice is that the Investing tab provides different views (available when you click Portfolio, Performance, or Allocations), each of which provides its own information:

- ✔ **Portfolio view** (see Figure 14-11) lists the investment accounts you've set up within Quicken, the securities on your watch list, and the major stock market indexes. In addition, the view provides a bit of high-level information about each of these items.

- ✔ **Performance view** (see Figure 14-12) graphs your investment account values and cost bases over a selected time period, and lets you compare these values with some external benchmark, such as the S&P (Standard & Poor's) 500.

- ✔ **Allocations view** (see Figure 14-13) provides charts and tables of information that let you see how your overall investments are allocated and how you've said they *should be* allocated. (To see your portfolio allocation, you need to have identified which asset category your individual investment securities fall into — and to have used the first Options button's Change Target Allocations command to set your allocations.)

Figure 14-11: Portfolio view of the Investing tab.

Figure 14-12:
Performance view of the Investing tab.

Figure 14-13:
Allocations view of the Investing tab.

The other thing I want to mention in passing are the asset allocation and portfolio analysis tools that are available when you click the Investing tab's Tools button. Through the Tools button, Quicken provides several useful commands:

✔ **Asset Allocation Guide** displays a web page that provides lots of solid information you can use to think smartly about how you allocate your investments between stocks and bonds and other choices. (This command is definitely worth a few minutes of exploration on your part.)

- ✔ **Buy/Sell Preview** lets you estimate the financial effect on your portfolio of buying and/or selling specific investments.

- ✔ **Capital Gains Estimator** calculates the unrealized capital gains and losses in your investment portfolio using the most current prices available to Quicken.

Asset allocation represents one of the best tactics you and I have to protect ourselves from crazy gyrations in the capital markets and from emotion-driven investment decisions. So let me throw out a random idea here. If you're interested in developing greater expertise about this asset allocation — expertise that goes beyond what's available from Quicken — I heartily recommend David F. Swensen's outstanding book *Unconventional Success: A Fundamental Approach to Personal Investment* (Free Press).

Part IV
Very Serious Business

Simplify your rental property bookkeeping by using the tips and tricks described in the article "Strengthening Your Rental Property Bookkeeping" at www.dummies.com/quicken2015.

In this part . . .

✔ Using Quicken Home & Business as a powerful-yet-easy accounting system for your small business.

✔ See how to use Quicken for Bookkeeping and Payroll.

✔ Get the lowdown on using Quicken Rental Property Manager to track rental real estate investments.

Chapter 15

Mind Your Business

- -

- -

The preceding chapters of this little book talk about using Quicken for your personal bookkeeping. But you may be interested to know that Quicken also does a truly excellent job at small-business accounting.

If you want to use Quicken for small-business accounting, you need to do just a couple of things. First, you want to make sure that you're working with the Home & Business version or the Quicken Rental Property Manager version of Quicken, because both these flavors of Quicken supply an extra menu of seriously useful business bookkeeping commands. Second — and this is only my humble opinion — you want to skim this chapter's discussions so that you get the business bookkeeping stuff set up right.

If you're not already working with Quicken Home & Business, you very possibly can upgrade to Home & Business by choosing Help⇨Add Business Tools or Help⇨Add Rental Property Tools. If those commands aren't available or don't make sense, contact Intuit by visiting http://quicken.intuit.com.

Setting Up a Business the Quicken Way

To use Quicken for small-business bookkeeping, you need to describe each business you or your spouse operates. If you work as a one-person consultant, and your spouse runs a tow truck business, you need to tell Quicken a little bit about both businesses. Quicken needs this information so that it can track each business separately and produce invoices for each business.

Describing your business (es)

To describe your business to Quicken, you need to give the business's name and identify the owner. Here's how you do this:

1. **Choose the Manage Business Information command.**

 Display the Business tab, click the Business Tools button, and choose the Manage Business Information command. Quicken displays the Manage Business Information dialog box.

 TIP

 If you don't have a Business tab, choose View⇨Tabs to Show and click Business, or choose Help⇨Add Business Tools.

2. **Tell Quicken that you want to add a business.**

 Click the Business Tools button and choose Manage Business Information from the menu Quicken displays. When Quicken displays the Manage Business Information dialog box, click Add. Quicken displays the Add Business dialog box, shown in Figure 15-1.

Figure 15-1:
The Add
Business
dialog box.

3. **Enter your firm's name in the Business Name text box.**

4. **(Optional) Enter a brief description in the Description box, which appears just below the Business Name text box.**

5. **Identify the business owner.**

 Use the Owner option buttons (Self and Spouse) to indicate who owns the business: you or your better half.

6. **Create a tag for the business.**

 You want the tag to be a memorable yet short acronym or abbreviation that you can use to mark transactions as connected to a particular business. Suppose that your family operates a consulting business and a

landscape design business. You might use the tags "Cons" (for *consulting)* and "Towing" (for *tow truck).*

7. **(Optional) Specify that this business is the default business.**

 You can tell Quicken that a particular business is the *default* business — in other words, that Quicken should assume that a business transaction relates to this business unless you tell it otherwise. To do this, select the check box titled Business Transactions without a Tag Belong to This Business.

8. **Save your business description.**

 Quicken returns you to the Manage Business Information dialog box, which now lists your newly described business venture (see Figure 15-2).

Figure 15-2:
The Manage
Business
Information
dialog box.

	Manage Business Information			✕

Manage Business Information

Business Name	Owner	Tag	Default Business
Big Bob's Towing LLC	Self	bigtow	✓

[Add...] [Edit...] [Delete]

(?) [Done]

9. **If you need to add more businesses, repeat Steps 2–8.**

10. **Click Done to close the Manage Business Information dialog box.**

The Manage Business Information dialog box provides two other useful buttons that I should mention briefly: Delete and Edit. You can click the Delete button to remove the selected business description, and you can click the Edit button to display the Edit Business dialog box, which allows you to change the selected business's description.

Designing business invoices

You need to add your business's name and address to the business invoice template that Quicken produces. To do this, display the Business tab, click the Business Actions button, and then choose the Invoices and Estimates⇨Design Forms command. When Quicken displays the Forms Designer window, click the Company Address Properties button (the button next to a double chevron) so

that Quicken displays the Company Address dialog box. Then enter your business and address. *Note:* You may need to click the Let's Get Started button the first time you want to access this dialog box.

I'm not going to discuss the Forms Designer window in more detail, but you may want to poke around the window a bit. You can use the window's buttons and boxes to customize with abandon the invoice form that Quicken produces. Note, too, that you may need (or want) to create and customize multiple invoice templates — if, for example, you're using Quicken for more than one business or if you want to use distinctly different invoices for different customers, products, or services. You can create a new invoice template by clicking the Forms Designer window's Layout button and then choosing New from the menu that Quicken displays.

Identifying invoice items

The stuff that appears on invoices — product or service descriptions, standard prices, and so forth — needs to be provided up front to Quicken. To do so, you set up invoice items.

Suppose that you're using Quicken to keep the books for a one-person tow truck business and that you bill your towing services by the hour, charging people $125 an hour for your services and the truck. To describe this standard invoice information, you set up a "towing" item by following these steps:

1. **Display the Business tab, click the Business Actions button, and then choose Invoices and Estimates⇨View All Invoice Items.**

 Quicken displays the Customize Invoice Items dialog box (not shown).

2. **Click the New button.**

 Quicken displays the New Item dialog box (see Figure 15-3).

3. **Name the item you're creating.**

 You might name an item for towing services "Towing" or an item for consulting services "consult." You just need to use an item name that's descriptive enough that you remember the item details when you see the item name.

4. **Categorize and tag.**

 Use the Category/Tag box to specify which income category should be used to account for the item.

 If you've set up two different businesses — consulting and tow-truck services — and use the tags "consult" and "towing" to differentiate, you enter the "consult" tag in the Tag field for consulting business items, and you enter the "towing" tag in the Tag field to specify tow-truck business invoice items.

Figure 15-3:
The New
Item dialog
box.

5. Describe the item in more detail, please.

Use the Description text box to provide the text you want to automatically appear on the invoice for the item. You can (and probably should) be quite descriptive. You can add more text to the invoice and edit the invoice item descriptions later, when you actually create the invoice, but Quicken automatically enters the item description for you. Therefore, you want to make Quicken type any long, detailed descriptions.

6. Flag any subtotal items.

Okay, here's a weird thing about items that appear on an invoice. Anything that you want to put in the body of your invoice is an item. Obviously, the services and products you sell need to be set up as items. But you also have to set up the other stuff that you want to put on the invoice — shipping charges, discounts, markups, and so on — as items.

After you understand this weirdness, subtotal items become clearer (I hope). The Subtotal of the Preceding Items check box, if selected, tells Quicken that the item simply adds up the preceding items shown on the invoice. Probably, by the way, the right item name for a subtotal item is subtotal and the right description is Subtotal or Total.

If you indicate that an item is a subtotal, by the way, you don't provide a category or tag. But that makes sense: Quicken grabs the category and tag information from the individual "real" items getting subtotaled — not the subtotal item.

7. (Optional) Add a blank line after the item.

To tell Quicken to add a blank line on invoices after an item, select the Print Extra Blank Line check box.

8. **Set the item price.**

 Use the Per Item Rate text box to specify a default price for the item. If you're setting up an item for a service, for example, you might enter the hourly billing rate in the Per Item Rate text box.

9. **Identify items that are subject to sales tax.**

 If an item is subject to sales tax — in other words, if you're supposed to charge sales tax on the item — select the Taxable check box.

10. **Give the percentage for any percentage-based items.**

 You may not need percentage items for your invoices. But if you regularly bill people for items that get calculated as a percentage of some other item on the invoice, you use a percentage item.

 Percentage items calculate an amount for your invoice by multiplying a percentage against the preceding item. If the preceding item shown on an invoice equals $1,000, a 10 percent "percentage" item adds another $100 to the invoice.

 Note that when you select the Percentage check box, the value you enter in the Per Item Rate text box isn't a dollar amount, but a percentage value. You enter 10 percent, for example, as **10**.

11. **When you finish describing an item, click the New Item dialog box's OK button.**

 Quicken returns you to the Customize Invoice Items dialog box.

12. **To add more items, repeat the preceding steps, or click the Customize Invoice Item dialog box's Done button.**

Working with Customers

You can invoice customers, record their payments, and monitor unpaid amounts after you've described your business, finalized your invoice form(s), and created an item list.

Setting up a Customer Invoices account

Quicken needs you to set up a Customer Invoices account to track the invoices you create. But this isn't difficult to do. Simply display the Business tab, click the Business Actions button, and choose the Invoices and Estimates⇨Create Invoices command. When you do, Quicken checks to see whether you've already set up an account to track amounts that your customers owe you. If you haven't, Quicken asks whether it can set up such an account. If you answer yes, Quicken asks whether it's okay to use a name like Customer Invoices. When you click the "Sure, I don't care what you name the account" button,

Quicken sets up the account for you. When Quicken sets up the Customer Invoices account, it also sets up a sales tax-payable account to track any sales taxes you collect from customers.

I'm not going to talk a bunch more about the Customer Invoices account, but let me make just three quick points:

- The Customer Invoices account is a regular Quicken account — sort of like a bank account. You see the Customer Invoices account listed, for example, on the Accounts bar and in the Accounts List window.

- You can enter or edit transactions directly by viewing the account in a register window (the same sort of register window I describe in detail in Chapter 4). Typically, however, you don't work directly with the register, because Quicken provides easy-to-use tools for recording customer invoices and payments (as described a bit later in this chapter).

- The Unpaid Invoices List is an easy way to see which customer invoices are open. (Often, these invoices are the only ones you truly care about.) To display this list, display the Business tab, click the Business Tools button, and then choose the Unpaid Invoices List command.

Invoicing your customers

To invoice a customer, follow these steps:

1. **Display the Business tab, click the Business Actions button, and choose Invoices and Estimates⇨Create Invoice.**

 Quicken displays the Invoice dialog box (see Figure 15-4). The Invoice window in Figure 15-4 shows a bit of information in its boxes, but don't get confused about that. In the steps that follow, I describe how to enter this information.

2. **Identify the customer and provide the address, if necessary.**

 If you're invoicing a customer for the first time, type his or her name in the Customer box in the upper-left corner of the Invoice window. Quicken copies the company name to the Bill To box. You can complete the address by adding the street information, city, state, and ZIP code.

 If you're invoicing a customer for a second (or subsequent) time, open the Customer box and select the customer from the list that Quicken displays.

 You can add customers on the fly — which is what I describe in the preceding step, and which means that you describe your customers with sketchy vagueness. Alternatively, you can also go hog-wild and describe each and every customer in painstaking detail. To go the painstaking-detail

route, choose the Business➪Customers➪Add Customer command. When Quicken displays the Edit Address Book Record dialog box, use its boxes to describe your customer. Note that you can use the Add Customer command at any time. You don't need to wait until you're ready to record an invoice.

3. Tag the transaction.

If you're using Quicken to track more than one business, and you've (very rightly) created a tag for each business, enter the appropriate tag in the Business Tag box.

Figure 15-4:
The Invoice
dialog box.

4. **Provide the Date, Due Date, Invoice #, and P.O. Number information.**

 Use the Date box to indicate the invoicing date. (Typically, the invoice date is the actual date you create the invoice.) Use the Due Date box to specify when you expect payment. Use the Invoice # box to give the invoice a unique number. Finally, if you're billing on purchase-order numbers, use the P.O. Number box to enter the customer's purchase-order number.

5. **Describe the individual items you're invoicing the customer for.**

 To enter an invoice item, click the Item column for the line you want to add and then select an item from the list Quicken displays. Quicken adds the category and description information you provided for the item, but you can edit this information, if you want. Next, specify the item quantity and verify the rate.

 You can initially fit ten items into an invoice, but if you need more room, click the Add Lines button.

6. **Add sales tax, if applicable.**

 If items on the invoice are subject to sales tax, enter the sales tax rate in the Tax box. Quicken calculates the sales tax for you by multiplying the sales tax percentage against each of the taxable items on the invoice.

 Note: Quicken tracks the sales tax you've collected by using a liability account. Quicken shows the liability account in the Tax Account drop-down list box at the bottom of the window.

7. **(Optional) Add customer messages or memo descriptions to the invoice.**

 If you want to add a message to the invoice, enter the message in the Customer Message box.

 If you want to record a bit of extra information about the invoice — information that won't appear on the invoice — enter that in the Memo box.

8. **Save the invoice.**

 You can save the invoice and close the Invoice window by clicking Save and Done. Or you can save the invoice and redisplay an empty Invoice dialog box so you can create another invoice by clicking Save and New.

Printing invoices

You can print invoices as you create them. Simply click the Print button on the Invoice dialog box. The Print button looks like a printer and appears in the lower-left corner of the dialog box. When you click the Print button, Quicken displays the Print Invoice dialog box. Click its OK button to print the invoice.

You can also print invoices in batches. To use batch printing, first create your batch of invoices (obviously). Next, display the Business tab, click the Business Tools button, and choose the Print Invoices/Invoices List command. When Quicken displays the Invoices List, verify that each invoice you want to print is marked with a check, click the Print button so that Quicken displays a menu of print commands, and then choose the List command. Quicken displays the Print dialog box. Click its OK button to print the selected invoices.

The Print Invoice and Print dialog boxes provide a bunch of buttons and boxes you can use to control how Quicken prints your invoices. If you have questions about how these printing options work, refer to Chapter 5. Chapter 5 describes how to print checks and check registers, but the process for printing those items closely resembles the process for printing invoices.

Recording customer payments

To record a customer payment, follow these steps:

1. **Display the Business tab, click the Business Actions button, and choose Invoices and Estimates⇨Receive a Customer Payment.**

 Quicken displays the Payment dialog box (see Figure 15-5).

Payment - Customer Invoices

Customer: Acme Explosives LLC	Amount: 500.00	
Deposit To: Checking	Check Number:	
Memo:		

DATE	BALANCE
7/31/2015	500.00

Existing Credits: 0.00 Total to Apply: 500.00
☐ Apply Existing Credits Unapplied Amount: 0.00

Outstanding Invoices

Pay	Date	Project/Job	Type	Invoice #	Orig Amt	Due Date	Amt Due	Payment
✓	6/30/2015		Custom...	101	500.00	7/30/2015	500.00	500.00
						Totals:	500.00	500.00

Clear Payments

? Enter Cancel

Figure 15-5:
The
Payment
dialog box.

2. **Select the customer.**

 Open the Customer drop-down list box and select the customer for whom you want to record a payment. After you select the customer and move to the next box, Quicken displays a list of any unpaid invoices the customer owes.

3. **Describe the payment.**

 You should enter the payment amount in the Amount box. That, I'm sure, represents a big surprise.

 Also, you probably should record the payment date in the Date box and the customer's check number in the Check Number box.

4. **Select the bank account into which you'll deposit the check.**

 This is easy. Open the Deposit To drop-down list box and select the bank account.

5. **Identify the open invoices that the customer is paying.**

 Quicken attempts to guess which unpaid invoices the customer is paying, marking each of those invoices with a check. Often, Quicken guesses correctly, but verify that each correct invoice shows a check mark. You can select and deselect invoices by clicking the check mark.

 If a payment pays partial amounts of unpaid invoices, you can click the Payment column in the Outstanding Invoices list and then edit the amount.

6. **Record the payment.**

 After you describe the payment and apply it to the correct open invoices, click the Enter button. Quicken records the payment and updates the invoice open balance(s).

Issuing credits and making refunds

Quicken provides commands and windows for issuing credits and for making refunds to customers.

To record a credit — a *credit* is essentially a backward invoice that says you owe your customer money rather than the other way around — display the Business tab, click the Business Actions button, and choose the Invoices and Estimates⇨Issue a Credit command. When Quicken displays the Credit dialog box (which is a mirror image of the Invoice dialog box), record your credit memo. You won't have any trouble using the Credit dialog box if you've previously used the Invoice dialog box. But if you have questions, refer to the steps for invoicing your customers earlier in this chapter.

To refund money to a customer because of an earlier credit memo, display the Business tab, click the Business Actions button, and choose the Invoices and Estimates⇨Issue a Refund command. When Quicken displays the Refund dialog box, identify the account you'll write the refund check on, specify the customer to which you want to issue a refund by entering his or her name in the Customer box, and then click Enter. Quicken records a check for you in the appropriate bank account register.

Business Bookkeeping Whistles and Bells

Quicken Home & Business (which I've spent the preceding paragraphs of this chapter talking about) provides a handful of additional business bookkeeping tools. I'm not going to describe these tools in any detail in this book because I don't think you'll use them. Nevertheless, I do want to give you a quick overview.

Jobs and projects

If you're really alert and have good eyes, you'll have noticed a Project/Job box in some of the figures of this chapter and some of the Quicken Home & Business windows. Just a quick note to explain: Most small businesses probably bill customers. But in some industries, you can find yourself billing jobs or projects that are in turn owned or managed by a customer. If this situation sounds like yours, you'll want to use the Customers⇨Create Project/Job command (available when you click the Business Actions button on the Business tab) to set up jobs or projects below your customers. When you invoice, you'll want to include not only the customer name on the invoice, but also the project or job.

Using finance charges, estimates, and statements

Three customer-invoicing commands (available on the Business tab when you click the Business Actions button and choose the Invoices and Estimates command) deserve a quick description: Create Estimates, Create a Finance Charge, and Print Statements.

The Create Estimates command allows you to create a dummy invoice you can give to a customer as a preliminary cost estimate of a job or service. The Estimate dialog box, not surprisingly, mirrors the Invoice dialog box. In fact,

if you ultimately need to invoice the customer for something you previously estimated, you display the Business tab, click the Business Tools button, and choose the Estimates List command. When Quicken displays the Estimates List window, select the estimate from the window that Quicken displays and click the Convert button.

The Create a Finance Charge command allows you to assess a finance charge on a past-due invoice. In essence, when you use the command, Quicken creates an invoice for the customer with a single item on it for the finance charge.

The Print Statements command lets you print customer statements that show the open invoices for a customer at a specific point in time. If you have customers for whom you need a statement, obviously, you need to use this command.

Managing vendor bills

If you display the Business tab, click the Business Actions button, and choose the Bills and Vendors command, Quicken displays a menu of commands that let you create a simple accounts-payable system for tracking your unpaid bills from vendors.

I'm not going to describe these commands here. You really shouldn't need to set up an accounts-payable system for a small business except in the special case in which someone foolishly decided that your business should use accrual-based accounting rather than cash-basis accounting. (If that's your situation — my apologies, but you need to get help from the nabob who sent you down the accrual-based-accounting path.)

If you record expenses just by writing checks — this is the way that Chapters 4 and 5 describe — you essentially keep your books by using cash-basis accounting. Cash-basis accounting usually works best for small businesses. It delays your income tax expenses, and it keeps your bookkeeping simpler.

Vehicle Mileage Tracker

Quicken Home & Business provides a handy utility you can use to keep a log of your business auto or truck use. As you're probably tired of hearing your accountant say, you need to keep such a log to prove your business-vehicle use.

I'm not going to describe the Vehicle Mileage Tracker here, though. You'll find the tool very straightforward to use. Simply display the Business tab, click the Business Tools button, choose the Mileage Tracker command, and poke around a bit.

Quicken Dirty Payroll

A lot of people who own small businesses or who have a household employee (a nanny, for example) need to deal with payroll. Although Quicken Home & Business doesn't provide payroll tools, I still want to provide some quick-and-dirty instructions for handling simple payroll situations with Quicken. Oh, sure, the instructions won't be fancy, but I promise you they will be fast and cheap.

Getting ready for payroll

To do payroll in Quicken, you need to set up a couple of payroll expense categories. Fortunately, doing so isn't particularly difficult.

I'm going to describe how you do this task for purposes of U.S. federal income and payroll taxes. If you employ people in a state that has a state income tax — California, say — you may also have to deal with state payroll taxes. But you can track and process these taxes the same way you process federal taxes. (Some counties and cities even have income taxes, but these taxes should also work the same way.)

Setting up the wages expense category

You need to set up a payroll expense category for tracking the wages you pay employees. Here's all you do:

1. **Choose Tools⇨Category List.**

 Quicken, with no hesitation, displays the Category List window.

2. **Click the New button.**

 Quicken displays the Set Up Category dialog box (see Figure 15-6).

3. **Enter Wages as the category name by moving the cursor to the Category Name text box and typing** Wages.

 If you told Quicken during setup that you'll use Quicken to track a business, Quicken may have set up the Wages category automatically.

4. **(Optional) Enter a description of the category.**

 If you want, you can type a description in the Description text box.

5. **Select the Expense option button.**

 This choice tells Quicken that you're setting up an expense category.

Figure 15-6:
The Set Up
Category
dialog box.

6. **(Optional) Describe the tax characteristics of this category.**

 To further describe taxable income and tax deduction categories, click the Tax Reporting tab and then select the Tax-Related check box.

 Optionally, if you want to be super-nit-picky and don't care about wasting your time, select the Standard List Item List or Extended Line Item List option button on the Tax Reporting tab and then choose the exact tax form and form line number the category gets reported on when you prepare your federal tax return. One caution: You won't know for an absolute certainty which forms and line numbers are used until the end of the year.

7. **Click OK.**

 Quicken adds the category to the category list and redisplays the Category List window.

Setting up the payroll tax expense category

You also need to set up a payroll tax category to track payroll taxes that the employer pays, including the company's share of Social Security taxes, the company's share of Medicare taxes, and any other employer payroll taxes (such as federal unemployment tax or the equivalent state employer taxes).

To set up a payroll tax expense category, follow the same steps I give you for setting up a wages expense category (in the preceding section). You can name the category *payroll taxes, taxes-payroll,* or something else that's even more clever.

Getting the taxes stuff right

You also need to do a couple of other things if you want to do payroll the right way in the U.S. of A.

Requesting (or demanding) an employer ID number

First, you need to file an SS-4, or Request for Employer Identification Number form, with the Internal Revenue Service (IRS) so that you can get an Employer Identification Number. You can get this form by calling the IRS or by visiting the IRS website (www.irs.gov).

In one of its cooler moves, the IRS allows you to apply for and receive an Employer Identification Number right online. Visit the www.irs.gov website, and click the Apply for an Employer Identification Number (EIN) Online link located on the left side of the page.

So what about Social Security, Medicare, and withholding taxes?

You need to do two things before you can figure out how to handle all those taxes. First, you need your employees to fill out W-4 forms to let you know what filing status they'll use and how many withholding allowances, or personal exemptions, they'll claim. You can get blank W-4 forms from the www.irs.gov website, too.

While you're visiting the IRS website, you also need to get a Publication 15 *Employer's Tax Guide* booklet (popularly known as *Circular E*). The *Circular E* booklet tells you how much you should withhold in federal income taxes, Social Security, and Medicare from employees' salaries, based on what they say about their filing statuses and the number of withholding allowances they claim on the W-4 forms mentioned in the preceding paragraph.

Paying someone for a job well done

After you set up the two needed expense categories within Quicken and after you collect the necessary tax information, you're ready to pay someone.

Figuring out the gross wages figure

Determining how much to pay your employees should be pretty easy. Does Raoul make $15 per hour? Did he work 40 hours? Then you owe him $600, because $15 times 40 equals $600. Is Betty's salary $400 per week? Then you owe her $400 for the week.

Calculating that deductions stuff

Your next step — after you know how much you're supposed to pay Raoul and Betty — is to figure out what Uncle Sam says you must withhold.

To determine this amount, you need both Raoul's and Betty's W-4s to find out their filing statuses and personal exemptions. Then just flip to the page in the *Circular E* that describes withholding for people claiming those filing statuses and weekly pay.

If Raoul is single and claims just one personal exemption, for example, you need to flip to the page that shows appropriate withholding amounts for single people receiving weekly payroll checks. That page shows a table that clearly indicates what you're supposed to withhold from Raoul's check for federal income taxes. The table might say that a single person making $600 a week who claims one withholding allowance should have $79 withheld for federal taxes, for example.

And Betty? Remember that fictional Betty's pay is $400 per week. If (say) Betty's filing status is married, she is filing jointly, and has three personal exemptions, you need to need to flip to the page in the *Circular E* that shows withholding amounts for a married person filing a joint return when the person claims three withholding allowances. Pretend, just for the sake of illustration, that the *Circular E* says you're supposed to withhold $18 from Betty's check each week.

You determine Social Security and Medicare amounts by multiplying the gross wage figure by a set percentage. Social Security is 6.2 percent of the gross wages because in 2014 (for example), the 6.2 percent applies on wages up to $117,000. The Medicare tax is 1.45 percent of the gross wages unless the Affordable Care Act "surtax" comes into play (as it does for a single person at $200,000 in wages), in which case the Medicare tax equals 2.35 percent of wages above this limit.

Figuring out someone's net wages

Table 15-1 summarizes the payroll calculations based on the examples developed in the preceding paragraphs.

Table 15-1	Payroll for Raoul and Betty		
Item	*Raoul*	*Betty*	*Explanation*
Gross Wages	$600	$400	Their pay
Withholding	$79	$18	From *Circular E*
Social Security	$37.20	$24.80	6.2% of gross wages
Medicare	$8.70	$5.80	1.45% of gross wages
Net Wages	$475.10	$351.40	What's left over

Does Table 15-1 make sense? If it doesn't, quickly skim the preceding four or five paragraphs. All I've really done in the table is reorganize some information, calculate the Social Security and Medicare taxes, and show how Raoul's and Betty's gross pay gets nickeled and dimed by the various taxes they owe.

Working with other taxes and deductions

If you have other taxes and deductions to make, and you know how the federal income taxes, Social Security taxes, and Medicare taxes work, you won't have any problem working with other taxes — whatever they are.

State income tax withholding, for example, works like federal income tax withholding. (You need to get the state's equivalent of the *Circular E* guide, of course.)

In general, you treat other taxes and the amounts that the employee pays similarly.

In fact, the only thing that you need to be careful about is what affects your employees' gross pay for income taxes but not their Social Security taxes — things such as 401(k) deductions and certain fringe benefits. If you have these kinds of things to deal with, and you need help, just ask your accountant. (Providing general answers that will work for everyone who reads this paragraph is just too difficult — and actually kind of dangerous, too. Sorry.)

Recording a payroll check

After you make the tax deduction and net wages calculation, you're ready to record the check. Suppose that you're going to record the check by using the Write Checks window. After you display the window, follow these steps:

1. **Enter the date of the payroll check in the Date field.**

2. **Enter the payroll check number in the Num field.**

3. **Enter the employee name in the Payee field.**

4. **Enter the net wages amount in the Payment field.**

5. **Describe the payroll details using Click the Split button.**

 Click the Split button. Then, when Quicken opens the Split Transaction dialog, describe the payroll details for the employee. Figure 15-7 shows how Betty Ready's payroll detail information from Table 15-1 should look. The $400 of gross wages shown in Table 15-1, for example, appears on the first line of the Split Transaction dialog box. After you complete describing the payroll details using the Split Transaction dialog box, click OK to close it.

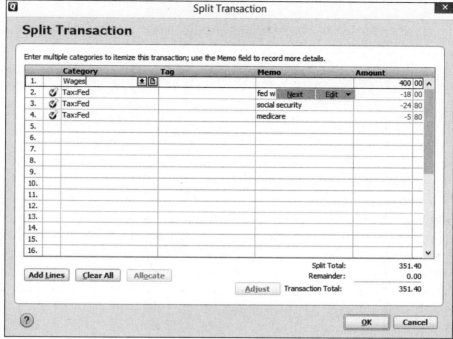

Figure 15-7:
The Split
Transaction
dialog box
recording
Betty's
$351.40
paycheck.

6. **To record the payroll check, click Record Check.**

Figure 15-8 shows how the completed payroll check looks. Note that the Category field shows the word Split.

You did it! You recorded a payroll check. Maybe it wasn't all that much fun, but at least it wasn't very difficult. (Chapter 5 describes how to print checks, just in case you're interested.)

Depositing taxes

Make no mistake: Uncle Sam wants the money you withhold from an employee's payroll check for federal income taxes, Social Security, and Medicare. Uncle Sam also wants the payroll taxes you owe — such as matching Social Security and Medicare taxes, and federal unemployment taxes.

Every so often, then, you need to pay Uncle Sam the amounts you owe.

Making the payments for these taxes is easy.

Figure 15-8:
A competed
payroll
check.

Depositing the employee withholding

To remit the payroll taxes you withhold from an employee's check, follow
these steps:

1. **Sign up for the U.S. Treasury's electronic funds tax payment system,
 also known as EFTPS.**

 You should visit the www.eftps.gov website a few weeks (at least
 a couple of weeks and preferably more) before you want to process
 payroll. Find the link that lets you sign up for the service, and carefully
 follow the onscreen instructions to create your EFTPS account. Note
 that you need to take this step only once.

2. Log on to www.eftps.gov.

This is easy. Click the link that indicates that you want to log on to the website and then provide three bits of information: your employer identification number, your PIN (personal identification number), and your password. Both the PIN and your password come in the letter that welcomes you to the EFTPS system.

3. Indicate that you want to make a payment equal to the payroll taxes that you withheld from the employee's check.

In the example case of Betty — in which withholding includes $18 of income taxes, $24.80 of Social Security taxes, and $5.80 of Medicare taxes — you initiate an EFTPS payment for $48.60. Again — and sorry to be so anal about this — but within Quicken, you need to categorize the check in the Wages expense category.

Don't categorize the check that remits the employee's portion of his or her taxes as falling into the payroll tax category. That would be a mistake. Yes, I know: It seems that payroll tax expense would be the right category. The withheld taxes are tax expenses of the employee, however — not tax expenses of the employer. The money represents a wage expense to the employer.

Betty's true earnings were $400: the $351.40 net payroll check plus the $48.60 of payroll-related and income taxes that she owed but that you, the employer, withheld.

Paying employer payroll taxes

You have to match any Social Security and Medicare taxes paid by the employee. To record the payment of these payroll taxes, you follow a similar set of steps to those in the preceding section. Indicate that you want to make another EFTPS payment equal to the payroll taxes you owe as the employer. (In the example case of Betty, in which withholding included $24.80 of Social Security taxes and $5.80 of Medicare taxes, you make a payment for $30.60 payable to the local bank.)

When you pay the employer's payroll taxes — such as the matching Social Security and Medicare taxes — you want to categorize the check as a payroll tax category. This money absolutely does represent a payroll tax expense to the employer.

Tax deposit tips

Let me make a handful of suggestions about making tax deposits easier and less painful. On the subject of tax deposits, let me also tell you that my fast-but-fancy payroll method has a weakness you should know about.

Tax deposit tip #1: Combine payments

Here's my first tip. In the preceding discussion, I suggest that you use one payment to pay the employee's taxes and another payment to pay the employer's taxes.

Specifically, I describe how to initiate a $48.60 EFTPS payment categorized as a wage expense and then how to initiate a second EFTPS payment for $30.60, which gets categorized as a payroll tax expense. But you could, in fact, save yourself a bit of fiddle-faddling by initiating one payment for $79.20 that combines both payments. If you do this, just be sure to split the transaction with $48.60 categorized as a wage expense and $30.60 categorized as a payroll tax expense when you go to record the tax deposit within Quicken.

Tax deposit tip #2: Combine employees

In the running example in this chapter, I describe how to deal with payroll taxes for a single employee.

I feel sort of dumb saying this, but you would (of course) often have more than one employee. And in that case, you probably would combine the payroll tax deposits for all the employees.

If you have multiple employees, you probably want to consider using a small-business accounting system such as QuickBooks or an outside payroll service bureau. Most of the payroll calculations and bookkeeping are pretty easy, but figuring out what you owe in terms of payroll tax deposits can be a bit messy if you have more than one employee to pay at a time.

Tax deposit tip #3: Don't delay your deposit

The system I describe in the preceding paragraphs doesn't keep track of what you owe in *payroll tax liabilities* (the withheld taxes, the company's matching of Social Security tax, and so on). And that's bad, obviously. You shouldn't just foolishly ignore any of your business or personal debts, of course. If you just deposit your payroll taxes immediately after every payroll, you should be fine.

Tax deposit tip #4: Know the De Minimis rule

While I'm talking about federal payroll tax deposits, I should cover another general but very useful rule related to when you need to make the deposit: If your accumulated federal payroll taxes are less than $2,500 for the quarter, you can pay the taxes with your quarterly 941 payroll tax return. (This is called the *De Minimis* rule — named after Congresswoman Dee Minimis, I think.) Don't rely on this rule, however, without checking with the IRS or your tax advisor.

Filing quarterly payroll tax returns

At the end of every quarter, you need to file a quarterly payroll tax return. (Specifically, you must file a Form 941 — which is a form you fill out to say how much you paid in gross wages, how much you withheld in federal taxes, and how much you owe for employer payroll taxes.)

If you don't own a business but have household employees — such as a nanny — you file a Form 942. You fill out this form to say how much you paid in gross wages, withheld in federal taxes, and owe in payroll taxes.

To get the gross wages totals and the balances in each of the payroll tax liability accounts, print a Cash Flow report for the quarter you need to report. You can do this by choosing Reports⇨Banking⇨Cash Flow. Quicken displays the Cash Flow report, but the dates will probably be wrong, so click the Customize button. Quicken displays the Customize Cash Flow dialog box.

Specify the range of dates as the start and end of the quarter for which you're preparing a quarterly report. Then click OK. Quicken produces a Cash Flow report, which you can easily use to fill out the quarterly payroll tax return.

You also need to report on the 941 tax form how much money you withheld from the employee's checks for federal withholding. You can do this manually (by looking through the payroll records) or algebraically (by comparing whatever the 941 or 942 shows as the total Social Security and Medicare taxes amount with the total payments made to the IRS).

You know what, though? If your accountant fills out the 941 or 942 for you, you don't even need to read the stuff in the preceding three sections. Your accountant won't have any problem completing the quarterly payroll tax return by using the Quicken report, and in fact — I kid you not — he or she will probably even enjoy it.

Even if you want to do payroll returns yourself in the future, have your tax accountant prepare the first return. Then you can use that return as a template for correctly preparing any future returns.

Computing annual returns and wage statements

At year end, you need to file some annual returns, such as the 940 federal unemployment tax return and the W-2 and W-3 wage statements. (You need to prepare these by hand. Perhaps to protest all the work that small businesses have to do to comply with tax laws, you could prepare these forms by hand, using a cheap ballpoint pen. Just an idea.)

As a practical matter, as long as you're doing payroll for a single employee, the only thing that's different about filling out these reports is that you need to use a Cash Flow report that covers the entire year — not just a single quarter. So you need to enter the range of dates in the Cash Flow report dialog box as January 1 and December 31.

The 940 annual return is darn easy if you've been wrestling with the 941 or 942 quarterly returns. The 940 annual return works the same basic way as those more difficult quarterly tax returns. You print the old payroll report, enter a few numbers, and then write a check for the amount you owe.

You need to prepare annual state unemployment summaries before preparing the 940. The 940 requires information from the state returns.

For the W-2 statements and the summary W-3 (which summarizes your W-2s), you just print the old Cash Flow report. Then, carefully following directions, enter the gross wages, the Social Security and Medicare taxes withheld, and the federal income taxes withheld in the appropriate blanks.

If you have a little trouble, call the IRS. If you have a lot of trouble, splurge and hire someone to do it. Again, any experienced bookkeeper can do the job for you.

Doing the state payroll taxes thing

I haven't talked about state payroll taxes — at least not in any great detail. I wish I could provide this sort of detailed, state-specific help to you. Unfortunately, doing so would make this chapter about 150 pages long. It would also cause me to go stark raving mad.

You still need to deal with state payroll taxes, however. State payroll taxes follow the same basic mechanics that you apply to federal payroll taxes. state income tax works the same way federal income tax works, employer-paid state unemployment taxes work the same way employer-paid federal unemployment taxes work, and employee-paid state taxes work the same way employee-paid Social Security and Medicare taxes work.

If you're tuned in to how federal payroll taxes work in Quicken, you really shouldn't have a problem with the mechanics of state payroll taxes.

Chapter 16

Managing Rentals

· ·

In This Chapter

▶ Describing rental properties and tenants

▶ Recording rent payments

▶ Keeping track of rental expenses

▶ Tracking rental profits

· ·

*T*he Quicken Rental Property Manager version of Quicken — the focus of this short chapter — provides everything available in the other versions of Quicken. The Rental Property Manager version also includes tools for tracking both your rental properties and your rental income and expense.

If you own rental properties — and I say this as a CPA who breaks down and cries several times each year when I see the messy financial records that most real estate investors keep — you definitely want to make the investment and buy Quicken Rental Property Manager. You'll have a much better handle on your rental property investments, the rental income the properties earn, and the rental deductions the properties produce.

Describing a Rental Property

To track rental properties with Quicken, you need to describe each property. To describe a property, follow these steps:

1. **Display the Rental Property tab.**

 If you purchased the Rental Manager version of Quicken, you should also have a Rental Property tab available in the Quicken window. If the tab doesn't show, choose View⇨Tabs to Show and click Rental Property. If you want to manage rental properties but didn't buy the Rental Manager version of Quicken, you may be able to buy and immediately turn on the

Rental Manager functionality by choosing Help⇨Add Rental Property Tools.

2. **Click the Properties & Tenants button and choose Add Property.**

 Quicken displays the Add Rental Property dialog box, shown in Figure 16-1.

Figure 16-1:
The Add
Rental
Property
dialog box.

The Properties & Tenants button also gives you access to another command, Show Property List, which you can choose to display a window that lists the previously added rental properties. You can edit a rental property that appears in this property list by selecting the property and then clicking the Edit button. You can remove a rental property that appears in this property list by selecting the property and then clicking the Delete button.

3. **Describe the property.**

 Describe the rental property you're going to track in Quicken. You'll want to name the property, using the Property Name text box. You can then create a tag for the property's income and expense transactions using the Tag text box. Optionally, you can enter the street, city, state, and ZIP code information in the appropriately labeled text boxes.

 Note: You use the tag to mark, or *tag*, each income or expense transaction for a specific property. By tagging the transactions in this way, Quicken easily produces a profit-and-loss statement by rental property.

You want a profit-and-loss statement by property to manage your real estate investments, of course. But you also need a profit-and-loss statement by property for your year-end income tax returns.

4. **Indicate whether the property is a single or multiple unit.**

Use the Property Type Information option buttons — Single Unit Property and Multiunit Property — to specify whether the property is a single-unit property (such as a single-family rental house) or a multiunit property (such as a fourplex or a strip mall).

5. **(Optional) Identify the multiple units.**

If you indicate in Step 4 that a rental property is multiunit, Quicken adds the Unit Information text boxes to the Add Rental Property dialog box. Use these boxes to name each of the rental units — using, for example, apartment letters, suite numbers, or similar identifying labels.

6. **(Optional) Track the net worth of the property.**

If you want to track the fair market value or your estimate of the fair market value of the rental property, select the Yes, I Want to Track the Value of This Rental Property button. Then, without laughing, enter the fair market value of the property in the Approximate Value text box.

Note: If you decide to track the net worth of the property, Quicken adds an asset account to the Quicken account list.

7. **Click OK.**

Quicken displays the Rental Property tab, or window, with the rental property you just created. (See Figure 16-2.)

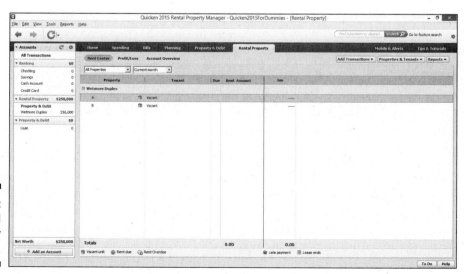

Figure 16-2:
The Rental Property window.

Describing Tenants

After you describe your rental property or properties, you need to describe the tenants that occupy the property or properties. To describe the tenants, follow these steps:

1. **Display the Rental Property tab.**

2. **Click the Properties & Tenants button and choose Add Tenant.**

 Quicken displays the Add Rental Property Tenant dialog box. (See Figure 16-3.)

Figure 16-3:
The Add Rental Property Tenant dialog box.

The Property & Tenants button also displays another tenant-related command, Show Tenants List. Choose the Show Tenants List command to display a window that lists the previously added tenants. You can edit and delete tenants that appear in the list by clicking the tenant and clicking either the Edit or Delete button.

3. **Describe the tenant.**

 Describe the tenant by clicking the Rent Details tab and then entering the renter's name in the Tenant Name text box and the monthly rent in the Rent Amount text box.

Choose the name of the bank account into which you'll deposit rent from the Account Name drop-down list box, and choose the property (or property and unit) the tenant occupies from the Property drop-down list box.

You can specify the rent due date — and I'm sure this is a big surprise — by using the Rent Due On drop-down list box.

Optionally, you can use the Contact tab of the Add Rental Property Tenant dialog box to collect and store the tenant's contact information, including work phone number, home phone number, email, and so on.

4. **(Optional) Document the lease agreement.**

You can use the Terms and Agreement tab to document the rental agreement, recording items such as the lease term, lease start date, late fee, and so forth.

You can use the Security Deposit tab to record the security deposit you collect at the start of the lease and any security deposit you return at the end of the lease.

5. **Click OK.**

Quicken displays the Rental Property tab or window. The names of any tenants you've added appear indented below the rental property they occupy.

Recording Tenant Rent Payments

After you describe your properties and your tenants, you can begin recording tenant rent payments as tenants pay you, the lord of the manor. Simply follow these steps:

1. **Display the Rental Property tab.**

No problem here, right? You just click the tab.

2. **Click the Add Transactions button.**

Quicken opens the a menu of commands related to working with your rental property record-keeping.

3. **Choose the Enter Rent command from the Add Transactions menu.**

Quicken displays the Enter Rent dialog box. (See Figure 16-4.)

Figure 16-4:
The Enter
Rent dialog
box.

4. Choose the tenant from the Tenant Name drop-down list box.

Quicken enters most of what else it needs to know to record the rent payment: the property, the rent amount, and so on. But confirm that this information is correct. You may want to edit the contents of the Memo text box, for example, or you may need to assess a late fee if the tenant has paid late.

5. Click Add to record the transaction.

Quicken adds the rent payment to your records, recording the rent check as a deposit in the specified bank account. Behind the scenes, Quicken tags the transaction as income related to a specific property — just as you want it to do.

Recording Rental Expenses

You record rent expenses in a fashion similar to that used to record rent income. Follow these steps:

1. Display the Rental Property tab.

2. Click the Add Transactions button.

3. **Choose the Enter Expense command from the Add Transactions menu.**

 Quicken displays the Enter Expense dialog box. (See Figure 16-5.)

Figure 16-5:
The Enter
Expense
dialog box.

4. **Choose the rental property from the Property drop-down list box.**

5. **Use the other fields in the dialog box to record the rent expense: the payee, category, and so on.**

 Quicken guesses at the bank account, so confirm this bit of information. You may want to edit the contents of the Memo text box, for example, and you may want to record a check number or payment method.

One other point: You don't have to use the Enter Expense dialog box to record expenses for a rental. Alternatively, you can record the expense directly in the register. If you use the "direct into the register" approach, however, you need to tag the transaction with the property's tag. If you have questions about how to record checks in a Quicken bank account, refer to Chapter 4.

Note: Tax laws now require you to send Form 1099s to your unincorporated vendors if, as part of your rental property business, you pay these people $600 or more in a year by check. Therefore, you probably want to collect completed W-9 forms (available from the www.irs.gov website) from any such vendors you use.

Tracking Rental Property Profits

I don't want to talk too long about the Rental Property Manager features. If I do that, you'll think that the tools are complicated to learn and use. The tools aren't complicated. They're really, really easy.

Before I quit, however, I do want to share one quick reminder: In Chapter 7, I talk about how to produce reports in Quicken, including how to produce reports specifically designed to track your rental properties. Peek back there.

Another thing to point out — and this is sort of redundant, but it's so darn important — is that the Rental Property Manager features let you track rental income and rental expenses *by properties,* using those tags that you create for each property. This tagging means you can produce reports that show profit by property. This "profit by property" measurement is really important. You use the segmented profit data to manage your properties — and to report what's happening with your rental properties on your tax return.

Working with tags

The Quicken tags aren't just for rental properties. In fact, tags (which used to be called *classes* in a previous version of Quicken) provide you a second method for organizing the data. Categories, of course, are the first data organization method, but tags are the second. They deserve your respect and admiration.

Because tags can get used for other purposes, Quicken's Tools menu provides a Tag List command. Choose this command, and Quicken displays the Tag List window. This window lists all the tags you've set up — and all the tags that the Quicken Rental Property Manager has set up for you. You can add still more tags by clicking the Add button. You can edit and delete existing tags by selecting a tag and then clicking the Edit or Delete button.

Part V
The Part of Tens

Go to www.dummies.com/extras/quicken2015 for an additional Part of Tens chapter with tips for mapping out a solid retirement plan.

In this part . . .

- ✔ Get answers to the most frequently asked questions about Quicken.

- ✔ Discover practical secrets for building personal wealth and avoiding financial disasters.

- ✔ Solve tricky Quicken and personal finance problems by using tried-and-true troubleshooting tricks and tactics.

Chapter 17

(Slightly More Than) Ten Questions I'm Frequently Asked about Quicken

. .

In This Chapter

▶ What are Quicken's best features?

▶ Does Quicken work for a corporation?

▶ What happens to stockholders' equity in Quicken?

▶ Does Quicken work for a partnership?

▶ Can I use Quicken to track more than one business?

▶ What kinds of businesses shouldn't use Quicken?

▶ Can I use Quicken for my real estate investments?

▶ Can I use Quicken retroactively?

▶ Can I do payroll with Quicken?

▶ Can I prepare invoices with Quicken?

▶ Can I import data from my old accounting system?

▶ What do you think of Quicken?

. .

When people find out that I've written a book about Quicken, they always ask a question or two. In this chapter, I list the most common questions and their answers.

What Are Quicken's Best Features?

Quicken has become more and more complicated over the years, so I think it may be fair to include a few sentences that review its most valuable and least valuable features. As far as what's best or most valuable, I would say that its checkbook feature is still clearly the most valuable. If you should use one feature in Quicken, it's the checkbook stuff. (To do so, set up a bank account for your checking account as described in Chapter 1, and then use Quicken to keep track of your balances, income, and expenditures as described in Chapter 4.)

I also have to say that I think that Intuit, the maker of Quicken, provides pretty neat stuff at its Quicken website, so I'd give that feature my vote as the second-best. I don't talk about the Quicken.com website a whole lot in this book. That's because you can have more fun and more success with the Quicken website by exploring it on your own.

Just because I'm super-compulsive — not only about my personal finances, but also about yours — let me say that I think that the Quicken financial calculators (I describe them in Chapter 10) are also really valuable. If you're willing and able to do just a bit of planning right now, you'll be truly amazed by the positive impact that planning has on your financial affairs a few years down the road.

So this leads rather nicely to another question: What are Quicken's least valuable features? I think the answer really depends on the person. I used to pooh-pooh the online banking because my bank caused me headaches, and my at-home dial-up Internet connection was unreliable. (For a while, I even suspected that carrier pigeons were involved in one link of the connection.) Now, however, with a fast cable modem connection, I really do like online banking.) The credit card stuff and cash account stuff don't do much for me. But you know what? Those tools may do wonderful things for you. It depends on the way you organize your finances.

I guess the bottom line, to me, is that the least useful features depend on what you don't need to do. But what you don't need to do will probably differ from what I don't need to do. I'm sorry that I don't have a more helpful criticism.

Does Quicken Work for a Corporation?

Sure. But let me talk for a minute about what's unique — at least from an accountant's perspective — about a corporation. (And just for the record, what I'm going to say here applies to regular corporations, to Subchapter S corporations, and to limited liability companies that have elected to be treated as regular corporations and as S corporations.)

In addition to recording assets (such as bank accounts and receivables) and liabilities (such as mortgages and trade payables), a corporation often needs to *track*, or keep records for, stockholder equity.

Stockholder equity includes the amount that people originally paid for their stock, any earnings the corporation has retained, cumulative income for the current year, and sometimes other stuff too. With Subchapter S corporations, for example, stockholder equity gets adjusted when the corporation pays distributions (also known as *dividends*) to shareholders.

"Ugh," you're probably saying to yourself. "Ugh" is right. Accounting for stockholder equity of a corporation is mighty complicated at times. It's so complicated, in fact, that Quicken can't track a corporation's stockholder equity.

I'm not saying that you can't use Quicken if you're a corporation, and I'm not saying that you shouldn't. (I do business as a Subchapter S corporation, and I used to use Quicken just for laughs.) Just remember that someone — probably your poor accountant — may periodically need to calculate your stockholders' equity.

Fortunately, the financial information you collect with Quicken provides, in rough form, much of the information that your poor accountant needs to do things manually.

But all this makes me remember something else. If your corporation enjoys revenue of $250,000 per year or more, or owns assets that total $250,000 or more, you must include a balance sheet with your corporate tax return. (This isn't something I just made up. It's actually the law.) Quicken isn't quite as robust about creating business balance sheets as a program like QuickBooks (Quicken's big brother). Accordingly, if your corporation grows so that its revenues or assets equal or exceed $250,000, consider retiring Quicken and upgrading to QuickBooks.

What Happens to Stockholders' Equity in Quicken?

Quicken doesn't exactly ignore a corporation's stockholders' equity. In an Account Balances report, the difference between the total assets and the total liabilities actually represents the total stockholders' equity. (Quicken labels this total Net Worth.) So to the extent that your total assets and total liabilities figures are correct, you know your total stockholders' equity.

Does Quicken Work for a Partnership?

Yep, it does. But a partnership that uses Quicken faces the same basic problem as a corporation that uses Quicken. In a partnership, the partners want to track their partnership capital accounts (or at least they should). A partnership capital account simply shows what a partner has put into and taken out of a business.

As noted in the preceding section, Quicken calculates a net worth figure for you by subtracting total liabilities from total assets. So to the extent that your total assets and total liabilities are accurately accounted for in Quicken, you know roughly the total partnership capital.

To solve this problem, you (or someone else) need to track what each partner puts into the business, earns as a partner in the business, and then takes out of the business. You can also just use the Quicken loan accounts for partnership equity accounts (and I've helped clients do this). Just don't freak out when your net worth shows as zero. Remember that the partnership equity accounts aren't really loans: They're capital.

One other thing to think about here concerns your partnership tax return. If your partnership books revenue of $250,000 per year or more, or owns assets that total $1,000,000 or more, you need to include a balance sheet with your partnership tax return. As mentioned in my earlier discussion about using Quicken for a corporation's accounting, Quicken isn't very good about creating the sort of balance sheet that needs to get included with a tax return. Accordingly, if your partnership grows so that its revenues equal or exceed $250,000 — or so that its assets equal or exceed $1,000,000 — consider upgrading to QuickBooks.

Can I Use Quicken for More Than One Business?

Yeah, but be very careful. *Very* careful. You must be especially diligent in keeping the two businesses' financial records separate.

Quicken provides a handy tool for keeping them straight: You can work with more than one file. Each file, in effect, is like a separate set of financial records. You can't record automatic transfers between accounts in different files; instead, you must record each side of the transaction separately. You can, however, keep truly separate business records.

To create a separate file, choose File⇨New.

If you've been using Quicken for a while, you can probably figure out for yourself how the File⇨New command works.

Keeping separate bank accounts is a must. If you keep separate records for two distinct businesses in Quicken, you need to set up separate bank accounts for them. In fact, my attorney tells me that in the case of a corporation, you must set up a separate corporate bank account for the corporation to be truly considered as an independent legal entity. Talk to your attorney if you have questions; attorneys can tell you the specifics that apply to a particular state and situation.

What Kinds of Businesses Shouldn't Use Quicken?

You're probably saying to yourself, "Quicken works for corporations (sort of), and it works for partnerships (sort of). Does that mean that it works for just about any kind of business?"

The answer is no. Quicken is a darn good product. In fact, for many small businesses, it's a great product. Quicken works especially well for service businesses: consultants, contractors, personal-service providers, and so forth. But it doesn't work in every situation.

The following is a three-part test that you can use to determine whether your business should use Quicken. If you answer yes to two or three of the

questions, you should seriously consider moving up to a full-featured small-business accounting system (such as QuickBooks).

✔ **Do you regularly need to produce business forms other than checks?**

- If you answer no, you're in good shape with Quicken, which produces checks easily. And if all you need is an occasional invoice, you can create it easily enough on your computer. To produce a handful of invoices per month, for example, you can use your word processor. If you want to, you can also use one of the super-sized versions of Quicken: Quicken Home & Business or Quicken Rental Property Manager. Both of these versions of Quicken not only do invoices, but also monthly customer statements. (I talk about these features in Chapter 15.)

- If you do produce a lot of forms besides checks and invoices — for example, purchase orders — you should probably consider moving to a small-business accounting system that produces the forms you want. If you've been using Quicken, for example, take a look at QuickBooks, another Intuit product. Another more powerful but wonderfully designed product you might try is Peachtree Accounting for Windows from Sage Software. You can probably buy any of these programs at the local office-supplies store. You can certainly buy the QuickBooks and Sage 50 Accounting (formerly known as Peachtree) programs by visiting `http://quickbooks.intuit.com` or `www.sage50accounting.com`. For reference, I can recommend these two books: *QuickBooks 2014 For Dummies*, by yours truly (earlier versions of QuickBooks have their own editions), and *Peachtree For Dummies*, 3rd Edition, by Elaine Marmel and Diane Koers.

✔ **Do you need to track assets other than cash, accounts receivable, or investments?**

For example, do you buy and resell inventory? Do you have a bunch of fixed assets (furniture, equipment, and stuff like that) that you need to track? An accounting system is usually helpful in tracking these items. Quicken doesn't do a very good job of tracking these other assets, so you may want to look at one of the other small-business accounting products — QuickBooks, for example.

✔ **Are you having problems measuring your profits with cash-basis accounting?**

I'm not going to get into a big, tangled discussion of cash-basis versus accrual-basis accounting. It wouldn't be any fun for you. It wouldn't be any fun for me, either. Nevertheless, you should know that if you can't accurately measure your business profits by using cash-basis accounting (which is what Quicken uses), you may be able to more accurately measure

your business profits by using accrual-basis accounting. To do so, use an accounting system that supports accrual-basis accounting. I should be totally honest with you and tell you that to measure your profits the right way, you (or your accountant) need to use — horror of horrors — double-entry bookkeeping.

If you're a Quicken user but realize that you're outgrowing the checkbook-on-a-computer scene, check out QuickBooks. (No, I don't get a kickback from Intuit.) Here's the deal: QuickBooks looks and feels a lot like Quicken. Also, it uses the data that you've already collected with Quicken, so you'll find that moving from Quicken to QuickBooks is only slightly more complicated than rolling off a log.

Can I Use Quicken for Real Estate Investing?

Yeah. Absolutely.

In a nutshell, all you need to do is set up an income category to track your rental income and then some expense categories to track your rental expenses. (In Chapter 2, in the section about changing a category list, I describe how to set up income and expense categories.)

To see which rental expense categories you need, either look at the Schedule E tax form that went with last year's tax return (if you've already been investing in real estate) or grab a Schedule E tax form from www.irs.gov (if you're new to real estate investing).

Now, before you stop reading and rush off to do the bookkeeping for your growing real estate empire, let me tell you one other critical thing: The Schedule E tax form on which you report your real estate income and deductions requires you to segregate your income and deductions by property. For example, if you have two rental properties — a duplex on Winston Street and a single-family cottage on Roosevelt Avenue — you'll need to break down your income and expenses by property.

To break down income and expenses by property, you use a Quicken feature called *tags*. Oh, yes, it all sounds complicated. But all you need to do is enter the tag name in the Tag field. For example, rather than just enter **rent** in the Category field when recording a rent payment from your tenants living in the Winston Street duplex, you enter **rent** (as the Category) and then also enter **Winston** (as the Tag).

By appending the tag **Winston** to the transaction, you can later easily produce a cash flow that shows income and expenses for the Winston duplex.

Just to make sure that you understand this, let me give you another example. Rather than record a check to pay the utilities expenses for the house on Roosevelt as **utilities,** enter **utilities** as the category and **Roosevelt** as the tag.

By appending the tag **Roosevelt** to the transaction, you can easily produce a cash flow later that shows income and expenses for the Roosevelt cottage.

A couple of other notes: The first time you enter a tag name in the Tag field, Quicken asks whether you want to set up a new tag. When you click "Heck, yeah," Quicken prompts you for a bit of information about the tag. After that, though, you just enter the tag without fanfare or embarrassment.

To produce a report that summarizes income and deduction information by tag, choose Reports⇨Banking⇨Cash Flow by Tag.

I talk a bit about the rental property management features of Quicken in Chapter 16.

Can I Use Quicken Retroactively?

Yeah. And the idea is better than it may seem at first.

Entering one year's worth of transactions doesn't take long in Quicken (as long as you have decent records to work with). If you're a millionaire, the task may take you a couple of days. (Of course, in this case, you can hire someone to do it for you.) If you're a regular, ordinary person, I bet you can get it done on a rainy Saturday afternoon.

After you enter all the information in a Quicken register, you can easily monitor your spending in various categories, track your income and outgo, and reconcile your bank accounts. I know one professional who uses Quicken records to do these things every year. Hey, it's not the most efficient way to do things. And it's not a very good way to manage business or personal financial affairs. But it works. Sort of.

Can I Do Payroll with Quicken?

Yes. See Chapter 15 for more details.

By the way, if you have only one or two salaried employees who always earn the same amount — a nanny, for example — you can rather easily use Quicken for payroll. But if you have a bunch of employees or even a single hourly employee, you'll probably want to either purchase a full-featured, real-live, small-business accounting program (such as QuickBooks) or use a payroll service (such as Paychex or ADP) to take care of the whole thing for you.

Intuit makes and sells QuickBooks, as you may guess by its name. You can get QuickBooks from the local software store, from one of the mail-order places, or from the Intuit website.

You can look up either payroll service — Paychex or ADP — in the telephone book. You can also look up either payroll service — Paychex or ADP — at www.paychex.com or www.adp.com, respectively.

Can I Prepare Invoices?

Not with Quicken Premier or Quicken Deluxe, but you can (very nicely, thank you) with Quicken Home & Business and with Quicken Rental Property Manager. If you want invoices, at least step up to Quicken Home & Business. This requirement may also be a symptom indicating that you should consider moving up to a full-featured small-business accounting system, such as QuickBooks.

Can I Import Data from an Old Accounting System?

Someone had to ask this question, I guess. (Imagine me taking a deep breath here.) Yes, you can import data from your old accounting system. To do so, export the old system's data to a file that matches the Quicken Interchange Format (QIF) specification. (A QIF file neatly organizes financial information in a well-documented structure so that other programs — and even people — can read and understand the data.) Then import this file into an empty Quicken file. Keep in mind, however, that this process isn't for the timid or fainthearted. I would also say that it isn't for people who have better things to do with their time.

My advice to you? Go to a movie. Mow your lawn. Read a trashy novel. Forget all about this importing business. Or, if you're really determined, look for a QIF conversion tool on the Internet. These tools do exist.

What Do You Think about Quicken?

I think it's great. But I bet your question isn't really whether Quicken is good or not. Heck, the package has something like 10 million happy users, so we both know that the package is pretty good, right? My guess is that what you really want is my opinion about using Quicken in particular business or personal situations.

It's tough to answer this question in a one-way conversation. Even so, let me give you some of the best reasons for using Quicken:

- ✓ You always know your bank account balances, so you won't ever have to wonder whether you have enough money to pay a bill or charge a purchase.
- ✓ Reconciling your account takes about two minutes. (I'm not joking.)
- ✓ You get a firm handle on what you're really making and spending.
- ✓ You can budget your spending and then track your spending against your budget.
- ✓ If you're a business, you can measure your profits as often as you want by using cash-basis accounting.
- ✓ If you're an investor, you can monitor your investments and measure their actual returns.

I hope these answers help. My guess is that if you think that a program such as Quicken will help you better manage your financial affairs, it probably will.

Chapter 18

(Almost) Ten Tips on How Not to Become a Millionaire

You read the chapter title right. But let me explain a couple of things. First, about 15 years ago, I wrote a book about how to save a million dollars for one's retirement. That sounds a little money-grubbing, I'll agree, but my argument then (and now) is that most people need to accumulate a nice-size nest egg for retirement because most of us can't or shouldn't completely count on things like pensions and Social Security for all our retirement needs.

If Congress does nothing — absolutely nothing — to save Social Security in the United States, the most recent reports from the Social Security Trustees show that about 20 years from now (in 2035), the government will need to reduce benefits to around 77 percent of the amount it pays today. For example, someone who may receive $1,000 per month today may instead receive $770 in the future. Although that difference isn't quite the financial meltdown some people think, it does mean that you and I really must prepare to augment our retirement income by having our own savings.

Anyway, as part of promoting this book, I spent several weeks on the road doing radio call-in shows, bookstore appearances, and television talk shows. I learned several things from that experience. First, I learned that after one

appears on some television show, it is, apparently, customary to remove the strange makeup that's applied for the cameras. This step is especially important if you plan to appear later in public.

I also learned something else in my travels and talking with people. Although everyone is interested in becoming a millionaire or in preparing financially for retirement, it turns out that most people are really more interested in how *not* to become a millionaire. In other words, they wanted me to explain in financial terms why people *don't* accumulate wealth.

At first, I thought that this was a little strange. But finally, somebody explained: "We all know we need to save and invest to build wealth. What we *don't* know are those things that prevent or sabotage our attempts to do this." People in the audience didn't want to make the same mistakes.

So that is what I want to cover here. I want to share with you my observations and research results about why people who know they should save at least some money for retirement don't end up building wealth. I've observed that eight really common problems or traps foul up most people.

Before I begin, note that one thing that happens when you start talking about compound interest and future values is that inflation makes comparing apples to apples difficult. In other words, I can say something like " . . . and then you'll have $3,000,000." But you then have to wonder what that amount will be worth after factoring in inflation. To deal with this annoying complexity, I adjust for inflation all the numbers I use in the following paragraphs. I subtract the inflation amount and give you only the adjusted-for-inflation numbers in current-day dollars. Note that the Quicken financial planners also let you adjust for inflation by selecting the Adjust for Inflation check box, which appears in most of the calculator dialog boxes.

Ignore the Fact That You Can Build Wealth by Investing in Ownership Investments and Earning Average Returns

You can build surprising wealth just by investing in ownership investments that produce average returns. By *ownership investments,* I mean basically stocks and maybe real estate. Here are three examples:

✔ Just by earning the stock market's average inflated adjusted return of around 6 percent, a 25-year-old saving $150 per month can build as much as $300,000 by age 65.

✔ Just by earning the stock market's average inflated adjusted return of around 6 percent, a 35-year-old saving $300 per month can build as much as $300,000 by age 65.

✔ Just by earning the stock market's average inflated adjusted return of around 6 percent, a 50-year-old saving $850 per month can build as much as $300,000 by age 65.

I want to stop here. An important truth here is that, sadly, most people miss this information. Consider what this means: You don't have to get fancy. You don't have to spend a bunch of time worrying. You don't need to spend a bunch of money on advisors, newsletters, or commissions — or even on books about using Quicken.

Compound interest is a powerful engine, and it creates wealth. And that means that you can build surprising wealth by investing in ownership investments and earning just average returns.

Note, too, that you can lock in average returns by choosing a low-cost index fund, such as The Vanguard Group's Index 500 or Total Stock Market Portfolio mutual fund.

If you choose an actively managed mutual fund or a mutual fund that charges average fees for managing your money, you basically don't have a snowball's chance in you-know-where of actually earning an average return over time. Over the long investment horizon required to prepare for retirement, if you go this route, chances are good that you'll actually earn a return that's equal to the market's return *less the expense ratio that the mutual fund manager charges and the trading costs the manager incurs.* Expense ratios for actively managed funds run about 2 percent annually. So rather than a 6 percent annual adjusted-for-inflation return, you'll actually earn a 4 percent annual adjusted-for-inflation return on actively managed mutual funds. That's brutal.

One final point: People see way more risk in this investing than really exists, particularly after the past few years. But over decades, which is how long you'll invest, the risk drops. If you had begun investing in the stock market in the mid-1920s and then continued systematically investing for 25 years through the crash of 1929, the global depression of the '30s, World War II, and the start of the Cold War, you would have earned about an 8 percent return on your money. Given that the inflation rate was just 2 to 3 percent over this same period of time, you still could have built wealth by investing in ownership investments producing average 5 to 6 percent returns. I honestly expect similar real returns over the remaining decades (I hope) of my life.

Ignore the Fact That You Can Get Much, and Maybe Most, of the Money from Tax Savings and Employer Matching

Okay. I'm moving on to another really important point. It's fine to say that you need to invest just $300 per month, and that produces the wealth you need. The big question is this: *Where do you get that money?*

You've got bills to pay and a rent or mortgage check to write. You want to enjoy at least a few of the material pleasures — like food and drink — that life offers up. Where in the world does someone come up with this kind of money?

Well, the answer is mostly from the tax man and your employer. No kidding. Because of the way that employer-matching provisions work in things like 401(k) and Simple-IRA plans and because of the way our progressive income tax system works, you can get a lot of money from your employer and from the government in the form of tax-deduction savings. You may even be able to get most of the money you need for your retirement savings from these sources.

Table 18-1 shows how someone who wants to save $300 a month might come up with the money. In fact, the first line of Table 18-1 shows how much you want to save: $300.

The second line of the table shows how much you might get from your employer in a 401(k) or Simple IRA plan. Note that an IRA obviously doesn't include employer matching. (This line shows up, therefore, as zero in Table 18-1.) But 401(k) plans commonly provide a 50 percent match on at least the first portion of your contribution. (This shows up as $100 in the table.) And basically by law, Simple IRAs provide a 100 percent match on the first portion of your contribution (which shows up as $150 in the table).

Table 18-1	Ways to Come Up with $300 Monthly		
	IRA	*401(k)*	*Simple IRA*
What you want to save	$300	$300	$300
What you can get from employer	$0	$100	$150
What you can get from tax man	$90	$60	$45
What you come up with yourself	$210	$140	$105

The third line of the table shows how much you might get in the way of tax savings. For example, if you're contributing $300 per month to an IRA, you might actually enjoy $90 per month in federal and state income tax savings if the tax rate you pay on your last dollars of income equals 30 percent. (This rate would be the case for many readers living in states with a state income tax.)

The fourth line of the table shows what you need to come up with yourself. The IRA is the worst case shown in the table. With an IRA and $300 per month of savings, you would need to come up with $210 yourself. The 401(k) plan looks better; with it, you need to come up with $140 yourself. The Simple IRA is the best case in the table. With it, you need to come up with only $105.

I don't want to overload you with data. But please note that this is an incredibly powerful insight. Much, and maybe most, of the money you need to build wealth can come from other people — specifically the tax man and your employer, if you work someplace that offers a 401(k) or Simple IRA plan.

Don't Tap Your Computer's Power to Develop Wealth-Building Insights

This is hard to describe in general terms because by definition, what the computer lets you do is get very specific. Consider this: Personal financial planning is essentially applied mathematics. What that means is that to make a decision, you often need to tally up the costs and benefits of Option A versus Option B, and then you need to make time/value of money calculations. (Practically speaking, this just means that you also need to figure in things like interest expense and investment income.) These sorts of tasks are the perfect applications for the personal computer.

When you use your computer to make better personal financial decisions, you develop powerful, wealth-building insights that often supply the rest of the money you need for your investing. More specifically, if you need to save $300 per month, and you can get $150 of this from your employer and through tax savings, you still need to come up with that last $150 per month. But what I'm saying is that your computer can, and should, help you find this money.

Here's one example: Have you heard about early mortgage repayment? It sounds like a good idea, at least on the surface. If you add an extra $25 per month to the regular mortgage payment on a typical mortgage, you often save about $25,000 in interest. (Maybe more. How much you save depends on the interest rate, the mortgage balance, and the remaining number of payments.)

Based on that bit of financial data, early mortgage repayment sounds like a pretty good idea. Lots of people — encouraged by financial writers — have started doing this. But is it a good idea? It depends.

To determine whether this is truly a good idea, however, you need to weigh your options. If you can instead put an extra $25 a month into a 401(k), you end up with about $100,000.

So there you have it: Option A, which is early mortgage repayment, sounds pretty good because $25,000 of interest savings is a lot of money. But Option B, the 401(k) option, is clearly better because, for no extra pain or hassle, you end up with $100,000.

But other important financial decisions and personal financial planning issues often provide you with similar opportunities for free money or extra wealth because you use your computer:

- ✔ **ARMs:** Sometimes adjustable-rate mortgages (ARMs) actually make you bear less risk and work better.

- ✔ **Buying a home:** Sometimes this isn't a good investment — even when it seems like it is.

- ✔ **Car leases:** They can be great deals or terrible deals. It all depends on the implicit interest rate that the lease charges.

In Chapter 10, I talk about how you use the Quicken financial planners to make better financial decisions. The Internet also provides a ton of tools, many helpful, for doing personal financial planning. I don't want to sound like your mother or some cranky uncle, but I urge you to use these sorts of computer-based financial tools to make wiser decisions. A little extra money here, a little there — and pretty soon, you've found that last bit of money you need to save for a comfortable retirement. No kidding.

Give Up, Because It's Too Late to Start Anyway

Another common trap that prevents people from saving money for retirement is they give up, thinking that it's too late to start. I have to tell you that, mathematically speaking, that's just dead wrong.

You may think that wealth-building schemes that rely on compound interest work only for young people. It's true that wealth building can be very easy for someone who's young. Often, young people need to make only a single,

clever decision in order to build wealth. For example, if a 25-year-old, pack-per-day smoker quits smoking and puts the money he saves into savings, he can rather easily build $1 million by retirement. All he needs to do is save his money in an IRA and select a small-company, stock mutual index fund. (Remember, I adjust for inflation; so really, this person will probably have between $3 million and $4 million of inflated dollars.)

You can't do that if you're 50 years old. I mean, you can't make one decision and expect that single good decision to grow to $1 million.

But there's another angle in all this: You aren't limited to making a single good decision. Oh, sure. That's easiest. But I really believe that if you make five or six or seven — maybe even ten — good decisions, you can still build substantial wealth by the time you stop working.

I don't think that surprises you if you're a mature investor. And I don't think it should discourage you. You possess more life experience and, I daresay, more wisdom, than someone who's 25. You can use your experience and wisdom to make a greater number of good decisions, and that can produce the wealth you need.

Get Entangled in at Least One "Get-Rich-Quick" Scheme

Get-rich-quick schemes don't work except for the person selling the scheme. And, in fact, they drain off energy and money you really should be using to build your investments. You know all this, of course. We all do. But I think that all of us have a tendency to assume that this one particular great investment or business we're presented with is different. Oh, sure, we know that other dummies get suckered, but "fill in the blank" is different.

I actually don't think trying the occasional flier is a bad idea. If you have some small percentage of your investment money chasing speculative returns, that's okay, but only as long as this iffy investing doesn't foul up your other, more important, boring-but-predictable wealth building for retirement. That's fair, right? If you or I want to try chasing down the hottest new mutual fund or try online day-trading or invest in some friend's start-up business, that seems okay. But you can't allow these get-rich-quick schemes to foul up your meat-and-potatoes investing.

Unfortunately, I see that most of the people who get involved in get-rich-quick schemes try to use this speculation as a replacement for true, disciplined investing. And I have never seen a get-rich-quick scheme that consistently works.

I offer one other comment: Many, and perhaps even most, of the best-selling books about money and investment techniques amount to just new get-rich-quick schemes. I'm not going to name names here. Neither my attorney nor the publisher will let me. But any book that promises you some way to magically and consistently double or triple the returns that other investors earn is a get-rich-quick scheme.

However, some wonderful books out there show you how to better manage your money. For example, Eric Tyson's *Personal Finance For Dummies,* 7th Edition, is a really good book about the basics. And I'm not just saying this to schmooze the publisher. (Both that book and this one are published by Wiley.) I also love basically everything that Andrew Tobias writes, plus John Bogle's books about mutual fund investing — *Bogle on Mutual Funds* (Irwin) and *Common Sense on Mutual Funds* (Wiley) — and Burton Malkiel's *The Random Walk Guide to Investing* (Norton). All these books provide good, fact-based advice that leads you in the right direction.

Fake It with False Affluence

I talk about this a bit in Chapter 3, but it's an important point and worth repeating. When people spend all their money trying to look rich, they don't have any money left over to save and invest. That means that most people have to decide — either explicitly or implicitly — whether they want to be rich or look rich. Weird, right?

Yet most millionaires live average lives. They live in average houses located in middle-class neighborhoods. They drive average cars.

Ironically, most of the people who live in big houses or drive expensive cars aren't rich. They may have high incomes, but they aren't rich. Yet that makes sense. You can't become rich if you're spending all your money trying to look rich.

Faking affluence is a trap that goofs up more people than you'd guess.

Give In to the First Big Temptation of Wealth Building

I think that when you boil everything down to its very essence, the big problem is that most people lack the commitment. We all must be culturally programmed this way or something. But most of us — I'm the same way — stumble over a couple of big temptations. So I mention these temptations here and in the next section.

Temptation #1: I can tell you, and so can any good financial planner, how to come up with an extra $100 or even $500 per month. Also, if you really do use Quicken in a disciplined way to manage your financial affairs, you'll find yourself freeing up money. You'll save a little bit of money here, waste a little less over there; pretty soon, you'll find yourself with a bit of extra cash. But you must have the commitment to save and invest that money. You and I have to decide to dedicate the next $100 or $500 to investments. If we do, we don't have to worry about financial security in retirement. And if we don't, we should worry. But anyway, that's the first temptation. When you find some extra money, you need to have the discipline to save and invest those funds. And if you do start to do this, you'll rather quickly amass thousands of dollars.

Give In to the Second Big Temptation of Wealth Building

Ironically, resisting Temptation #1 leads rather quickly to . . .

Temptation #2: After you collect an extra $5,000 or $25,000 or $50,000 in your portfolio, you need to have the commitment necessary to let that money grow. That seems obvious, of course. But I've also noticed that a lot of people don't do this. A lot of people, after they amass a nice little pot of money, decide it's time to abandon a strategy that has worked wonderfully. They decide to buy a bigger house or a boat. Or they change investment strategies, maybe by investing in some friend's or family member's new business. Or they turn their money into a hobby — perhaps deciding that they're going to use their retirement money to try out this online investing thing or leveraged real estate investing.

It's your money, of course. You get to do with it whatever you want. But I am going to be honest with you and say that if you really want to build up a nice nest egg for retirement, you need to be committed enough to resist these two big temptations.

Chapter 19

(Almost) Ten Troubleshooting Tips

After writing about Quicken for almost 25 years, I've had a revelation of sorts. People want not only specific, step-by-step information about how to use the program, but also troubleshooting advice. They want techniques and tactics that they can use to solve the inevitable problems they encounter while using Quicken in real-life settings. What follows is my list of the best troubleshooting techniques that I can offer you.

Tactics #1 and #2: Use the Quicken Help File and This Book

I know what you may be thinking: You have some problem that you can't solve by using Help, and it's either a bug or some glaring error in the Quicken documentation. And, of course, you've looked through this book, and it says nothing — absolutely nothing — about your question. In fact, upon further reflection, you may be thinking that you've encountered some problem that you can't possibly solve by consulting the Quicken Help file or this book.

Maybe you're right.

But in my experience (when I talk with people who have problems), about half the time, the problem is that people don't know enough about Quicken to know what to do. People simply experience a mechanical problem, and they can't make the program work because they haven't used Quicken enough to figure out how it works. Therefore, the right way to solve this sort of problem is to find out more about Quicken and try again. For example, if you're having problems printing a report, just finding out more about printing and reports often solves your problem.

In most cases, though not all, you should be able to find the information in this book by using either its index or table of contents.

Usually, you should be able to find the information (perhaps in a slightly less friendly form) in the Quicken Help file. To find information in the Quicken Help file, choose Help⇨Quicken Help to display the Help window, click the Search Quicken Help tab, and then enter the word or phrase that you want to look up.

Tactic #3: Visit the Quicken Product Support Website

Another really good resource for troubleshooting is the Intuit product support website for Quicken. This website, available at `http://quicken.intuit.com/support`, supplies a rich database of troubleshooting information.

To use the website, you select the version of Quicken you're using. After you click your version, you see a web page that lists common categories of problems or questions. You select a category, and you're on your way. The product support website then displays a list of troubleshooting articles that may help you solve your problem.

Tactics #4 and #5: Check the Microsoft or the Hardware Vendor Product Support Website

Keep in mind the possibility that your problem may not be a problem with Quicken at all, but a problem with your computer and its hardware or with Microsoft Windows. If your problem stems from the hardware or the operating system, you can consult the hardware or software maker's product support website for troubleshooting information. The Microsoft product support

website, which is phenomenally rich in information, is available at `http://support.microsoft.com`. You can usually find the hardware maker product support website easily by using a good Internet search engine. For example, to locate Dell Computer's product support website, type something like **Dell Computer product support** in a search engine such as Google (at `www.google.com`).

You can find troubleshooting information about Intuit products at the Microsoft product support website. If the solutions that the site offers aren't very reassuring, at least you can find out whether others have experienced the same problem. Microsoft may suggest that you contact the vendor (which is Intuit) or that you upgrade to a newer version of the Quicken software. But knowing that the problem you've encountered is a real problem that Microsoft has logged in its product support knowledge base (that's what Microsoft calls it) and described in some technical detail is often useful.

Tactic #6: Contact Intuit Directly

In addition to the option of using the Intuit product support website, you can contact Intuit directly by visiting the Quicken support page and clicking the Contact Us button. The URL for Intuit support is `http://quicken.intuit.com/support`.

If you're willing to wait for your help, you should also know that free support is available by e-mail (consult the Intuit support website for current details). Finally, the Intuit site also offers a free chat service 24 hours a day, 7 days a week.

Tactic #7: Try the Quicken Live Community

If your problem with Quicken isn't really a program bug or can't be easily solved by getting more information, you can sometimes find an answer by consulting other Quicken users. One of the easiest ways to do this is to browse the Quicken Live Community forums at `https://qlc.intuit.com`.

You may not need this background information, but I'm going to point out a few important things about forums. Community groups really amount to free-form — and sometimes meandering — discussions among users. You can't necessarily expect to have your question answered. And good community forum etiquette suggests that if you're going to ask questions, you should also try to answer questions.

Tactic #8: Install and Use Antivirus Software

Okay, this shouldn't really be Tactic #8. This tactic deserves a higher ranking than that. But that's beside the point. The point is this: If you can't solve a problem, and you have Internet access, and you've been downloading files or accepting e-mail messages with attachments from strangers, your computer may have a virus. And it may be that your Quicken problems (particularly Quicken problems that you can't solve in other ways) stem from the virus.

In this case, I'd buy, install, and use antivirus software such as Norton AntiVirus or McAfee VirusScan. Consider one of these software programs just another part of the price of Internet connectivity. To locate online stores where you can download antivirus software, use www.google.com to search for *Norton AntiVirus* or *McAfee VirusScan*. You can also try Microsoft's free antivirus software, Microsoft Security Essentials, available at http://windows.microsoft.com/MSE.

Tactic #9: When All Else Fails . . .

If you use a CPA or enrolled agent to prepare your federal and state income taxes, you can probably get a quick (and perhaps free) answer from him or her. CPAs and enrolled agents, as you may guess, have spent years learning about and working with accounting systems. Commonly, the problems people have with Quicken aren't technical software problems but accounting or bookkeeping conundrums. So what you think is a Quicken bug may, er, really be an operator error.

Let me also mention that even if you don't have a CPA or enrolled agent prepare your tax return, you may want to find one whom you can ask for help and then pay him or her. Even if you're using Quicken for a small business or for real estate investing — something a wee bit complicated — an hour or so of personalized training is often all you need to get all your questions answered.

Part VI
Appendixes

For help choosing the right version of Quicken, read the "Straight Talk on Quicken Flavors in 2015" article at www.dummies.com/extras/quicken2015.

In this part . . .

- ✔ Protect yourself from a Windows 8.1-triggered nervous break-down with a quick-and-dirty overview of how to use Microsoft's new operating system.

- ✔ Look up easy-to-understand definitions of common personal finance and Quicken terms and impress your friends . . . or at least your family.

Appendix A

Quick-and-Dirty Windows 8.1

• •

*I*f you're new to Microsoft Windows 8.1, you need to know a few things about the Windows 8.1 user interface. Although this appendix doesn't reveal anything earthshaking, it does provide a quick-and-dirty overview of some basics you need to know to get around.

If you've used other Windows applications and have already spent at least a little bit of time using Windows 8 or Windows 8.1 (and so know how to start programs and how to stop Windows), you probably don't need to read this appendix because you already know the material it covers.

I won't bore you with technical details. The information here, though, will enable you not only to operate Quicken, but also to converse easily about the newest versions of Windows at cocktail parties, over lunch, or with the guy at the computer store.

If you want more information, you may want to read a book such as *Windows 8.1 For Dummies,* by Andy Rathbone (John Wiley & Sons, Inc.).

If you're working with Windows Vista or Windows 7, much of what this appendix talks about also applies to your use of Quicken 2015.

What Is Windows 8.1?

Windows 8.1 — and when I use the term *Windows 8.1* here, again, I mean any version of Microsoft Windows 8.1 — is an operating environment that manages your *system resources* (things like memory, your monitor, your printer, and so on).

Applications (programs such as Quicken) run on top of Windows 8.1. In other words, you start Windows 8.1 by turning on your personal computer (PC). Then, after Windows 8.1 is running, you can start applications, such as Quicken.

Windows 8.1 provides a standard graphical interface. In English, Windows 8.1 provides a common approach for using *visual elements* — tiles, icons, buttons, check boxes, and so on. (This appendix describes how the major pieces of this graphical interface work.)

Windows 8.1 enables you to run more than one application at a time. You may, for example, run Quicken; a tax preparation package; and a Windows accessory program, such as a web browser.

Starting Windows 8.1

Starting Windows 8.1 is easy. You just turn on your personal computer (PC). If you can find the on–off switch, you're set.

If you can't find the on–off switch, or it doesn't seem to work, don't feel silly. Ask someone who has used that computer. Sometimes the switch is on the front of the computer and is labeled On–Off (which makes good sense, of course). Sometimes, I'm afraid, manufacturers stick the on–off switch on the back of the computer or label the switch something really stupid, such as 0 and 1. Sometimes, too, people plug a computer and all its peripherals (printers, modems, and all that junk) into a power strip that needs to be turned on to turn on the computer. So just ask someone. (If you bought the computer, of course, you can just telephone the place you bought it from.)

Just so you don't feel like a complete imbecile, I have to tell you something: I once had to call someone to find out how to click the stupid mouse that I got with my laptop computer.

Figure A-1 shows a typical Windows 8.1 Start screen. The Start screen is what you see after Windows 8.1 starts.

In earlier versions of Windows, you didn't see a Start screen after you started Windows. Rather, you saw the *desktop*. You can still get (and easily get) to the desktop by clicking the rectangle labeled Desktop, which appears in the lower-left corner of the Start screen.

Starting Programs

To start a program like Quicken, you click the Quicken tile — which, after you've installed Quicken, appears someplace on the Start screen.

By the way, the tiles (those colorful rectangles) that appear on the Start screen are big — almost the size of small candy bars. Accordingly, you may need to scroll the Start screen left or right (using the left- and right-arrow buttons) to see the tile you want to click.

To practice this starting-a-program business, try starting the Quicken program by following these steps:

1. **Locate the Quicken tile on the Start screen.**

 The Quicken tile will probably be visible, but you may need to use the left- and right-arrow keys to locate the tile.

2. **Click the tile for the program you want to start.**

 Windows 8.1 opens Quicken. Figure A-2 shows the Quicken program window showing the home tab. (A *program window* is just the window that a program like Quicken displays.)

A tidbit about the Windows 8.1 desktop

If you're a longtime Windows user, you may want to just skip working with the Start screen and its childlike world of giant tiles. And you can do this by clicking the Desktop tile. The Quicken installation program installs itself both as a tile on the Start screen and as a familiar-looking icon on the Windows desktop. The Windows 8.1 desktop works in a way comfortingly similar to older versions of the Windows desktop. For example, the desktop includes a *taskbar* that you can click to move among the programs you're running and that you can use to start some very popular programs, such as Internet Explorer. The only thing that one really misses (at least in the beginning) is the Start button, which in older versions of Windows listed the programs you could click to start. And that deletion really hints at the big interface change the Microsoft Windows 8.1 designers came up with: Out with the Start button (and its textual list of programs) and in with the Start screen (and its graphical "game board" of colorful tiles).

Figure A-2:
The Quicken window.

Choosing Commands from Menus

To set something in motion in Windows 8.1, you usually need to choose *commands* from menus.

I don't know why they're called commands. Perhaps because you often — but not always — use them to command Windows 8.1 and applications to do things ("Hello, Windows 8.1? I command thee to start this application" or "Quicken, I command thee to print this report").

Most application windows have a *menu bar* — a row of menus across the top of the window. Predictably, not every menu bar contains the same menus, but they're often darn similar. Some of the commands on the Quicken menus, for example, mirror commands on the Internet Explorer menus.

This menu similarity isn't some nefarious conspiracy. The common command sets make things easier for users.

If you choose to read the next sections, don't worry about what particular commands or menus do. Just focus on the mechanics of choosing commands.

Choosing commands with the furry little rodent

Oftentimes, the easiest way to choose a command is to use the mouse.

To select one of the menus by using a mouse, move the *mouse pointer* — the small arrow that moves across your screen as you physically roll the mouse across your desk — so that it points to the name of the menu that you want to select. Then click the mouse's left button. Windows 8.1 or the application program displays the menu. Figure A-3 shows the Quicken File menu, for example. Now click the command that you want to choose. For example, if you want to click the first command listed on the menu, which happens to be New Quicken File, you click those words.

If you inadvertently display a menu, you can *deselect* it (that is, make it go away) by clicking anywhere outside the menu box.

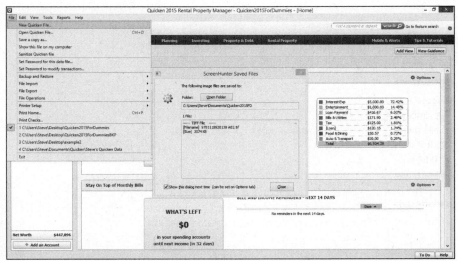

Figure A-3:
The Quicken File menu.

Choosing commands by using Alt+key combinations

Another way to choose a command is to use an *Alt key* (cleverly labeled Alt), usually located at either end of the spacebar:

1. **Press the Alt key.**

 Doing so tells Windows 8.1 or the application that you want to choose a command by using your keyboard. After you do this, Windows underlines one of the letters in each menu name, as shown in Figure A-4. When you press the Alt key, for example, Windows underlines the letter *F* in File.

2. **Press the letter representing the menu that you want to choose.**

 Doing so tells Windows 8.1 or the application program which menu contains the command you want. Press *F* to select the File menu, for example.

3. **Press the underlined letter of the command you want to choose.**

 Each command on a menu is usually underlined, too, if you've pressed the Alt key. Accordingly, you can tell the program which command on a menu you want to choose by pressing the underlined letter of that command. If you've chosen the File menu, for example, you can choose the last option on the File menu, Exit, by pressing the letter *X*. (You can try choosing Exit if you want, but then restart Quicken so that you can continue to follow along, okay?)

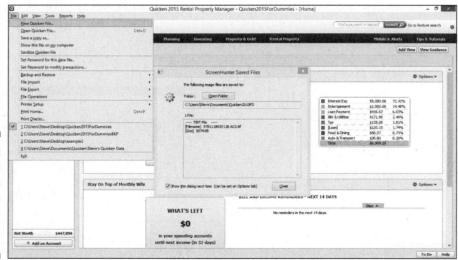

Figure A-4:
The Quicken File menu again — this time with underlined letters.

Windows 8.1 and Windows 8.1 applications often offer yet another way to choose menu commands. After you press the Alt key, you can use the left- and right-arrow keys to highlight the menu that you want. Then press Enter. Windows 8.1 or the Windows 8.1 application displays the menu. Use the up- and down-arrow keys to highlight the command that you want to choose. Then press Enter.

If you want to deselect a menu but still leave the menu bar activated, press the Esc key once. To deselect the displayed menu and at the same time deactivate the menu bar, press the Esc key twice.

Context menus or shortcut menus

A quick point: Many Windows 8.1 applications display a menu, called a *context menu* or *shortcut menu,* if you right-click some part of the program window.

Within Quicken, if you right-click anything, Quicken displays a context menu of commands you might use to do something to or with the right-clicked object.

Using shortcut-key combinations

For many menu commands, Windows 8.1 and Windows 8.1 applications offer shortcut-key combinations. When you press a shortcut-key combination, Windows 8.1 or the Windows 8.1 application program simultaneously activates the menu bar, chooses a menu, and chooses a command.

Windows 8.1 (and application programs such as Quicken) displays the shortcut-key combination that you can use for a command on the menu beside the command.

If you take a peek back at Figure A-4, for example, you see that two of the commands listed on the File menu are followed by cryptic codes. Following the File⇨Open Quicken File command, for example, you can just barely make out the code Ctrl+O. And following the File⇨Print Home command, you can see the code Ctrl+P. These codes are the shortcut-key combinations. If you simultaneously press the two or three keys listed — the Ctrl key and the P key, for example — you choose the command. (Shortcut-key combinations often use funny keys — such as Ctrl, Alt, and Shift — in combination with letters or numbers. If you're not familiar with some of these keys' locations, check your keyboard.)

Disabled commands

Oh, jeepers, I almost forgot to tell you something. Not every menu command makes sense in every situation. So Windows 8.1 — and every Windows 8.1 application — disables commands that would be just plain kooky to choose.

To show you when a command has been disabled, the program displays the disabled command in gray letters; commands you *can* choose show up in black letters. Figure A-4 shows no disabled commands, but on other menus, if you keep your eyes peeled, you see that Windows 8.1 or the Windows 8.1 applications sometimes disable commands that make no sense to use just now.

Let me make one other point about choosing commands in the Windows 8.1 environment. Windows 8.1, as the screen shots in this book show, makes your computing experience as visual and graphical as possible. Accordingly, if Windows 8.1 or a program designed for Windows 8.1 can replace a boring old menu command with a clickable picture or icon, that's how it appears.

The Internet Explorer program does this visualization quite a bit. I'm not going to show you a picture of this program here in the pages of this book, but if you start the Internet Explorer program, you can see (in the lower right and left corners) buttons with arrows that point left and right. And if you click one of these buttons, you move to the last web page you were viewing or the next web page you just moved back from. Quicken 2015 doesn't make fetishlike use of command icons. But if you poke around Windows 8.1 much — or if you work with other Microsoft programs, such as Internet Explorer — you'll see what I mean. Oh, baby, will you see what I mean.

Working with Dialog Boxes

Windows 8.1 (and Windows programs like Quicken) uses a special type of window, called a *dialog box,* to communicate with you. In fact, after you choose a command, Windows 8.1 and application programs often display a dialog box to get the information they need to carry out the command.

Dialog boxes have these unique design elements: text boxes, check boxes, tabs, option buttons (also called *radio buttons),* command buttons, and list boxes.

Text boxes

Text boxes provide spaces in which you can enter text. To see what a text box looks like (and I'm assuming that you've still got Quicken running), choose the Edit⇔Find command. Quicken, responding nicely to your deft touch, displays the Quicken Find dialog box (shown in Figure A-5). The text box is the box to the left of the button labeled Find and in the figure shows the date 6/30/2014.

If the *selection cursor* — the flashing line or outline that selects the active element of a dialog box — isn't already in the text box, you need to move it there by clicking in the text box. Then type the text. If this "active element"

mumbo-jumbo seems too technical, just press Tab a bunch of times and watch the dialog box. See that thing that moves around from box to button to box? It selects the active element.

Figure A-5:
The Quicken
Find dialog
box.

You can move the selection cursor in several ways:

- Click inside the text box.

- Press Tab or Shift+Tab until the selection cursor is in the text box. (Pressing Tab moves the selection cursor to the next element; pressing Shift+Tab moves the selection cursor to the preceding element.)

- Press the Alt+*key* combination, if available. In Figure A-5, the text box holding the date is unlabeled. But if the text box were labeled, as some text boxes are, the program typically underlines one of the letters in the label. In Figure A-5, for example, the label Find (which labels another box) has the letter *i* underlined. In this case, you can press Alt+I to move the selection cursor to that box.

If you make a typing mistake in the text box, press the Backspace key to erase incorrect characters. Other editing tricks are available, but I don't describe them here. (After all, this chapter is just a quick-and-dirty overview of Windows 8.1.)

You also can move the *insertion bar* — the vertical line that shows where your type gets placed — by using the left- and right-arrow keys. The left-arrow key moves the insertion bar one character to the left without deleting any characters. The right-arrow key moves the insertion bar one character to the right without deleting any characters.

Check boxes

Check boxes work like on–off switches. A check box is "on" if the box is selected with a check mark. A check box is "off" if the box is empty. Figure A-5, earlier in this appendix, shows the Search Backwards check box turned on.

To turn a check box on or off with the mouse, click the check box. If the check box is on, your click turns off the check box. If the check box is off, your click turns on the check box.

You also can use the spacebar to select and deselect a check box. After you move the selection cursor to the check box, press the spacebar to alternately select and deselect the check box. Toggle, toggle, toggle.

Tabs

Figure A-5 doesn't use them, but sometimes *tabs* appear in dialog boxes. Click a tab to see it when a dialog box has multiple tabs.

Option buttons

Option buttons (or *radio buttons*) are sets of buttons representing mutually exclusive choices. Figure A-5 doesn't show option buttons, but take a peek at the dialog box shown in Figure A-6. If you want to follow along, display this dialog box by selecting Quicken's Edit⇨Preferences command and then clicking the Write Checks entry in the list of preferences. The Preferences dialog box does show a set of Printed Date Style option buttons — 4-Digit Year and 2-Digit Year — to let you specify how you printed dates appear.

You can select only one option button in a set. Windows 8.1 or the Windows 8.1 application identifies the selected button by putting a *bullet,* or darkened circle, inside the button. In Figure A-6, for example, the 4-Digit Year option button is selected. The easiest way to select an option button is to click the option button you want.

Command buttons

Every dialog box has command buttons. *Command buttons* tell Windows 8.1 or an application program what you want to do after you finish using a dialog box.

Figure A-5, earlier in this appendix, shows command buttons labeled Find, Find All, and Close. If you were really working with the Quicken Find dialog box (and you're not; you and I are just playing around here), you'd click Find or Find All after completing the rest of the dialog box. If you didn't want to use the Find dialog box after all, you'd click Close.

Figure A-6 shows two command buttons: OK and Cancel. If you click OK, you tell the Windows application to follow your command. If you click Cancel, you tell the application (basically), "Oh, never mind."

To choose a command button, click it, or move the selection cursor to a command button and then press Enter.

The small box marked with an *X* that appears in the upper-right corner of dialog boxes and windows is a command button too. You can click this command button, called a *Close box,* to cancel a dialog box or close a window. If you've been following along on your computer with me and you started the Notepad program, for example, you can click the Close box to close that program.

List boxes

List boxes list a series of possible choices. And to select an entry in a list box, you just click the entry you want.

Note, though, that Windows 8.1 serves up two flavors of list box: a regular list box (which is always displayed) and a *drop-down* list box, like the one shown in Figure A-7. (This particular list box appears if you select the Calendar and Currency entry in the Select Preference Type list of the Preferences dialog box, click the Fiscal Year option button, and then click the Starting Month box.)

Figure A-7:
The Preferences dialog box with the Starting Month drop-down list box "dropped."

Drop-down list boxes initially look like text boxes with a down-arrow key at the right end of the box before you "drop" them. To drop the list down, you click the down arrow. After you do this, the list box looks and works like a regular list box. You select an entry, for example, by clicking it.

And a final point: Unfortunately, sometimes a list is too long for the list box to display completely. (This is *not* the case in Figure A-6.) When this minor tragedy occurs, you can use the PgUp and PgDn keys to page through the list.

You also can use the *scroll bar* — the vertical bar with arrows at either end. Just drag the square scroll-bar selector up or down. You also can click the arrows at either end of the scroll bar, or you can click the scroll bar itself. (This last trick moves the scroll-bar selector toward the place where you clicked.)

Stopping Quicken in Windows 8.1

To stop an application program such as Quicken, either click the program's Close box — the button with the *X* in it that appears in the top-right corner of the application window — or choose File➪Exit.

A Yelp for Help

Help, a separate application within Windows 8.1, has powerful tools to help you find out more about Windows 8.1 and application programs, such as Internet Explorer and Quicken. To access Help, select the Help menu or click the ? icon.

The Quicken 2015 Help menu (see Figure A-8) lists nine commands: Getting Started Guide, Quicken Help, View Guidance, Quicken Live Community, Quicken Support, Submit Feedback on Quicken, Privacy Preferences, Log Files, and About Quicken. In the following paragraphs, I briefly describe how each command shown in Figure A-8 works.

Figure A-8:
The Quicken
Help menu.

The Getting Started Guide command

The Getting Started Guide command displays windows that list Quicken Help topics related to getting the Quicken program set up and to getting started using Quicken.

The Quicken Help command

If you choose Help⇨Quicken Help, the Help program displays a window (shown in Figure A-9) that has two tabs: Contents and Search Quicken Help.

Figure A-9:
The
Contents tab
lists major
Help topics.

The Contents tab lists some of the major Help topic categories. To display the topics within a particular category, double-click the Help topic category. Help expands the list to show the topics within each category. Double-click a topic to display the Help information on that topic.

You can click the Search Quicken Help tab (shown in Figure A-10) to search the Help topics. To use the Search tab, enter your search words, or *keywords,* in the first text box and then select the Help topic in the last list box.

Figure A-10:
The Search
Quicken
Help tab lets
you search
for Help
topics by
keywords.

The View Guidance command

The View Guidance command tells Quicken to turn on Quicken Qcards, which are little sticky-note-like things that provide tips and helpful nuggets of information about working with Quicken.

The Quicken Live Community command

The Quicken Live Community command connects you to an Intuit-sponsored Quicken support-forums website (`https://qlc.intuit.com`) so that you can discuss Quicken problems and solutions with other Quicken users.

The Quicken Support command

The Quicken Support command opens a web page at Intuit's product support website for Quicken. There's lots of good information here.

The Submit Feedback on Quicken command

The Submit Feedback on Quicken command opens a web page that you can use to submit suggestions, share comments, or report bugs. If you have something to say about Quicken to Intuit, this command is the way you do it.

The Privacy Preferences command

This command displays information about the ways that Intuit attempts to keep your financial data secure and about the business practices that Intuit employs. The command also provides a couple of check boxes you can use to tell Intuit whether you're cool with its collection of usage statistics. If you're not, you clear some check boxes; then your copy of Quicken won't share information with Intuit about how easily Quicken connects to your online banking vendor and so on.

The Log Files command

The Log Files command displays a web page with links you can click to easily access the log files that Quicken maintains. You may want to use this command if some part of the Quicken program goes haywire, you need to call Intuit's technical support, and then the technical support folks want or need to know what in the world happened.

The About Quicken command

The About Quicken command displays a dialog box that lists the application's complete name (such as Quicken Premier 2015). To remove this dialog box from the screen, click OK.

The Add Tools commands

Though Figure A-8 doesn't show them, some versions of Quicken Help menus include one or more Add commands. Depending on the version of Quicken that you're working with, you might see commands such as Business Tools, Rental Property Tools, Retirement & Other Planning Tools, or even More Investing & Tax Tools.

These commands let you upgrade automatically to more expensive versions of Quicken.

The Register Quicken command

The Register Quicken command opens a web page you can use to register your copy of Quicken by answering questions such as what your name is, where you purchased Quicken, and what the cube root of 1331 is.

Quitting Windows 8.1

To quit Windows 8.1 (and I grant that this may just be the screwiest feature of the new Windows), you move the mouse into the upper-right corner of the screen so that Windows displays the Charms bar, which is a slide-out menu of five icons: Search, Share, Start, Devices, and Settings. Click the Settings icon and then click the Power button you see. When Windows 8.1 displays the pop-up menu, choose the Shut Down command. Unbelievable.

If you exit Quicken the wrong way

If you exit Quicken by turning off (or resetting) your computer, the file that Quicken uses to organize your financial records gets . . . well, wasted. Quicken rebuilds the file when you restart, but this process takes a few seconds.

Don't exit Quicken (or Windows 8.1) by turning off your computer. Doing so may not cause serious problems (let me say, though, that Windows 8.1 isn't always as forgiving as Quicken), but it is bad form — akin to eating the last potato chip or leaving the gas tank empty in your spouse's car.

Appendix B

Glossary of Business, Financial, and Computer Terms

· ·

940 Payroll Tax Form: The annual federal unemployment tax return. A 940EZ version is supposed to be EZ-er to fill out.

941 Payroll Tax Form: The quarterly federal payroll tax form that tells the IRS what federal employee payroll taxes (Social Security, Medicare, and federal withholding tax) you've collected and remitted.

942 Payroll Tax Form: The quarterly payroll tax form that tells the IRS what domestic employee payroll taxes an employer has collected and remitted.

account: In Quicken, a list of the increases and decreases in an asset's value or in a liability's balance.

account balance: The value of an asset or the outstanding principal owed for a liability. The value of a checking account, for example, is the cash value of the account. The balance of a mortgage liability is the principal you still owe.

account transfer: An amount you move from one account (such as a checking account) to another (such as a savings account).

account type: Different Quicken versions, or types, of accounts. There are accounts both for keeping records of the things you own — checking, saving, money market, cash, brokerage, IRA or Keogh, 401(k), dividend reinvestment plan, other investments, house, and vehicle — and for keeping records of the amounts you owe (credit card and liability).

Accounts bar: The list of accounts and hyperlinks that appears in a vertical list along the left edge of the Quicken program window. If you click an account hyperlink, Quicken displays the account in a register.

accounts payable: In a business, the amounts you owe your trade creditors — your landlord, the office-supplies store, the distributor from which you purchase your inventory, and so on. People who prefer monosyllabic speech often refer to accounts payable as *A/P*.

accounts receivable: In a business, the amounts your customers or clients owe you. People who prefer monosyllabic speech often refer to accounts receivable as *A/R.*

amortization: The itsy-bitsy principal payments you make over the course of repaying a loan. Eventually, these principal reductions pay off the loan.

ASCII: An acronym for *American Standard Code for Information Interchange.* People often use the term to refer to a type of computer file. ASCII files contain just regular old text — letters, numbers, symbols from the keyboard, and so on — and have no fancy formatting.

backing up: Making a copy. If something terrible happens — fire, hard drive failure, thermonuclear exchange — you still have a copy on removable media (such as CDs, DVDs, or flash drives) safely stored away from your computer, preferably offsite.

balancing an account: The steps you take to explain the difference between what your records show as a balance and what the bank's records (statements) show as a balance. Also referred to as *reconciling an account.*

bookkeeper: Someone who keeps the *books,* or financial records.

brokerage account: A Quicken account specifically set up to track brokerage transactions that you use to invest in securities. Unlike a mutual fund account, a brokerage account includes a cash element. See also *account type.*

budget: A plan that says how you will make and spend money.

capital account: The money a sole proprietor leaves in or contributes to the sole proprietorship; also, the money a partner leaves in or contributes to a partnership.

capital gain: What you earn by selling an investment for more than you paid. Capital gains (and losses) receive special treatment on your income tax return.

capital loss: What you lose by selling an investment for less than you paid.

category: In Quicken, how you summarize income and outgo. You may use a category, such as Wages, to summarize your payroll check deposits. You may use categories (such as Housing, Food, and Fun) to summarize your checks.

category group: A group of categories that you monitor as a group. You create category groups so that you can monitor them. See also *supercategory.*

category list: The list of categories you can use. Quicken suggests category lists for home users and for business users as part of the setup.

certified public accountant (CPA): Someone who's taken a bunch of undergraduate and often even graduate accounting courses, passed a rather challenging test, and worked for at least a few years under an established CPA doing things like auditing, tax planning and preparation, and consulting. Really exciting stuff, in other words.

chart: A picture that shows numbers. In Quicken, you can produce pie charts, bar charts, line charts, and so on.

check date: The date you write your payment instructions, or check. Technically, the check date is the date on which your payment instructions to the bank become valid.

check form: The preprinted form that you use to provide payment instructions to your bank: "Okay, Mammoth National, pay Joe Shmoe $32 from my account, 00704-844." Theoretically, you could use just about anything as a check form: a scrap of paper, a block of wood, and so on. In fact, rumor has it that someone once used a cowhide. It's easier for your poor bank, though, if you use check forms that follow the usual style and provide OCR (optical character recognition) characters along the form's bottom edge.

Circular E: Instructions from the IRS to employers. This publication tells stuff like how much federal income tax to withhold. Call the IRS and request a copy if you need one. Or visit the IRS website (`www.irs.gov`).

class: The old name for what Quicken now calls *tags*.

cleared: When a check or deposit has been received by the bank. An *uncleared* transaction hasn't been received by the bank.

commands: What you use to tell Quicken what it should do. You can click an option on a menu that says (in effect), "Quicken, I command thee to print a report." Note that in addition to using menu commands to navigate within Quicken, you can use the buttons, QuickTabs, and hyperlinks that appear within the Quicken windows. Just thought I'd mention this.

controller: A business's chief accountant — and usually the butt of most accountant jokes; also known as a *comptroller.*

corporation: A legal business entity created by state law, owned by shareholders, and managed by directors and officers. As a business entity, a corporation has unique advantages and some disadvantages. Ask your attorney for more information. But know that for small businesses, a limited liability company (LLC) is usually better. See also *LLC.*

credit card account: A Quicken account specifically set up to track credit card charges, payments, and balances. See also *account type.*

deleted transaction: A transaction that Quicken has removed from the register.

disc/disk: The thingamajig in your computer on which Windows stores your programs (such as Quicken) and your data files (such as the Quicken file for your financial records). A hard drive inside your computer can store a great deal of information; removable storage devices (such as CDs, DVDs, and flash drives) typically store a lot less data than a hard drive can.

exit: To shut down, terminate, or stop a program. By the way, you want to always do this the right way, which means by using the File menu's Exit command or by clicking the program window's Close box. Don't just turn off your computer.

EFTPS: The electronic tax deposit system maintained by the U.S. Treasury which IRS regulations require you to use for making payroll tax deposits if you operate a small business or withhold taxes for domestic help. I include this entry in honor of the IRS employee I talked to this year who didn't know what the EFTPS system is and suspected my client for using it.

file: Where data is stored. But just to be nitpicky, what Quicken calls a file is actually the name used for a special group of several files. You don't need to worry about this unless you create multiple files.

filename: The name of a file in which Quicken stores data.

financial wizards: People who believe that they know so much about the world of finance that it's actually their God-given duty to share their expertise with you. See also *wizard*.

find/Find: A tremendous bargain, as in "At $22,000, the five-bedroom house was a real find." In Quicken, it's also an Edit-menu command that you can use to locate transactions. See also *search criteria*.

fiscal year: An accounting year. Most of the time, a fiscal year is the same as the calendar year, starting on January 1 and ending on December 31. Some businesses and foreign taxpayers use a different fiscal year, though. (Why they do that is way, way beyond the scope of this book.)

folder: What Windows uses to organize the files on your hard drive. Some people call folders *directories*.

formatting: Hey, this word is too complicated for a book like this, isn't it? Let me just say that formatting means doing some things to a disc so that you can write files to that disc. It can also mean setting up some nice typesetting "looks" in your printed documents.

Help: A program's online documentation, which you can almost always access by pressing F1; also, a verbalized cry for assistance.

hyperlink: A bit of clickable text (and sometimes a clickable picture) that you can use (by clicking, of course) to move to some other Quicken feature or some other web page. Quicken, as you may have noticed, scatters hyperlinks everywhere. And I mean everywhere. A hyperlink is also called a *link*.

index fund: A mutual fund that buys all (or nearly all) of the assets in the category it invests in — and so delivers, at very low cost, the average return for the category.

internal rate of return: An investment's profit expressed as a percentage of the investment. If you go to the bank and buy a certificate of deposit earning 3 percent interest, for example, 3 percent is the CD's internal rate of return. I don't want to give you the heebie-jeebies, but internal rates of return can get really complicated really fast.

liability account: A Quicken account specifically set up for tracking loans, payments, the principal and interest portions of these payments, and the outstanding balance. See also *account type*.

limited liability company: See *LLC*.

LLC: An abbreviation for *limited liability company*. LLCs are popular with tax accountants and tax attorneys because they sort of give you the best of both the corporation and partnership worlds. For small businesses and real estate investments, LLCs are nice because (compared with corporations) they offer both simplicity and less paperwork.

memo: A brief description of a transaction. Because you also give the payee and category for a transaction, it usually makes sense to use the Memo field to record some other bit of information about a check or deposit.

menu: In Quicken, a list of commands; in a restaurant, a list of things you can order from the kitchen.

menu bar: A horizontally arranged row, or bar, of menus. Yes, it does sound like a place where menus go for a drink after work.

missing check: A gap in the check numbers. If your register shows a check 101 and a check 103, for example, check 102 is a missing check.

mutual fund account: A Quicken account specifically set up to track a mutual fund investment.

online banking: An extra service you can buy from your bank. With online banking, you record a payment in your Quicken register and then transmit the payment information to your bank so that it can make the actual payment. Online banking also lets you transfer money electronically between your accounts — and grab your statement electronically.

Online Bill Payment: An extra service you can buy from Intuit, the folks who bring you Quicken. With Online Bill Payment, you record a payment in your Quicken register and then transmit the payment information to Intuit's computer or to your bank. Intuit or your bank then uses this information to make the actual payment.

online investing: Downloading transactions from many (and maybe even most) of the online brokerage services right into your investment accounts. If you're buying and selling securities, downloading these transactions (rather than entering them by hand) saves you time. This feature is particularly valuable for people who want to see how quickly they can lose everything they own through day trading.

partnership: A business entity that combines two or more soon-to-be-former friends. In general, each partner is liable for the entire debts of the partnership.

password: A word you have to give Quicken before Quicken gives you access to a file. The first password, "Open sesame," was used by Ali Baba.

payee: The person to whom a check is made payable. (If you write a check to me, Steve Nelson, I'm the payee.) In Quicken, however, you can fill in a Payee field for deposits and for account transfers.

power user: Someone who's spent far more time than is healthy fooling around with a computer. Power users are good people to have as friends because they can often solve your worst technical nightmares. Note, however, that most people who describe themselves as power users aren't.

QIF: An acronym for *Quicken Interchange Format.* Basically, QIF is a set of rules that prescribes how an ASCII file must look if you want Quicken to read it. If you're a clever sort, you can import category lists and even transactions from ASCII files that follow the QIF rules.

Quicken: The name of the checkbook-on-a-computer program that this book is about. You didn't really need to look this up, did you?

Quicken.com: The Intuit Corporation website especially for Quicken users. Visit this website, my friend. It's really good.

Quicken Premier: A supercharged version of Quicken that includes a bunch of extra whistles and bells, including a really neat program for locating great mutual funds (called, cleverly enough, Mutual Fund Finder) and a Home Inventory System program. This book is about Quicken Rental Property Manager, but users of Quicken Basic, Quicken Deluxe, Quicken Home & Business, and Quicken Premier can apply this book to their products. (All the products are similar in their core functionality.)

Quicken Quotes: An online service that you can use to grab up-to-date price information on stocks and bonds. This book doesn't talk much about Quicken Quotes.

QuickFill: A clever little feature. If Quicken can guess what you'll type next in a field, it types, or *QuickFills,* the field for you. QuickFill enters transactions, payee names, and category names.

register: Another name for the transaction list — a register shows the increases and decreases in an account balance.

report: An onscreen or printed summary of financial information from one or more registers.

restore: Replace the current version of a file with the backup version. You may need to do this after a fire, hard drive failure, or thermonuclear exchange. See also *backing up.*

savings goal accounts: A Quicken pseudo-account. In effect, a savings goal account is a compartment in a banking account where you can "hide" or set aside money that you're saving for a special purpose. A new car. A boat. A trip to Montana. Whatever.

scroll bars: The vertical bars along the window's right edge and the horizontal bars along the window's bottom edge. Use them to scroll or page through your view of something that's too big to fit on one page.

search criteria: A description of the transaction that you want to locate. See also *find/Find.*

sole proprietorship: A business that's owned by just one person and that doesn't have a separate legal identity. In general, businesses are sole proprietorships, partnerships, corporations, or limited liability companies.

split transactions: A transaction assigned to more than one category or transferred to more than one account. A split-check transaction, for example, might show a $50 check to the convenience store paying for both groceries and automobile expenses such as motor oil. (Now, that's what I call one-stop shopping!)

stockholders' equity: The money that shareholders have contributed to a corporation or allowed to be retained in the corporation. You can't track stockholders' equity with Quicken.

subcategory: A category within a category. The suggested Quicken home categories list breaks utilities spending into Cable TV, Gas and Electric, Telephone, and Water subcategories.

supercategory: A group of categories that you monitor as a group. You create supercategories so that you can monitor a batch or bucket of categories all at once. See also *category group.*

tabs: The clickable labels that look like file-folder tabs and that appear near the top of the Quicken program window, below the menu bar and icon bar.

tag: Another way (formerly known as a *class)* to summarize Quicken data when categories just aren't enough. This book doesn't talk about tags much. Sorry.

target retirement fund: What almost everybody should use for retirement investments but almost nobody does . . . alas.

tax deduction: For an individual, an amount that can be deducted from total income (such as alimony or IRA contributions) or used as an itemized deduction and deducted from adjusted gross income (such as home mortgage interest or charitable contributions). For a business, any amount that represents an ordinary and necessary business expense. Be sure to consult your tax advisor if you have any questions about what is or isn't a valid tax deduction.

tax-deferred account: A not-currently-taxable account — IRAs, for one example, and 401(k) plans for another. To deal with this real-life complexity, Quicken lets you tag any account as being tax-deferred. As a practical matter, however, probably only investment accounts and the occasional bank account are tax-deferred.

technogeek: Someone who believes that fooling around with a computer is more fun than anything else in the world.

transaction list: The list of increases and decreases in an account balance. Quicken displays a transaction list in a window that looks remarkably similar to a crummy old paper register: your checkbook. To print a copy of the register that you see on your screen, press Ctrl+P and then press the Enter key.

transposition: Flip-flopped numbers, such as 23.45 entered as 24.35 (the 3 and 4 are flip-flopped as 4 and 3). These common little mistakes have caused many bookkeepers and accountants to go insane.

W-2: The annual wages statement that employers use to tell employees what they made and to tell the IRS what employees made.

W-3: A summary form of W-2s. When employers send a stack of W-2s to the IRS, they also fill out a W-3 form that summarizes all the individual W-2s. W-2s and W-3s aren't much fun, but they're not hard to fill out.

Windows: The Microsoft Windows operating system. Quicken for Windows relies on Windows to do a bunch of system stuff, such as print. Refer to Appendix A for more information.

Windows 7: The last decent version of the Microsoft Windows operating system and the version that preceded Windows 8. See also *Windows.*

Windows 8/8.1: The latest editions of Windows available — and editions that many, many people hate because they're really designed for tablet computers, not the desktop or laptop computers that most people are running Windows on.

wizard: A little program that walks you through the steps of completing some tasks that some programmer thinks you're too dense to figure out on your own. Although a wizard sounds bad, it actually isn't. Quicken supplies a bunch of cool wizards, including wizards for setting up accounts and setting up how you want to record a paycheck, planning for retirement, planning for your kid's college expenses, reducing your debts, and so on.

Index

• *J* •

jobs, 117, 284. *See also* business accounting

• *K* •

Keough accounts, 232

• *L* •

liability accounts. *See also* scheduled transactions
 automatic entries, 208
 balance adjustments, 219–220
 charts, 211
 escrow account options, 216–218
 interest rate changes, 211–213
 loan deletions, 213–214
 loan details, 204–205, 207, 210–211
 payments, 215–216
 principal-interest breakdown adjustments, 219–220
 reminder settings, 209
 setting up, 204–205
 tracking liabilities, 26, 353
 transaction splits, 208
LLCs (limited liability companies), 351, 353
Loan Calculator, 161–164

• *M* •

Macintosh, exporting data to Windows, 21
Maturity Dates for Bonds and CDs reports, 114
McAfee VirusScan website, 330
Medicare tax, 293
memos
 checks, 62, 74, 79, 89, 353
 defined, 353
 searching, 79
Microsoft Excel, 97, 120
Microsoft Money, 21–22
Microsoft product support website, 328–329

Microsoft Windows 8.1
 Alt key commands, 338–339
 closing boxes/windows, 343
 commands, 336–337
 context menus, 339
 data imports from Macintosh, 21
 defined, 357
 desktop option, 334
 desktop versus tiles, 336
 dialog boxes, 340–344
 disabled (grayed-out) commands, 339–340
 file management, 21
 Help access, 345
 keyboard commands, 338–339
 menu bars, 336–337, 353
 mouse, 337–338
 opening programs, 335–336
 overview, 333–334
 program windows, 336
 quitting, 348
 scrolling, 335, 344
 shortcut keys/menus, 339
 starting, 334–335
 stopping applications, 344
 tabs, 356
 tiles, 335
mini-reports, 120
Missing Checks reports, 113, 117, 353
money market accounts, 256–259
mortgage-refinancing calculations, 164–165
mutual funds
 choosing, 230
 defined, 353
 diversification strategies, 168
 examples, 161
 investing in, 228–230
 target retirement funds, 230, 356

• *N* •

Net Worth reports, 114
940 form, 295–296
941 form, 295–296
942 form, 295–296
Norton AntiVirus website, 330

About the Author

Stephen L. Nelson is a CPA in Redmond, Washington. Nelson has an undergraduate degree in accounting, a Master of Business Administration degree in finance, and a Master of Science degree in taxation. He's spent three decades helping individuals, real estate investors, and businesses manage their finances — usually, in part, by better use of computer systems such as Quicken.

As corny as it sounds, Steve truly enjoys writing books that make using personal computers easier and more fun. In fact, a substantiated rumor that appeared first in *The Wall Street Journal* says Steve has written more than 150 computer books.

Steve is the best-selling author on the Quicken product. In fact, John Wiley & Sons, Inc., recently tallied up Steve's *Quicken For Dummies* sales — and darned if the publisher hasn't printed more than 1 million copies!

Author's Acknowledgments

I want to acknowledge the help of two groups. First, a huge thanks to the wonderful folks at Intuit who helped me by providing the beta software and other friendly assistance for this and past editions of this book, especially Roger Kimble, Dale Knievel, Laura Messerschmitt, Aaron Patzer, Kjirsten Petersen, and Jayme Ringer.

Another big thank-you goes to the editorial folks at John Wiley & Sons, Inc., including Kevin Kirschner (project editor), Kathy Simpson (copy editor), and Katie Mohr (acquisitions editor). Thanks also to David Ringstrom for his technical assistance and superb attention to detail. Finally, thanks, too, to the composition crew who made it a book.

Publisher's Acknowledgments

Project Editor: Kevin Kirschner

Acquisitions Editor: Katie Mohr

Copy Editor: Kathy Simpson

Technical Editor: David H. Ringstrom

Editorial Assistant: Claire Johnson

Sr. Editorial Assistant: Cherie Case

Project Coordinator: Melissa Cossell

Cover Image: ©iStockphoto.com/OJO_Images